Just Water

REVISED EDITION

Ecology and Justice

An Orbis Series on Integral Ecology

Advisory Board Members
Mary Evelyn Tucker
John A. Grim
Leonardo Boff
Sean McDonagh

The Orbis Series on Integral Ecology publishes books seeking to integrate an understanding of Earth's interconnected life systems with sustainable social, political, and economic systems that enhance the Earth community. Books in the series concentrate on ways to:

- Reexamine human–Earth relations in light of contemporary cosmological and ecological science.
- Develop visions of common life marked by ecological integrity and social justice.
- Expand on the work of those exploring such fields as integral ecology, climate justice, Earth law, ecofeminism, and animal protection.
- Promote inclusive participatory strategies that enhance the struggle of Earth's poor and oppressed for ecological justice.
- Deepen appreciation for dialogue within and among religious traditions on issues of ecology and justice.
- Encourage spiritual discipline, social engagement, and the transformation of religion and society toward these ends.

Viewing the present moment as a time for fresh creativity and inspired by the encyclical *Laudato Si'*, the series seeks authors who speak to ecojustice concerns and who bring into this dialogue perspectives from the Christian communities, from the world's religions, from secular and scientific circles, or from new paradigms of thought and action.

JUST WATER

Theology, Ethics, and Fresh Water Crises

REVISED EDITION

By

Christiana Zenner

*(Author of Just Water: Theology, Ethics,
and the Global Water Crisis by Christiana Z. Peppard)*

ORBIS BOOKS

Maryknoll, New York 10545

 ORBIS BOOKS
Maryknoll, New York 10545

 Fathers and Brothers
MARYKNOLL™

Founded in 1970, Orbis Books endeavors to publish works that enlighten the mind, nourish the spirit, and challenge the conscience. The publishing arm of the Maryknoll Fathers and Brothers, Orbis seeks to explore the global dimensions of the Christian faith and mission, to invite dialogue with diverse cultures and religious traditions, and to serve the cause of reconciliation and peace. The books published reflect the views of their authors and do not represent the official position of the Maryknoll Society. To learn more about Maryknoll and Orbis Books, please visit our website at www.maryknollsociety.org.

Library of Congress Cataloging-in-Publication Data

Names: Peppard, Christiana Z., author.
Title: Just water : theology, ethics, and global water crises / by Christiana Zenner.
Description: Revised edition. | Maryknoll, NY : Orbis Book, [2018] Series: Ecology and justice, an Orbis series on integral ecology | Includes bibliographical references and index.
Identifiers: LCCN 2018014083 (print) | LCCN 2018030177 (ebook) ISBN 9781608337637 (e-book) | ISBN 9781626982970 (pbk.)
Subject: LCSH: Human rights—Religious aspects—Catholic Church. | Right to water. | Human ecology—Religious aspects—Catholic Church.
Classification: LCC BT738.15 (ebook) | LCC BT738.15 .P47 2018 (Print) | DDC 261.8/8—dc23
LC record available at http://lccn.loc.gov/2018014083

Contents

Acknowledgments . . . . *ix*

Prelude: Writing Water . . . . *xiii*

Chapter 1
Theology and Ethics for the New Millennium:
The Catholic Church from Globality to Planetarity 1

Catholic Theologies Turn to the World 2
An "Effective Theology" 5
Environment and Ecology in Catholic Social Teaching 10
Pope Francis and Laudato Si':
    On Care for Our Common Home (2015). 13
The Thorny Problem: Universal Moral Claims and
    Particular Contexts 15
Embodied Experience and the Turn to Ecology. 19
Diversity, Plurality, and Marginality in Theology and Ethics 24
Conclusion: Theology, Ethics, and Fresh Waters 26

Chapter 2
A Primer on Global Fresh Water Crises. .28

A Primer on Global Fresh Water Trends .30
Conclusion: Facts, Frameworks, and Fatigue in
    Pursuit of Just Water 48

Chapter 3
Water: Human Right or Economic Commodity? 51

Message in a Bottle 52
What Kind of Thing Is Water?. 59
Bolivian Water War?. 62
Conclusion: Valuing Water. 67

Chapter 4

A Right-to-Life Issue for the Twenty-First Century. 68

Catholic Social Teaching: The Church's "Best-Kept Secret" 69
Fresh Water in Catholic Social Teaching—Eight Insights 72
Conclusion: A Right-to-Life Issue for the Twenty-First Century. 84

Chapter 5

The Agriculture/Water Nexus 86

Making Water Visible from Seed to Supper:
    Virtual Water and Water Footprints 86
A Brief History of Agriculture, from Prehistory to
    the Produce Aisle. 89
Ecological Consequences: Depleted Groundwater and Soils. 100
Rethinking Industrial Agriculture in the Face of
    Hydrological Reality 108
Water, Agriculture, and Theological Ethics 112
Conclusion: Radicalism and Incrementalism 116

Chapter 6

Climate Change and Water in the Anthropocene 118

Geology, the Anthropocene, and Climate Change 118
Climate Change, Scientific Uncertainty, and Matters of Faith 123
The Climate/Water Nexus. 131
Conclusion: Anthropogenic Climate Change and Water 145

Chapter 7

Water from Rock: Standing Rock and *Laudato Si'*. 146

The Dakota Access Pipeline, Standing Rock, and Mni Wiconi 148
Laudato Si': The Value(s) of Water and a Papal Turn to
    Indigenous Knowledge 157
Water Justice and Indigenous Knowledge between
    Laudato Si' and Standing Rock. .161
Conclusion: Who Speaks for Water? .164

Chapter 8
The Jordan River. 168

    The Shape of the Jordan River Today. 169
    Religious Rhetoric and Riparian Reality 176
    Conclusion: Bodies of Water. 184

Chapter 9
Women, Wells, and Living Water 191

    Current Biblical Hermeneutics and the Woman at the Well. 193
    Deconstructing and Historicizing Water 196
    "Her Daily Toil": Women and Water Worldwide 201
    Conclusion: Thirst 205

Coda: Lessons in Liquidity 209
Notes. 214
Further Resources. 241
Index. 249

Acknowledgments

Returning to a previously published volume in order to update ideas, analyses, and normative assessments is an intellectual enterprise as well as a personal one. I am grateful to Orbis Books for the opportunity, both for their belief in this book from the outset with editors Sue Perry and Jim Keane, and now with Jill O'Brien. Robert Ellsberg has been a source of humor, insight, and goodwill throughout. Maria Angelini and copyeditor Teresa Jesionowski made correcting the manuscript into a fun task. Thank you, all.

I proposed a revised edition of *Just Water* because data and social developments needed attention; the encyclical *Laudato Si'* had entered Catholic environmental and social discourse in ways that amplified my initial claims about the magisterial Catholic Church's advocacy on matters of fresh water (and, happily, confirmed much of what I had hypothesized in the first edition), and scholarly conversations and publications between 2014 and 2018 enriched my thinking and reshaped some of its contours. As a result, many claims put forward in the first edition of *Just Water* became more precisely honed while others were jettisoned entirely: for example, all chapters dealing directly with theology and Catholic social teaching have been revised to include *Laudato*

Si'. The chapter formerly dedicated to hydraulic fracturing has been replaced by a chapter on extractive industry and indigenous values at Standing Rock in light of *Laudato Si'* and US legacies of settler colonialism. The public health and environmental racism conflagration in Flint, Michigan, has been incorporated into chapter 9. Criticisms of the Anthropocene concept now appear in chapter 6; that chapter as well as others were reordered for a more elegant flow. Other minor adjustments and updates to data percolate throughout the chapters.

As in the first volume, several chapters reflect and rework previously published material:

"Fresh Water and Catholic Social Teaching: A Vital Nexus," *Journal of Catholic Social Thought* 9, no. 2 (Summer 2012): 325–51.

"Troubling Waters: The Jordan River between Religious Imagination and Environmental Degradation," *Journal of Environmental Studies and Sciences* 3, no. 2 (2013): 109–19.

"Commentary on *Laudato Si'*," in *Modern Catholic Social Teaching: Essays and Commentaries*, edited by Kenneth Himes, SJ (Washington, DC: Georgetown University Press, 2018).

"*Laudato Si'* and Standing Rock: Water Justice and Indigenous Ecological Knowledge," chapter 12 in *Theology and Ecology Across the Disciplines*, edited by Celia Deane-Drummond and Rebecca Artinian-Kaiser (New York: Bloomsbury, 2018).

I gratefully acknowledge the permission granted by Bloomsbury Press to adapt and reprint "*Laudato Si'* and Standing Rock" in its entirety from *Theology and Ecology Across the Disciplines,* appearing here as "Water from Rock: Standing Rock and *Laudato Si'*" (chapter 7).

The first version of *Just Water* aimed for legibility to and (quite frankly) approval from my tenure committee—while also striving for salience within scholarly conversations and accessibility to broader audiences. Perhaps only a neophyte would aspire to such varied aims, but the project seems to have worked well enough for what I hoped the book might be, even while there is always more to be said and much that could be said in far greater and more critical detail. I remain grateful to the institutions, communities, and individuals in whose company and conversation I inhabited the voice of the first edition of this book. These entities include Fordham University, Villanova University, Dominican University, and the Cathedral of St. John the Divine. Intervening years have seen many more lectures, conversations, and personal as well as professional developments; so I add my thanks to the following institutions that graciously hosted me in one capacity or another and provided a platform for discussing ideas contained in this revised version of *Just Water:* Barry University, Nazarene College, University of the Pacific, Georgetown University, Trinity Church Wall Street, MindBodyGreen and 1Hotel Brooklyn, the College of St. Benedict and St. John's University, Siena College, Viterbo University, Yale Divinity School, and the Catholic Theological Society of America.

Individuals acknowledged in the first edition of *Just Water* are honored here implicitly for the integrity and support they offered at the time. Then and since I have received excellent research assistance from Meg Stapleton-Smith, Vanessa Williams, Christine McCarthy, Steven Payne, and Dorothy Chang. I am deeply grateful to Karina Martin Hogan and J. Patrick Hornbeck II for sensitive leadership of our department in transitional times. In the four years since *Just Water* was first published in 2014, many relationships deepened with laughter or seriousness; others dissipated by geography and dynamisms of self-development. I honor much that Michael Peppard and I worked on as colleagues and co-parents, and I am consistently and ebulliently delighted by our remarkable daughter who embodies enormous spunk and tenacity in the face of intractable problems such as fresh water scarcity, climate change, and middle school. Colleen and Jason Wachob have steadily advocated for the salience and desirability of my work, goaded me onto Twitter, and continue to remind me to trust the process. Thanks to Twitter, my scholarly and social lives are immeasurably enriched by flights of rigor and fancy on this open platform, where water folks have kept me laughing and pondering fluid topics through the tenure process in a Department of Theology. Raul Pacheco-Vega is possibly the world's most patient co-author and assuredly a beacon of intellectual generosity as well as a dear friend. Thanks are due to Drew FitzGerald, whose talent in naming companies (JUST water) at first irked and then prompted me to consider more fully the implications of social good capitalism, despite the fact that bottled water is a direct object of critique in chapter 3. The ladies Zenner and their spouses have been present and a source of great laughter and solidarity in ways I never would have imagined five years ago: what a gift! My home-front tribe of Susan Burlazzi, Kirsten Aghen, Kimberly Kraus, and Lou Ann Hesch have made so very many things possible: thank you. Ben Dunning, Bob Davis, Jeni Rinner, Jennifer Boutin Carroll, and Richmond Eustis: infinite are the blessings of your friendship. I love that you love my nerdy jokes.

This version of *Just Water* is ultimately dedicated to a core group of brilliant, insightful women without whom there would have been no revision of life or publications: Kathryn Reklis, Leigh Marcus, and Meghan Clark. Thank you for reminding me that my versions matter, and how magnificent are the fluid dynamics of the heart.

Prelude

Writing Water

This book is an interdisciplinary analysis of the significance of fresh water in an era of economic globalization that draws on multivalent resources within a range of disciplines, including theology, ecology, ethics, Catholic social thought, environmental humanities, religion and science, social theory, and human geography. Aimed at the educated nonspecialist as well as scholars who work across disciplinary boundaries, *Just Water* seeks to inform readers of important aspects of global fresh water crises while also providing trenchant, ethical analysis and principled recommendations about fresh water use and scarcity in the twenty-first century. The goal is to render water visible in complex, nuanced ways, and at the same time to offer tools for adjudicating contemporary ethical problems posed by the looming century of fresh water scarcities. As the chapters in this book make clear, there are a number of vital issues pertaining to fresh water: from the hydrological optimism of industrial agriculture to the effects of climate change; from the challenge of new, extractive technologies to the disproportionate burdens that domestic water procurement places on women worldwide.

As a professor of theology, science, and ethics, I employ the Christian tradition—and particularly Catholic social thought—as a primary tradition of moral interlocutors throughout the book. For this reason, chapter 1 explains the relationship between theology and ethics in the twenty-first century and specifies how fresh water is an apt substance for consideration. Readers who are interested primarily in understanding how to think about global fresh water scarcities might move directly to chapter 2, which is a detailed yet brief and digestible primer on global fresh waters. It is necessary reading for all subsequent chapters. Chapter 3 depicts a central debate in the political economy of water: Is fresh water a human right or an economic commodity? This groundwork leads into chapter 4, which develops a set of principled insights about the value of fresh water from recent Catholic social teaching. Building on this interdisciplinary foundation are chapters that articulate key twenty-first-century challenges for fresh water supply: agriculture (chapter 5) and anthropogenic climate change (chapter 6). Subsequent chapters amplify and deepen the analysis by focusing on the claims that "water is life" heard at Standing Rock, in conversation with the papal encyclical *Laudato Si'* (chapter 7), the idea and reality of the contemporary Jordan River (chapter 8), and how water's burdens intersect both symbolically and practically with gender, and with histories of racial difference and social class (chapter 9). The Coda outlines key principles and insights gleaned from the book as a whole, but the nature of this text prevents comprehensive summary.

There is also always more to be said about fresh water, which brims with associations and meanings and tends toward diffusion. For ease of navigability and coherence to interdisciplinary audiences I have tried to minimize supplemental discussion of internal scholarly debates, and this means I have limited scholarly citations in the endnotes. This decision surely confers greater navigability on the narrative, but it also means that some relevant texts and debates are not directly referenced, and so until a different sort of book is published I will have to trust that those who are specialists on any of the given topics will infer the array of interlocutors looming behind each paragraph. Should nonspecialists desire further information on various topics, a list of additional resources is at the end of the book, organized under broad thematic categories.

Just Water is a rigorous, interdisciplinary analysis of a slippery topic. At best, it may offer some resources for resisting—or ameliorating—the often invisible, and always egregious, pains of the shackles of contemporary economic globalization and environmental degradation. One hermeneutic should be clear from the outset: fresh water is vital, and the burdens of its pollution or absence are experienced most acutely by those whose bodies unjustly bear its weight.

Chapter 1

Theology and Ethics
for the New Millennium

The Catholic Church from Globality to Planetarity

More than any other period in human history, the twentieth century incarnated globality. It was a period in which political, economic, and technological power manifested in profound and complicated ways, as ideologies and totalitarian tendencies led to the Holocaust, World War II, and nuclear détente. DNA was discovered; hormonal birth control was invented; women won the right to vote in some parts of the world; and the entire human genome was mapped. Tens of thousands of species, from plants and microbes to nematodes and charismatic megafauna like the Arizona jaguar or the California brown bear, were extinguished from the face of the earth as a direct result of human activity. Many colonized peoples and nations across the globe asserted and regained political independence from their European colonizers. Human rights were invented and civil rights were sought against the constraints of traditional injustices based on race, class, sex, or creed. Economic globalization amplified and diversified patterns of power and privilege; natural resources were extracted at an unprecedented rate and scale, and finance was decoupled from the gold standard and became speculative. The computer and the Internet revolutionized communications. Human knowledge of the world grew secular, thanks to advances in the natural sciences—and also differently religious than in previous centuries. Fundamentalism and atheism flourished.

Photographs of the earth from space revealed this planet to be a small, blue orb amid a vast darkness, and astrophysicists confirmed that earth is a much smaller part of the cosmos than previously imagined. Evolutionary biology and the ecological sciences have crested into public consciousness and presented human beings as potent parts of planetary earth systems dynamics. And now, in the first half of the twenty-first century, the idea of globality has opened into *planetarity*: a recognition of the breadth and depth of earth systems and ecosystems, as well as the massive-scale impacts and presumptions of capitalist-oriented, fossil-fuel-driven societies.

Such factors form a matrix on which Western, Christian religious traditions have developed their theologies in the mid- to late-twentieth century and are now grappling with the realities of the twenty-first. It may seem odd to begin a book on water with a tour of major trends and concepts in Catholic theologies of the twentieth and twenty-first centuries. But there are real—if indirect and contested—ecological and social outcomes that follow from various concepts and paradigms by which philosophies, religions, cultures, and societies organize their perceptions of reality. This chapter provides an intellectual history of how Catholic theology turned to the world and, more recently, the planet—in conversation with important themes such as economic globalization, diversity and pluralism, and embodiment and ecology.

Catholic Theologies Turn to the World

After the 1950s, the Roman Catholic Church faced down the fact of its immersion in—and necessary relationship with—the shape of the contemporary world. The twentieth-century Catholic Church, both institutionally and theologically, pivoted around the Second Vatican Council (1962–65). As a result of that three-year conclave of reflection, Catholic theologians were charged with turning "towards the world" to engage with particular dynamics of social, political, economic, scientific, and cultural life. In the words of *Gaudium et Spes*, one of the Pastoral Constitutions of the Second Vatican Council: "We must therefore recognize and understand the world in which we live, its explanations, its longings, and its often dramatic characteristics. . . . Today, the human race is involved in a new stage of history."[1] Catholic theologians, in various ways and various contexts, began to articulate how the church could no longer reasonably view its institutions and theological dogma as entirely separate from economics, politics, and society.

The Second Vatican Council is known for inaugurating not only a shift in liturgical sensibilities—allowing the Mass to be said in the vernacular and the priest to face the congregation, for example—but also in theological methodology. Fodder for theological reflection began to surface, so to speak, as theologians were encouraged to read the "signs of the times" in the service of the world church. The laity's contributions to theological reflection became more pronounced: women received doctorates in fields traditionally open only to men and claimed a place in theological and ethical discourse within and outside of the patriarchal institution. To some degree, the Catholic Church also became more aware of its own pluralities—beyond the confines of white, European, male leadership—as priestly vocations declined in Europe and North America, and the demographics of religious affiliation shifted dramatically toward the global South.

Global complexity, diversity, power, and knowledge also shaped the formal practices of theology in the twentieth century. For example, the fallibility of human knowledge has been a persistent issue, as scientific knowledge and social scientific analyses have challenged claims of theological objectivity and universalism. Another important development is that as new idioms and insights emerged from interactions among the church, its mottled history, and vexing social issues, theology and ethics have become tightly intertwined. New, specific issues were explored in formal, magisterial reflection (on topics such as birth control, nuclear proliferation, communism, and capitalism). Dominant forms of theological, moral, and ethical reflection were both invigorated and transformed, because these new issues presented problems that transcended traditional modes of analysis. For many theologians, no small part of twentieth- and now twenty-first-century inquiry is to explore whether the "method of responding and the operative theological presuppositions are adequate to the task," as James Keenan, SJ, nicely put it.[2]

One persistent question for twentieth-century Catholic theology and ethics was: What does it mean to be a good neighbor, to recognize and respond to one's fellow humanity in need? The quandary, presented in the parable of the Good Samaritan in the Gospel of Luke in the New Testament, has been a source of theological reflection for millennia. Karl Rahner, a towering figure in Catholic theology in the twentieth century, suggested that this question is encountered by every generation. But because every generation is in some ways unique, love of neighbor

> exhibits a true historicity. . . . Concrete love of neighbor, necessarily and constantly, takes on ever new forms in history, one after another, in accordance with the diversity of human beings and their varying historical situations. But history and historical development are not simply the development, the unfolding, of what is known to have gone before. History is always providing surprises. The same will be true, then, for the history of Christian love of neighbor. . . . This is why the Church too is constantly encountering new surprises in this area—colliding with demands and tasks for the love of neighbor alive within it with which it has never had to reckon before, tasks which it has simply never preached from the pulpit in the

"good old days"—tasks whose moment for Christianity has come but slowly to Christian consciousness.[3]

While the wisdom and witness of past generations are an important legacy, Rahner recognized that theological reflection "will constantly be confronted with new situations—with which it has never had to reckon until now, situations that have not always been represented in traditional, customary Christian religious discourse."[4] So while the injunction to love one's neighbor retains a timeless and universal sheen in Christian tradition, it is only within the particularities of history, geography, and culture that human beings can figure out what it means to love appropriately and well. The obligation should not be taken lightly, says Rahner, for in the Catholic tradition "love for God only comes to its own identity through its fulfillment in a love for neighbor."[5] In the twentieth and now twenty-first centuries, Keenan suggests theological ethics must examine "structures in the world, above all, with regard to globalization."[6]

An "Effective Theology"

Epochal events of the twentieth century left their mark on Catholic theology. The profound suffering and evil that occurred during World War II, coupled with the Vatican II charge to engage the "signs of the times," led to a growing interest in how well-honed theological claims contained ethical meaning in discrete historical contexts, including even social and political implications. This development—known generally as political theology—amplified the earlier, modernizing methodologies of *la nouvelle théologie*, which was an intellectual movement that had sought to expand theological reflection beyond a strict neo-Scholasticism. Teachers such as Karl Rahner, M. D. Chenu, and others shaped the mid-twentieth-century Catholic theological milieu; their influence continued to grow through the work of European political theologians such as J. B. Metz, as well as theologians from across the Atlantic. Indeed, some of the young men who went to Europe for their theological training during the 1950s and 1960s from Central and South America brought to their theological studies a vast array of experience with suffering—not the suffering of World War II and the Holocaust, but rather rampant poverty, economic stratification, and ongoing political oppression. Many of these priests encountered economic theory and sociology that illuminated some of their experiences at home, recognizing a descriptive truth in Karl Marx's diagnosis that capitalist systems of social, economic, and political power rely on the ongoing oppression of an underclass. These priests had seen and lived in and ministered to the deplorable conditions of impoverished people, and they began to read the story of Jesus's life, crucifixion, and resurrection as a rebuttal of those forms of oppression, calling Christians to work for justice in the current world.

Gustavo Gutiérrez first articulated these claims in book-length form with his justly famous analysis of poverty and theology, *A Theology of Liberation: History, Politics, Salvation* (1971). Poverty, according to Gutiérrez, must be understood not just as a spiritual condition but also—indeed, primarily—as a historical, material, and dehumanizing reality. Economic, social, and political structures enshrine patterns of privilege and poverty, but they run counter to the Gospel message. As Jon Sobrino wrote, the result of God's word being a historical event is that "the Son of Man is present in the poor of this world" in an ongoing way.[7] And the late Salvadoran priest Ignacio Ellacuría, who was murdered in 1989 for his views, wrote:

> Christians must insist that history is the locale of God's revelation, and that this revelation is meant to show us here and now that God is revealing himself in history. . . . Christianity must take seriously the thrust and import of the Word made flesh in history. . . . There is no access to God except through this sign in history.[8]

Ellacuría, like many of his fellow priests and theologians, gave a straightforward reason for this interpretation. Grounded in the Vatican II imperative to engage the "signs of the times," Ellacuría asserted that

> one should not be scandalized to find that the Church is continually learning what its concrete mission is by taking fresh readings of revelation in the changing reality of human history; and that it proclaims salvation in different ways, depending on different situations.[9]

Liberation, then, is to be understood in both the ultimate Christian theological sense of salvation as well as proximate social and economic senses. It does not equal a call to arms, but it does demand justice. In this approach, Jesus is understood as the savior, the enactment of salvation in history. He is the man scorned, beaten, oppressed by the dominant religious and political power structures of his day. The revelation continues in the lives of the poor to the present day and in the ethical demand to care for the least among us. For liberation theologians love of God is fundamentally interwoven with love of neighbor in an era characterized by economic, social, and political disparities. Because the poor are especially vulnerable, there is a "preferential option for the poor," an obligation to improve the lives of those who exist on the margins of society.[10] As Sobrino frames the obligation: it entails Christian recognition of "a certain basic minimal [ethical] content: a just life worthy of a human being. We might call it an economic and sociological opportunity."[11]

This is a vision informed by sociological and economic analysis, but its aims are not politically utopian. It is neither a call to violent revolution nor an endorsement of communism: it "does not allow for a cool and calculated strategy aimed at the overthrow of the oppressor and the acquisition of power by the poor."[12] Nor do liberation theologies expect that human efforts will bring about a perfect world. The insight is simpler, more basic, and thus more profound: creedal statements of belief must manifest as praxis. One must walk the walk, not just talk the talk. In Ellacuría's words, liberation theology is an "effective theology," where theology and ethics become inextricable.[13] It is theology as action oriented to the well-being of vulnerable populations, especially people living in poverty.

Not everyone has been convinced of these claims. Critiques of liberation theology query: Does liberation theology inappropriately focus on salvation as a historical, material event? Does it succumb to Marxist ideology? Does it sanction violence? Dialogue on these matters has been both civil and severe. In the 1980s, the Vatican's Congregation for the Doctrine of the Faith (under the direction of Joseph Ratzinger, who later became Pope Benedict XVI) questioned and sought clarification on aspects of liberation theology. But it is now clear that the legacy of liberation theology is vital for Catholic theology in the twenty-first century. By linking theological reflection with rigorous analysis of economic and social structures of globalization, liberation theology took seriously the "signs of the times." It allowed theologians to speak not just about individual charity, contrition, or sinful acts, but also about power, privilege, and structures of sin.[14] By emphasizing how the love of neighbor must take shape in history, it reframed relationships between ethics and theology and drew vital connections between faith and action. In the summary analysis of Elizabeth Johnson:

> Naming God the liberator does not just craft one more symbol to add to the treasury of divine images. It puts a question mark next to every other idea of God that ignores the very concrete suffering of peoples due to economic, social, and politically structured deprivation. Thus, this call for the praxis of justice is important not just for the faith of Latin Americans but for the faith of the worldwide church. In a particular way it challenges the complacency of Christians in the affluent countries of

the Northern and Western hemispheres to acknowledge and take responsibility for our participation in institutional and structural injustice in the global economy.[15]

The pursuit of justice is a basic implication of liberation theology as an "effective theology." The reverberations of this insight will likely frame the work of theologians and the institutional Catholic Church throughout the twenty-first century.

Already, insights from liberation theology have been woven into the fabric of Catholic teaching at the highest levels. Official Catholic social teaching, for example, has incorporated notions such as the preferential option for the poor, subsidiarity, and solidarity into its formal operating principles. At the top of the Vatican hierarchy, since 1967 many papal encyclicals have called for adjustments to global economic systems in light of their negative consequences on the lives of the poor (see chapter 4). Therefore, those who would eschew or minimize the insights of liberation theology would do well to take heed of magisterial authorities, especially addresses by Pope Emeritus Benedict XVI and Pope Francis: Consider Pope Benedict XVI's 2013 Message for the World Day of Peace:

Fifty years after the beginning of the Second Vatican Council, which helped to strengthen the Church's mission in the world, it is heartening to realize that Christians, as the People of God in fellowship with him and sojourning among mankind, are committed within history to sharing humanity's joys and hopes, grief and anguish, as they proclaim the salvation of Christ and promote peace for all. In effect, our times, marked by globalization with its positive and negative aspects, as well as the continuation of violent conflicts and threats of war, demand a new, shared commitment in pursuit of the common good and the development of all men, and of the whole man. It is alarming to see hotbeds of tension and conflict caused by growing instances of inequality between rich and poor, by the prevalence of a selfish and individualistic mindset which also finds expression in an unregulated financial capitalism.[16]

Indeed, as Elizabeth Johnson aptly observes, "rarely has the core project of a theology been so quickly and widely adopted into mainstream social teaching" in the Catholic Church.[17] What does this mean for Christians who strive to attend to social responsibility in everyday life? One approach is to cultivate a resolute attention to the lives and needs of people who exist on the underside of history—an attention that begins with listening. Maureen O'Connell, for example, suggests that

> with our faces turned to the faces of those who suffer, we discover that our ability to articulate universal truths about human nature and life in community is constantly evolving and dependent on the wisdom that we gain through relationships with people quite different from ourselves. . . . Political compassion forbids those who seek a global approach to ethics to glaze over these shortcomings but rather compels them to examine them for the insights they hold.[18]

This interweaving of theology and ethics in the concrete contexts of human life and global economic structures has become a persistent theme in the first decade of Pope Francis's leadership as pontiff of the Catholic Church.

Environment and Ecology in Catholic Social Teaching

Paul VI was the first pope to address the UN on matters of environmental degradation, as Marjorie Keenan notes in her anthology of papal teachings on the environment.[19] The idea that collective human activities damage nature and could subsequently entail the possibility of the self-destruction of humankind emerged in the papal encyclical *Octogesima Adveniens* (1971) and has recurred throughout subsequent Catholic social teaching. Numerous addresses, letters, and encyclicals during the papacies of John Paul II and Benedict XVI developed these themes. But it is inaccurate to depict Catholic magisterial tradition before 1990 as self-consciously or consistently concerned with matters ecological. As Columban priest and missionary Sean McDonagh observed in 1990, "It is a fact of recent history that the Church has been slow to recognize the gravity of the ecological problems of the earth."[20]

A fuller ecological focus can be dated to that same year, when John Paul II identified a "lack of due respect for nature" in his papal *Message for the World Day of Peace*, a speech in which the pontiff clearly noted that the "ecological crisis" is "a moral problem" and identified a "human vocation to participate responsibly in God's creation."[21] Also in the 1990 message, John Paul II stipulated themes of interconnectedness and responsibilities to future generations ("we cannot interfere in one area of the ecosystem without paying due attention both to the consequences of such interference in other areas and to the well-being of future generations");[22] identified the importance of recognizing that the earth is a gift from God and thus a common heritage meant for the benefit of all; called for solidarity between industrialized and developing nations; restated the fundamental need to respect life; and asserted that there is a "right to a safe environment" that "must be included in an updated Charter of Human Rights" and attained through international collaborations.[23] These themes have percolated through subsequent papal documents, including especially the encyclicals *Sollicitudo Rei Socialis* (1987) and *Centesimus Annus* (1991), both promulgated by John Paul II, and to a lesser degree *Evangelium Vitae* (1995).

In 2002, John Paul II collaborated with the environmentally minded Ecumenical Patriarch Bartholomew, who has since assuming the Patriarchate of the Orthodox Church made ecological issues a signature theological and pastoral charism. The two leaders cosigned the "Common Declaration on Environmental Ethics," expressing serious concern about human suffering and "the negative consequences for humanity and for all creation resulting from the degradation of some basic natural resources such as water, air and land, brought about by an economic and technological progress which does not recognize and take into account its limits."[24] Constructively, they noted that "Christians and all other believers have a specific role to play in proclaiming moral values and in educating people in ecological awareness, which is none other than responsibility towards self, towards others, towards creation." They asserted: "What is required is an act of repentance on our part and a renewed attempt to view ourselves, one another, and the world around us within the perspective of the divine design for creation. The problem is not simply economic and technological; it is moral and spiritual."[25] In 2015, Pope Francis's encyclical *Laudato Si'* foregrounded the ecological charism of the Orthodox patriarchate, and Francis and Bartholomew issued a joint statement on September 1, 2017, which is now shared by both churches as the decreed Day of Prayer for the Environment.

In 2004 the Pontifical Council for Justice and Peace (PCJP) promulgated the official *Compendium of the Social Doctrine of the Church*, which devoted one chapter to the intersection of Catholic social teaching (CST) and the environment.[26] Pope Benedict XVI continued the trajectory after his election in 2005 by linking ideas of authentic or integral development, human ecology, and environmental degradation and sensitivity to the vulnerable and suffering in an era of economic globalization and technical power. In particular, chapter 4 of his encyclical *Caritas in Veritate* (2009) addressed "the development of people, rights and duties, and the environment."[27] Concern for environmental degradation as a part of disordered economic and political relationships, an emphasis on interrelated human and environmental ecologies, and the obligations of highly developed nations to take up duties of effectual solidarity are all themes that appear in *Caritas in Veritate*.[28]

The twentieth century also saw a proliferation of statements on the intersection of environmental and social well-being by regional bishops' conferences. When Pope Francis issued *Laudato Si'* (*LS*), scholarly commentators quickly observed that in citing a variety of bishops' conferences, Pope Francis seemed to be modeling a participatory and regionally specific environmental and social epistemology—always framed, of course, within broader Catholic teachings about God and human beings.

Pope Francis and *Laudato Si'*: *On Care for Our Common Home* (2015)

Initial years of Pope Francis's leadership of the Catholic Church were characterized by steady commentary and moral exhortation on problems of poverty, economic structures that privilege the rich over the poor, and concern for ecology. His especially potent charism for ecological issues was signaled, first, by his selection of the name "Francis," and his musing in the inaugural papal address that, "these days we do not have a very good relationship with Creation, do we?"[29]

Prior to his election to the papacy, Cardinal Bergoglio had witnessed and engaged situations of extreme poverty and the impacts of environmental degradation during his years in South America, and his pastoral experiences overlapped temporally with the rise of liberation theology. While Bergoglio's historical relationship to liberation theology is complicated, the pope has also made clear his commitment to stances such as the preferential option for the poor and critiques of structural (especially political and economic) forms of oppression that exclude many people from meaningful opportunities and basic conditions of human dignity. Francis notes that "twenty percent of the world's population consumes resources at a rate that robs the poor nations and future generations of what they need to survive."[30] Soon after assuming the pontificate, Francis met with liberation theologian Gustavo Gutiérrez and sought input from former Franciscan priest Leonardo Boff.[31] The convergence of the pope's personal-pastoral charism and the trajectory of magisterial reflection on ecology and environmental degradation since the 1990s has proved potent. As McDonagh suggests: "Given this history, it was quite logical that Pope Francis would write an encyclical encompassing his critique of global poverty and his concern for what is happening to the earth."[32] The encyclical was met with critical acclaim, and Pope Francis now holds the honor of being the first pope to release myriad quotes from an encyclical over Twitter, while also addressing the encyclical to "every person living on this planet."[33]

Of course, although a charismatic pope has a particularly powerful pulpit, scholars and practitioners outside of the magisterium—and in varying relationships of proximity or distance, embrace, or détente with regard to official church leadership—have long identified important themes and offered trenchant, constructive analyses on topics related to environmental concern, often informed by developments in the natural and social sciences. For example, although official Catholic teaching has been resolutely anthropocentric (that is, focused primarily on human well-being) in the modern era, scholars decades ago began to argue persistently that Catholic teachings on creation are not only anthropocentric but are also theocentric, whereby care for the earth as a gift of God is a moral responsibility and wherein there is also room to appreciate nature as such because it is created and deemed good by God. Scholars working in ecological theology and Catholic social teaching, as well as in Christian and comparative theology more generally, have created robust contemporary discourses at the intersections of theology, ecology, and ethics. To name only a few, Thomas Berry, Elizabeth Johnson, Denis Edwards, Sean McDonagh, Celia Deane-Drummond, Rosemary Radford Ruether, Ivone Gebara, Leonardo Boff, Ilia Delio, John Hart, and John Haught have been consistent voices in Catholic theology who have advocated for ecological consciousness.[34]

It is also important to note that the ecclesial and social contexts into which *LS* was launched cannot be separated from Catholic demographic trends in general and institutional failures in particular. The world's Catholics constitute roughly half of all Christians and 16 percent of all religiously affiliated people.[35] These numbers are significant and globally dispersed, so it is important to note that patterns of Catholic adherence are shifting around the world. In Latin America, there is a significant number of people who report as Catholic (69 percent), but this is still a decline from previous years due to the rise of evangelical Protestant churches and the slow growth of religiously unaffiliated groups, and the Pew Research Center reports that "much of the movement away from Catholicism and toward Protestantism in Latin America has occurred in the span of a single lifetime."[36] Pew also reports that "among all US adults who were *raised* Catholic, half (52 percent) have left the church at some point in their life," and there is steady decline of Catholic affiliation in Europe as well as a rise in Catholic adherence in sub-Saharan Africa.[37] In terms of institutional failures, the Catholic Church (especially but not exclusively in the United States and Ireland) has faced major challenges to its integrity as a result of priestly sex abuse crises and various institutional complicities in covering up or protecting abusive priests. Disgust and disillusionment about priestly power and evasion of legal responsibility have led many people to question whether an institution that did not protect the vulnerable (in this case, children) from sexual predation has the authority to issue calls to ethical behavior on other matters.

The Thorny Problem:
Universal Moral Claims and Particular Contexts

Given the diversity of cultures and religions worldwide, with knowledge of the evils wrought upon human beings by totalitarian ideologies, racial bias, and economic colonization, how can one speak universally—about human nature, or morality, or flourishing, for example? Many astute theologians and ethicists have pondered this problem as they became aware of how notions of universality, often inherited from previous generations, have reified existing patterns of power and privilege. In order to speak of any universal realities, theology and ethics must be in conversation with, and accountable to, particular contexts and embodied experiences; in an era of profound diversity and plurality, it is insufficient to expound grand theories about humanity or human nature. Certainly, moral philosophers and theologians have long understood that the particular application of moral norms requires certain forms of prudential judgment, but it is also the case that, historically, those judgments have tended to be based on an idea of human nature that reflects the particular (often privileged) experience of narrow groups of people but nonetheless calls those descriptions "natural" or "universal" or "objective" or "obvious."

The quandary here, which Protestant theological ethicist Traci West puts squarely in her discussion of racism and women's lives, is that

> particular moral concerns can seem volatile and dependent upon varying circumstances. Universal ones seem like stable, unifying concerns that are completely independent from messy particularities. As Christians transform the ethical principles rooted in traditions of faith into daily actions that help to shape our society, exactly how is the link made between individual (particular) concerns and common (universal) ones?[38]

Although there is much to be said about different theological and ethical approaches to this issue, for the purposes of this chapter the focus will be on several theologians whose work has been influential in the Catholic Church. One approach that Catholic theologians have explored to remedy this problem can be found in the work of the late Dutch priest Edward Schillebeeckx. By the late 1970s, Schillebeeckx was a major thinker at the intersection of theology, philosophy, and social theory. During the course of his life, his theological writings garnered extraordinary praise as well as stringent criticism. Particularly noteworthy for our purposes is a revealing little essay, "Coordinates for an Anthropology," in which Schillebeeckx was vexed about making universal, theological claims in an era of globalization, diversity, and plurality. Aware of the twentieth century's excesses and indignities, he thought that one should avoid blithe, simplistic appeals to a universal human essence. With evident frustration and skepticism, he wrote:

> What is striking everywhere in our society is a facile speaking about the human subject, humanity in general, and universality. . . . Whoever is unaware of this ideological implication when analyzing basic human experiences . . . discovers a hierarchy of values in basic human experiences, values which are then called "universally human."[39]

Too often, observed Schillebeeckx, human beings are tempted to generalize about humanity from our own particular experiences. Certainly, experience teaches us quite a lot, and important lessons must be drawn from the challenges of living. Sometimes those lessons have implications far beyond the moral domain of individual action. However, Schillebeeckx warned, there is a danger: individual or cultural experience cannot always be generalized. And Western, European theology had been particularly susceptible to the illusion that it spoke for all of humanity. Liberation theology provided an important wake-up call to those who would listen; in Schillebeeckx's analysis, "Especially with the emergence of liberation theology . . . Western theologians came to the realization that their own theology has just as much sociocultural bias as any other."[40]

In other words, long-standing Western assumptions about human nature or universal features of humanity must be interrogated: Do they reflect the conditions of all persons, not just those in the lineage of European thought, other privileged communities, or self-interested positions of power? Without such interrogation, it is all too easy to assume that individual persons' or cultures' experiences are normative, universal, and even "natural." This is the source of Schillebeeckx's frustration with the language of human nature. But even so, Schillebeeckx did not want to give up on the idea that some commonalities to human experience could be articulated. True, any account of universal features of humanity had to be stripped of ideology (or any particular experience that paraded as universality). But it did not follow for him that the alternative was a relativistic embrace of plurality and diversity. Rather, he believed that despite our global diversity, there remain some shared features of human being and becoming. They ought to be articulated with caution, care, and considerable nuance. But how?

Schillebeeckx's remediating approach was to eschew the explicit language of "human nature" and "universality." Instead, he identified several domains in which human beings experience life. These "constants," as he called them, are basic. They include physical, embodied existence; immersion in a geographical location and environment; existence in a particular time period; and several other aspects. Each anthropological constant signals—though does not exhaust—a different dimension of human experience, without constraining its expression to a particular culturally bound form, and without concluding in advance what kinds of norms must necessarily follow.[41] In his view, they "point to [general], permanent human impulses and orientations, values and spheres of value." Yet what do those values mean for action? Schillebeeckx specifies that norms for action can arise only "in the context of . . . particular circumstances."[42] Thus, instead of asking the classical question, "What is human nature?" for Schillebeeckx the better question is, "What is a livable humanity?"

Any viable answer must consider these "anthropological constants" and the particular context in which they take shape. Hence it is only within the interplay of anthropological constants and context that "specific norms in the changing process of history" can be identified.[43]

What makes Schillebeeckx's work unique and important here is his concise attempt to navigate the paradox between the universal "anthropological constants" and the particular, local realities that shape human experience in concrete ways, because he navigated this dialectic earlier, and often more adroitly, than most theologians of his generation (and many since). One important consequence to highlight in Schillebeeckx's reasoning is that attention to the local or particular does not necessarily lead to relativism. Instead, Schillebeeckx insists that a cluster of "constants" exists. Parallel to liberation theologians' convictions that theology must be effective, even ethical, Schillebeeckx argues that anthropological constants reveal what is required for a "livable humanity" and what is central to theology. Yet these constants are always only understood, experienced, and mobilized into norms through a resilient attention to social, historical, and geographical realities. Context matters, but still, some things are universal. Embodied experience within ecological context is one such category.

Embodied Experience and the Turn to Ecology

Twentieth-century Catholic theology (as with Christian theology more generally) was also characterized by renewed attention to the bodily aspects of human experience. The sacramental theologian Louis-Marie Chauvet, for example, insisted that people "go to God not in spite of the heavy ambiguity of their humanity but at the very core of it; not in spite of their bodies—of desire, of tradition, of culture, of universe—but in their very bodies."[44] Theology, he suggests, cannot be disembodied. Although there are many tensions about the role of the body in Christian theology and ethics, the idea of embodiment also has an august history in Catholic tradition, with roots in classical Christian doctrines of both creation and incarnation. The significance of embodiment has been nuanced in the latter half of the twentieth century and the early part of the twenty-first in crucial ways by feminist theologians and ethicists and by those who take seriously the knowledge generated by modern science—especially with regard to ecology and environmental degradation. In a globalizing world characterized by ongoing white male privilege, colonial legacies, capitalist extractive tendencies, and rampant environmental degradation, theology—especially if it is to be an effective theology—must begin with the fundamental insight that bodies matter. In the twenty-first century, ecology is a frame within which embodiment discourses take robust ethical shape.

Ecology is the study of relationships among living beings, physical entities, and dynamic systems in a given domain or environment. Ecological theology is the attempt to articulate theological claims in light of that information. Ecological and environmental ethics represent the normative analysis and recommendations for frameworks and principles that can guide human actions. Thus, for example, ecological theologians remind us that embodiment—the condition of constitutive materiality—is not merely a human or creaturely phenomenon but also an ecological datum, since it is but a small step from our porous bodies to the created, evolving world that sustains us. How then ought we to relate to the world of which we are part? What social, political, and economic structures help or hinder environmental sustainability or ecological flourishing? The latter questions are classically ethical and have gained momentum as central claims in Catholic social teaching. Most dramatically, the promulgation of *LS* by Pope Francis has prompted the Catholic Church and also much of the world to consider how ecological responsibility, human flourishing, and religious faith are related: that encyclical, which is addressed to "every person living on this planet," is exceptionally clear that ecology is focused on relationships— between God and human beings, among human beings in various types of social structures, and between human beings and the earth that sustains us. These concerns are both theological and ethical. (I have written extensively about *LS* elsewhere, as noted in "Selected Additional Resources.")

Ecology helps reconfigure anthropology in several ways. First, in a cosmological frame: Denis Edwards reminds us that "scientific cosmology and evolutionary biology offer fundamental resources for an ecological theology of the human. They tell us a story of the human that was not available to theologians of the past. They situate the human in relation to the history of the universe and the history of life on earth."[45] In such a frame, *Homo sapiens* is a newcomer to the history of life on earth; yet through the generative dynamics of the Big Bang and the law of conservation of matter, it is the case that "quite literally, human beings and all creatures on this planet are made of stardust."[46] Second, human beings experience the world in our bodies. This is a quotidian reality, not just a philosophical claim, for we breathe the air surrounding us. We drink the water available to us. And, as the science of toxicology shows, we absorb the chemicals around us (see chapter 5). Through mouth and skin, we siphon the world in: Our gastrointestinal tracts, for example, are contiguous, open systems with the outside world. Whether we choose to recognize it or not, we are embodied and in relationship. Human beings are, literally and materially, shaped by our contexts. The world inscribes itself in us.

Such insights resonate with the first of Schillebeeckx's seven anthropological constants: the "relationship to human corporeality, nature, and the ecological environment."[47] Schillebeeckx was aware of human beings' reliance on the natural world; of human immersion in, and potential for destruction of, ecosystems; and of the ambiguous potential of technology.[48] He warned that we ignore this first anthropological constant at our own peril:

> If we take no account of this human reference in our
> action, then in the long term we shall dominate nature

or condition men [*sic*] in so one-sided a way that in
fact we shall destroy the fundamental principles of our
own natural world and thus make our own humanity
impossible by attacking our natural household or our
ecological basis.[49]

The capacity for human beings to degrade ecological bases of
our own existence is a theme that is now central in CST, since
the encyclicals of Benedict XVI and Francis. *LS,* after all, is sub-
titled "On Care for Our Common Home."

Scholars who employ the methods and insights of womanist,
Mujerista, queer, and feminist theology and ethics also continue
to shape the growing body of ecological theology and environmental ethics with crucial insights. Insofar as feminist theology
entails, in the words of Susan Ross, "a reverence for the earth
and for the body," feminist theologians can often adroitly depict
and expound on the significance of embodiment and ecological
sensibility while critiquing hierarchical, patriarchal, and dualistic
worldviews.[50] Feminist theorists point out that all human beings
are bodied creatures, living in and dependent on a material,
supple, and contingent world in which structures of power are
shaped by patriarchy and exploitation of the planet. For example, Rosemary Radford Ruether has offered consistent critical
insights into the theological and ethical significance of embodied interrelationships; Protestant theologian Sallie McFague, in
her book *The Body of God,* was an early voice pointing out how
reality is "composed of multitudes of embodied beings who
presently inhabit a planet that has evolved over billions of years
through a process of dynamic changes marked by law and nov-
elty into an intricate, diverse, complex, multileveled reality, all
radically interrelated and interdependent."[51]

A significant part of the task of ecological theology and
environmental ethics is to make visible the often uninterro-
gated assumptions about who human beings are in relation to

the natural world, as well as what sources of knowledge we take to be authoritative. All knowing, including ecological knowing, develops out of particular places and historical moments. Thus Ivone Gebara, in her book *Longing for Running Water: Ecofeminism and Liberation*, argues that "what we know, how we know it, and how we make it known are all related to the way in which we lead our lives and how we value our own lives and all lives."[52] In Gebara's analysis, we often do not recognize this truth "because it seems obvious that we live in a given place and that in that place we breathe, eat, walk, and sit. Furthermore, our senses are seldom educated to perceive this interdependence's great importance."[53] But what is simplest is sometimes also most profound. Thus Gebara advocates a "contextual epistemology":

> Contextual epistemology upholds the tension between the local aspect of human knowing and its universal character. Knowing anything is knowing it from within some concrete context. And it is precisely this local character, this quality of being spatiotemporally limited, that opens out into universality. Universality does not mean that a concrete knowing is valid for all human groups, but rather that all knowing has a universal localness about it. . . . In this sense, to speak of feminist and ecological epistemology is already to envision, perhaps in embryonic form, an understanding of the world that stands somewhat apart from our traditional notions.[54]

Likewise, my analyses suggest that fresh water is precisely the sort of substance—indeed, perhaps the substance par excellence—that illuminates the embodied, universal, and contextual character of human and ecosystemic existence. The presence or absence of clean, fresh water always shapes the realization of human, societal, ecosystemic, biotic, and planetary potentiality on many levels of scale and in a wide swath of contexts.

Diversity, Plurality,
and Marginality in Theology and Ethics

The human intellect—particularly the power of reason—is a crucial and valuable feature of human nature, one that renders our species distinct in some ways from other forms of life. Theologians such as Augustine and Aquinas theorized in great detail about the integral relationship between the human soul (classically understood as the seat of the intellect) and the sensate, corporeal body. But as some historians, ethicists, and theologians began to point out in the twentieth century, a hierarchical dualism between soul and body has permeated traditional accounts of what it means to be human. In binary fashion, the soul is usually seen as a superior power, associated with the intellect, rationality, and masculinity. The body, by contrast, is depicted as inferior and associated variously with emotions, porosity, death, and femininity. The binary as portrayed in these broad strokes is simplistic, but its various nuanced forms and historical manifestations have been very powerful.[55] (Even Charles Darwin, who revolutionized the very idea of human nature, could opine without apparent reproof that "the chief distinction in the intellectual powers of the two sexes is shewn by man's attaining to a higher eminence, in whatever he takes up, than woman can attain.")[56] Such assumptions have been roundly challenged since the mid-twentieth century, for a range of reasons, including feminist activisms and scholarship in decrying philosophical viewpoints that claim objectivity but instead reify masculinity, rationality, and patriarchy as normative ideals. These approaches have unmasked theological presuppositions that—under the guise of objectivity—lead to imbalanced, incomplete accounts of human nature and human flourishing. The most promising remedies to long-standing gaps in theological and moral anthropology have come from women and other scholars at the margins of normative, white, male, academic theology.

However—as black feminist, womanist, and Mujerista theologians have pointed out—some early expositors of feminism replicated the problem of exclusion. If theology were to be anything besides a transfer of power from the image of the white male to the image of the white female, then several things were necessary: epistemic humility, a healthy skepticism of universalizing language, and the ability to listen to and recognize the validity of others' experiences, particularly those persons who exist at the margins of society and who do not have a voice in elite discourses. This cannot be done from a place of pretend neutrality: white scholars in particular must beware the tendency to replicate the colonizing impulse of extracting insights from others without sufficiently honoring and amplifying the voices whose experiences undergird these "marginal" statements of theological truths. Calling out the privileges afforded to white scholars, such as myself, is an essential part of honest theological and ethical epistemology in the twenty-first century. It is the only way to stand and work in integrity and solidarity.

When such stances are adopted, the historical, culturally coded nature of mainstream theological discourses also becomes evident: far from being objective and given, they are instead constructed and negotiated (usually by people in positions of power and privilege). Scholarship from the so-called margins is committed to revealing such power dynamics and rectifying epistemological occlusions. Of course, experiences of marginalization vary depending on context, but some common themes emerge. Women of color tend to be disenfranchised from society by the intersecting factors of race, class, and gender. In an era of economic globalization, women and children in the global South bear the brunt of the world's productive labors and burdens. To attend to the particularity of people's lived experience is an important bulwark against the submersion of theology by ideology.

The aim is not to enshrine a vague, postmodern relativism, as some skeptics will claim. The aim is rather to address—responsibly, rigorously, and with full attention and accountability—"the unsteady interchange between particular differences and universal commonalities."[57] This does not mean that anything goes. To the contrary, many theologians who employ these methodologies point out that although deconstruction is an important move, it is not sufficient. Thus, for example, Emilie Townes has argued that particularity can be a "conscious touchstone" for "universality, but does not exhaust it."[58] Skepticism is warranted with regard to totalizing discourses about human nature, but the language of universal moral claims still matters. This paradoxical claim may strike some feminists and social theorists as dangerous; Margaret Farley has acknowledged how "concern for a ground of moral obligation may seem anachronistic and even harmful in a time when most of Western ethical theory has discredited or at least moved beyond so-called foundationalist interests."[59] But, despite the historical occlusions, some grounds for universal, moral obligation can be cautiously identified—though they may be far fewer and farther between than previously imagined. At the same time, only by paying attention to the diversity of embodied experiences in this world will activists, ethicists, and policymakers be able to speak cogently about whatever universals may persist; only then can members of society pursue a frank, honest, inclusive conversation about desirable and just paths of action.

Conclusion:
Theology, Ethics, and Fresh Waters

This book is about the ways in which theological and ethical paradigms for fresh water have emerged in distinct ways in several sets of discourses, and what might be learned at their intersections. Primary analysis in this book focuses on different ways that Catholic theologies and ethical pronouncements relate to emerging physical and social-scientific data on fresh water issues. In one sense, this book explains global fresh water crises and proffers ethical principles as well as concrete policy measures. At the same time, this book is not just about water. It is also an attempt to navigate the slippery relationship between universals and particulars (or constants and contexts) that has so vexed theology, ethics, and global discourse in the late twentieth and now twenty-first centuries. There are better ways to proceed than by ethical pinball between two dismal extremes of hegemonic universalism or relativistic impasse. Hence, *Just Water* strives to demonstrate a value universalism that is mediated by context. The challenge hovers in the dialectic: to specify values that can honor both universality and particularity and to navigate carefully their translation into norms.

Before proceeding further, it is important to come to a shared appreciation of some of the potent dynamics of global fresh water scarcities in the twenty-first century. The next chapter therefore presents a primer on fresh water, including key data and analytic concepts for aspects of global fresh water crises. Just as chapter 1 represents a foundation for understanding theology and ethics in the new millennium, so does the primer on fresh water offer a necessary foundation for understanding global fresh water scarcities and key conceptual tools that scholars currently use to understand the dynamics of this complex, slippery, and vital substance.

CHAPTER 2

A Primer on Global
Fresh Water Crises

Fresh water is the substance that constitutes a fundamental baseline of human existence. At birth, each person is composed of roughly 75 percent water and remains predominantly watery until death. Our aqueous bodies can survive not even a week without intake of fresh water. In individual, ecological, societal, civilizational, and evolutionary terms, fresh water is a foundation of existence. It is no exaggeration to say that in an ultimate sense, water charts human history. And threats of global fresh water scarcity have now catapulted into mainstream public consciousness in the United States and Europe. The evidence is, of course, in front-page features in the *New York Times* or the *Economist* that proclaim the dawn of an era of fresh water scarcity and global water crises. Manufacturers and many global businesses now recognize that the absence of a long-term water strategy is a recipe for financial failure. The World Economic Forum has since 2015 decreed fresh water scarcity to be among the top threats to global financial stability. Generals and governmental officials now identify climate change's waterborne impacts as key security threats. Pundits proclaim that wars of the future will be fought over water, not oil. And water-mediated inequalities are now visible, spawned in places from Detroit and Flint, Michigan, to Cochabamba, Bolivia. Meanwhile, bottled water sales continue to bring in millions of dollars for multinational corporations, even as "take back the tap" campaigns spring up at universities. Nongovernmental aid organizations, including numerous religious outreach projects, provide fresh water supply or infrastructure to people in need. Pope Francis has affirmed and strengthened the assertions of his predecessors that fresh water is a fundamental human right, even a right-to-life issue. And on World Water Day 2012, then-US Secretary of State Hillary Clinton asserted that "ensuring that everyone has the clean water they need to live and thrive has to be a high priority for all of us."[1]

In this century, there is already good reason to worry about shifting availability of fresh water supply. In North America alone, several consecutive seasons of drought in major agricultural regions have taken a toll on farmers' livelihoods and food prices. The state of California has faced droughts that result from diminished mountain snowpack, limited flows of the Colorado River, and increased agricultural demand. Studies demonstrate that snowmelt is decreasing over time, leading to more limited surface water. Aquifers that quench the thirst of farms and suburbs are rapidly declining in the Midwestern United States and on the Texas–Mexico border, as in many other places worldwide. Large-scale pollution of waterways as a result of extractive industries (including but not limited to fossil fuels) has occurred in South America, the Athabascan tar sands in Canada, and many other places worldwide. Non-point pollution from industrial agriculture has made parts of the Mississippi River toxic and created algal blooms in Lake Erie, as well as dead zones in the Gulf of Mexico.

The ascending furor over fresh water is in some ways a unique product of this particular historical moment: the Internet and digital communications have opened new ways for individuals, communities, institutions, and societies to communicate and connect on issues pertaining to economic globalization, water pricing and access, and pollution of fresh water sources. Coalitions seeking to support fresh water access for populations and ecosystems have sprung up around the world and include transnational institutions like UN-Water; water justice advocacy organizations like Blue Planet Project and Food and Water Watch; journalistic endeavors and think tanks like Circle of Blue; and a wide range of blogs and public forums where people with an Internet connection and a concern about fresh water can process information, congregate, and strategize. Still, although awareness and advocacy regarding fresh water has gone global in new ways, it is also fair to acknowledge that fresh water has long been an enduring human concern. For millennia, individuals and societies have focused on its availability or absence, and for good reason: without fresh water, there is no life. What is new in this millennium is the fear that, on a global scale, societies and individuals really could run out of it.

This book engages the topic of fresh water crises from the starting point of two foundational observations. First, fresh water is a baseline requirement for survival and flourishing—for human beings, societies, civilizations, and ecosystems—and, second, it is nonsubstitutable. In philosophical terms, it is *sine qua non* (an essential condition) and *sui generis* (unique in its characteristics). As a substance that is sui generis and sine qua non, fresh water is an ultimate variable in survival at all levels of scale. This kind of radical dependence can be invisible—and thus, unremarkable—when clean, fresh water is readily available. However, when clean, fresh water is scarce or difficult to obtain, or when waterways are polluted or run dry, then human bodily dependence and vulnerability are revealed. This chapter aims to provide readers with conceptual tools necessary to talk with sufficient skill about water crises, before we turn to ethical analysis.

A Primer on Global Fresh Water Trends

As a primer, this chapter is intended to be generally comprehensive but certainly not exhaustive: it is focused on trends and so will not be specific to all scenarios. Topics identified here generally receive fuller treatment in later chapters, where critical and constructive methods for ethical analysis are further developed, often in conversation with Catholic social teaching or theological discourses. Additional references on the general topic of fresh water can be found at the end of the book.

Crises—Plural

It is increasingly common to hear that the world is running out of fresh water, or that there is a global fresh water crisis. To some degree, this very general statement may be true. In other ways, it is profoundly simplistic, so much so as to be deceptive. Although more will be said about planetary dynamics of fresh water molecules in the chapter on climate change, what is important to remember at the outset of this book is that *there is no such thing as a global fresh water crisis in the singular.* Fresh water crises are always *plural:* that is, there are multiple causes and effects of the seemingly infinite variety of fresh water challenges around the world. It is one thing to proclaim that the world is running out of water. It is another thing entirely to specify how, and why, in what contexts, and with what effects on what sorts of populations and entities that rely on a given fresh water supply. It is best to refer to global fresh water crises in the plural; that way, we can begin to talk about the kind of crises, the sorts of proximal and distal causes, and the kinds of downstream consequences. Only then will viable, place-based solutions be found that are attentive to the variables shaping water scarcity in a given region or community.

But If You Must:
A Short Definition of "the Global Fresh Water Crisis"

Still, there are a few trends that stand out in the contemporary reality of fresh water scarcity. Fresh water is essential for every human being, society, and ecosystem. There is no substitute for it. Yet it represents less than 2.5 percent of all available water on earth. Current global rates of fresh water extraction and consumptive use are unsustainable, and the demand for fresh water continues to rise. Stated most succinctly: Causes of global fresh water scarcity are myriad and complex but can be traced to increased demand for fresh water, coupled with unsustainable rates of extraction and consumption of fresh water (especially from nonrenewable groundwater sources such as deep aquifers). These dynamics have emerged decisively since the mid-twentieth century.

How Much Fresh Water Is There in the World?

This blue planet seems watery, but of all the water in the world, 97.5 percent is salt water, while only 2.5 percent is fresh water. Of that tiny proportion of fresh water, 70 percent is locked in ice caps and the polar regions. Nearly 30 percent is groundwater (about which more will be said shortly), and a mere 0.3 percent of all fresh water is surface water, or what we tend to think of as the "renewable" water supply.[2]

Current Demand for Fresh Water

Twentieth-century human thirst exceeded all previous withdrawals of fresh water on a global scale. According to UN-Water, "Water use has been increasing at more than twice the rate of population increase in the last century," and the rate of withdrawal is expected to increase even more in the twenty-first century.[3] In the past fifty years, fresh water withdrawals have more than tripled. One estimate holds that contemporary "demand for fresh water is increasing by 64 billion cubic meters per year."[4] There are several interrelated reasons for this increase, including the global economic development that has led to improved standards of living for many people. Improved standards of living are, in general, a good thing. But as more and more people achieve a level of affluence, more demand is placed on fresh water supply; as analysts Peter Rogers and Susan Leal observe, "Affluence drives up consumption." Leading the way "with the largest water footprint," they explain, is the United States; and "as the better-educated and higher-paid populations of China and India ascend into the middle class, they are increasing their water footprint, too."[5]

Consumption can be illuminated further by the notion of "virtual water" or, more specifically, the "water footprint," which is a measure of how much water is consumed in the generation or production of a given product. Think, for example, of two products that are demanded by residents of economically affluent societies: meat and microchips. Each is the kind of thing that people buy when they are not living at a subsistence level, but rather when they have some expendable income. Beef is an agricultural product: to produce a pound of beef requires approximately 1,799 gallons of water (for the cow to drink, of course, but also to grow the grain that feeds the cow, to process the beef product, and so forth). Microchips are industrial products: one microchip requires roughly 32 gallons of water to be produced. Certainly this is a smaller water footprint than the pound of beef, but it is still significant when considered in light of the prominence of computing and digital communication devices around the world.[6] In other words, as societies become more economically prosperous, the consumption of water tends to increase with demand for products of both agriculture and manufacturing.

Water Use by Sector: 70–22–8

Currently, the vast majority of the world's fresh water goes to agriculture (70 percent), followed by industrial uses such as manufacturing (22 percent), and trailed distantly by domestic uses (8 percent).[7] There is considerable variance for particular countries or regions. Industrialized nations, for example, tend to devote more water to industry; low- and middle-income nations tend to devote the vast majority of their water to agriculture. Climate and hydrology are also factors. Still, global fresh water withdrawals by sector can be summarized with the ratio of 70–22–8 (agriculture–industry–domestic). These proportions are helpful in recalling that not all uses of water are equally detrimental or consumptive of fresh water supply.

Key Terms:
Water Withdrawals, Consumptive Use, and Nonconsumptive Use

"Water use" is a general term that needs further definition. The important concepts for our purposes are water withdrawals, consumptive versus nonconsumptive uses, and groundwater depletion.

Water withdrawals refer to water that is taken out of, or diverted from, its source. Most uses of fresh water involve water withdrawals. But not all uses have the same outcomes; we must ask further questions. What is it being used for? Where does the water go thereafter—that is, how much of it returns to the watershed? Of that which returns to the water system, how much is potable or reusable?

Nonconsumptive use means that after water is withdrawn, it is returned in a usable way to the watershed. Many domestic uses of water are nonconsumptive: the water is reintegrated into the ecosystem or municipal water supply in some fashion.

Consumptive use of fresh water, by contrast, means that water does not return to the watershed in any usable or recognizable form once it has been withdrawn. It is permanently removed from its source. Agriculture and some forms of industry are highly consumptive of fresh water: once withdrawn, it is gone for good. Consumptive uses thus contribute in rather direct ways to the depletion of fresh water supply, water scarcity and, eventually, crisis.

How would these terms function in the present day? First, water is withdrawn or diverted from its source. Next, it is directed to some purpose (say, domestic, agricultural, or industrial). That withdrawn water can be used consumptively, nonconsumptively, or—as is most often the case—some combination of both. Some water may be returned to the watershed (and may be of varied quality), while some of that water is permanently removed and does not return to the local hydrological cycle in any meaningful way.

Domestic and even some industrial uses of water tend to be more nonconsumptive than consumptive. In the domestic sector, for example, water for bathing and cooking is often returned to the watershed or water system. In the industrial sector, thermoelectric cooling consumes only about 3 percent of the water withdrawn for that purpose. The remaining amount of water—in this case, nearly 97 percent—returns to the watershed. So it is that "much of the water used for domestic and industrial purposes is eventually returned to a water body, e.g., toilets are flushed and cooling water in thermoelectric power plants is returned to rivers. . . . In total, the domestic, industrial and energy sectors account for less than 10 percent of global water consumption."[8] Thus, while domestic and industrial sectors together account for 30 percent of all water withdrawn worldwide, they *consume* only about 10 percent. And while agriculture accounts for 70 percent of fresh water withdrawals, it accounts for nearly 90 percent of global fresh water consumption. In agriculture, little of the water withdrawn is returned to the system. Instead, it is transformed into fruits, grains, and other agricultural products.[9] Because agriculture consumes more water than it returns, it contributes to the depletion of fresh water supply. Pollution and other negative impacts on water quality are important and relate in complex ways to the quantity of available, potable water. But for the purposes of this discussion, the crucial distinction is between consumptive and nonconsumptive uses of fresh water.

Where Does the Water for Agriculture Come From?

Because nearly all of the water withdrawn for agriculture is consumed, it is in the realm of agriculture that unsustainable practices are particularly evident and prevalent. One major culprit is the hydrological optimism that accompanied the application of hydraulic technologies for agriculture in the twentieth century. It was a heady, exciting time for hydraulic engineers: technological innovation, financial incentive, and political will led to the development of major infrastructure projects for fresh water, beginning in the United States and spreading around the world through policy trends, financial incentives, and loan conditions set by transnational institutions such as the World Bank and the International Monetary Fund. Twentieth-century hydraulic prowess and hydrological optimism are enshrined most visibly in the mammoth concrete carapaces of large dams; behind them, rivers pool into placid, sprawling reservoirs. Less glitzy than large dams—but every bit as significant—are the subtler capillaries of irrigation networks and hydraulic pumps. The increased power and efficiency of the latter facilitates the extraction of groundwater. Irrigation canals then siphon those waters into dry soils, such that deserts transform into croplands. In the western United States, for example, the growth of both agriculture and urban centers in Los Angeles or Arizona was made possible only through the implementation of large-scale hydraulic technologies.

The point is not that the twentieth century invented irrigation. (In one form or another, hand-hewn irrigation systems long provided a more reliable water supply than rain alone could provide.) Rather, during the twentieth century, technological and engineering advances revolutionized the scale and efficiency of irrigation systems. That legacy bequeathed fertility to places like California's Central Valley, as well as parts of Texas, Nebraska, India, Russia, and more, such that into the present day a significant proportion of global agriculture is sustained almost entirely by irrigation. This raises the question: Where do societies get the water that flows through irrigation canals to fields? Sometimes, it comes from impoundment—that is, storing seasonal precipitation (rain or snow) behind dams during wet seasons and, later, releasing it down canals to farmers. Often, though, fresh water for agriculture comes from deep below, that is, "groundwater." Groundwater supplies—including the water found in aquifers—were largely untapped until the past hundred years. And it was access to this largely untapped, underground water supply, made possible by new hydraulic technologies, that contributed to the hydrological optimism and agricultural expansions of the twentieth century.

Aquifers:
What They Are and Why They Matter

Aquifers are underground geological formations that are natural holding areas for fresh water. They come in all sizes and are composed of a range of types of sediments. The Ogallala Aquifer, for example, lies beneath the vast area between Nebraska and Texas. Other aquifers undergird Beijing and Mexico City, parts of Israel and the West Bank, and Wisconsin—just to name a few. Aquifers matter enormously as sources of groundwater.

Recall that 2.5 percent of all water on earth is fresh water. Of that, 30 percent is groundwater. It is groundwater that was "discovered"—that is, accessed—in new ways in the past hundred years. Groundwater is often extracted by advanced hydraulic pumps, and then it can be dispersed in arid regions via irrigation canals, delivered to acres of farmland, and piped through municipal faucets. Extraction of groundwater has thus increased the overall available supply of fresh water, which has led to a range of outcomes, including greater agricultural production than in previous eras. The problem is that many aquifers do not recharge on any humanly meaningful time scale. Most aquifers take upward of ten thousand years to refill—an extraordinarily long time. Many aquifers take much, much longer to refill—on the order of millions of years. Maryland's Patasco Aquifer, for example, was recently found to be over one million years old. It makes sense, then, that water experts often refer to the water in aquifers as "fossil water" and the extraction of this water as "water mining." Once we use it, we lose it.

And although the precise amount of fresh water in aquifers is notoriously hard to quantify, a growing body of scientific evidence shows that many aquifers are sputtering. This evidence comes in the form of salination (when the water inside an aquifer turns brackish), sea-water intrusion (which ruins the aquifer as a source of fresh water—a particular issue for coastal aquifers), and subsidence of land atop the aquifers (creating sinkholes). Subsidence provides one clear, visible sign of invisible aquifers: cities built atop these aquifers actually start to sink because there is no longer enough pressure to support them. Mexico City and Beijing are prominent examples. Insofar as societies are tethered to the continued, unsustainable extraction of a finite supply, this dependence on fresh water from aquifers is literally sinking civilizations. For these reasons, aquifers are the most important things you've never seen. They cradle most of the earth's groundwater, much of which is nonrenewable on humanly meaningful time scales.

Current extraction of a finite water supply from aquifers far outpaces the renewal rate. As water expert Jeremy J. Schmidt has aptly observed, "For years water was considered as renewable as sunlight or wind, and the potential for its development seemed limitless"; but we now recognize that while some uses of fresh water are renewable, fresh water supply is "as finite as many other resources."[10] Groundwater depletion therefore represents a large part of twenty-first-century global fresh water crises.

The Domestic Sector: Does It Make a Difference?

Many people, especially in societies that are focused on individual freedoms, quite reasonably assume that fresh water problems are caused by individual wastefulness and conclude that a solution to global fresh water scarcity means reducing personal consumption of fresh water. Many water conservation campaigns endorse this line of thinking. For example, in the mid-1980s, I was a kid living in the suburbs of Denver. The semi-arid front range of Colorado has had its share of water drama, drought watches, and seasonal water restrictions, and one summer I saw a message about water conservation zoom through the suburbs, pasted on the side of a bus. This campaign took aim at the water use of Denver domiciles. It was memorable: two sets of clean feet—his and hers (one set hairy, another nicely manicured)—posed suggestively beneath a shower curtain. "Sing shorter songs!" the caption exhorted. From this ad I gleaned several points, including the suggestion that residents can use less water and use it more efficiently—for example, taking shorter showers, installing water-conserving spigots, running the dishwasher only when full, or turning off the tap when we brush our teeth.

Being attentive to domestic water habits is part of what experts call "harnessing demand." It is a way to lessen demand on water supply—taking shorter showers, as it were. This type of approach to water scarcity is important for municipal and regional conservation efforts, especially during droughts and in semi-arid and arid regions. It also helps people to maintain mindfulness about fresh water's importance. But even with increased water virtue and mindfulness, shorter showers won't solve global fresh water crises, because domestic water use is a small piece of a large puzzle. Admittedly, it would be nice if shorter showers did the trick: it's a straightforward action that individuals can take, and it is psychologically satisfying to view fresh water crises as rectifiable by individual choice and behavior. However, responsibility for fresh water can't reside in the domestic sector, which accounts for only 8 percent of global fresh water withdrawals. Again, while fresh water challenges may be ameliorated in partial ways by harnessing domestic demand, most fresh water crises will not be solved by attending solely to the largely nonconsumptive uses of the domestic sector.

To truly engage global fresh water dynamics, sectors and patterns of consumptive water use must be addressed within frameworks of political economy and sustainability. As author and activist Derrick Jensen has aptly noted, these are issues that go far beyond the scale of individual action. Jensen, a regular columnist in *Orion* magazine, hit the mark with a pithy and memorable essay titled "Forget Shorter Showers."[11] He argues that environmental action needs to be channeled away from an obsession with individual domestic habits and toward a fundamental rethinking of the industrial economy. Yet it remains easier for corporations and political entities to target individual responsibility (say, via an ad on the side of a bus) than to rethink structural, political, and economic incentives toward water use in other sectors. This is why, in Jensen's exhortation, we should "forget shorter showers": focusing on individual habits distracts people from the broader tasks of reassessing and revamping the industrial economy in which we participate. But the fact remains that fresh water is a social, political, and structural issue that requires nuanced attention to agricultural and industrial sectors, as well as other types of highly consumptive uses. The arrangements of the political economies of fresh waters need to be reconfigured to maximize accountability (of corporations and other large-scale water users) and long-term sustainability of groundwater and surface water. Granted, this new kind of hydro-logic is full of tangles, there is no one-size-fits-all calculation for how it would look, and it is not nearly as picturesque as sharing a shower.

Technological Innovation: Is It the Answer?

Unfortunately, not even technology is a panacea for fresh water issues. Technology is a marvelous tool. People are often rightly optimistic that technological interventions can help with remediation or management of some aspects of complex environmental problems. Yet when it comes to fresh water, many people seem to hope or expect that technology will play a significant—sometimes even salvific—role. Economists, for example, insist that a market reality of decreased supply can spur technological innovation, and engineers are hard at work in responding to specific problems with new inventions. Many people suggest that, given the quantity of salt water in the oceans, the obvious answer to fresh water scarcity worldwide is to desalinate the oceans. In other words: surely human ingenuity and technological development can innovate toward a solution! While human creativity is wonderful, technology is not a panacea, for several reasons. First and foremost, there is no substitute for fresh water, which is sui generis (nonfungible). No other substance will suffice to replace fresh water's life-mediating properties, and it is highly unlikely that an alternate compound will be invented that fulfills these properties. So even in a situation of increased demand and even with ingenious innovation in materials science, a substitute for fresh water is unlikely to be found.

But finding a replacement substance for fresh water is, after all, quite the lofty goal. Aren't there other ways that technology could mitigate fresh water scarcity, such as desalination? This observation is entirely correct: already, technological interventions are increasing efficiency, decreasing waste, reclaiming polluted water, and thereby making a finite fresh water supply go further than ever before. Meanwhile, more sensitive technologies and practices are constantly in development around the world. In the future, for example, it is not just likely but virtually guaranteed that polluted water will be reclaimed as gray water and used in the agricultural and domestic spheres in ever more efficient and effective ways, as is already the case in places like Israel and Sweden. Singapore already fully recycles its domestic water, from sewage to tap, to great functional effect. In the realm of agriculture, methods and mechanizations for hydrating crops (such as drip irrigation) will continue to reduce the amount of fresh water lost to evaporation.

As noted above, there is also hope that technology might enable us to turn salty water into fresh water: while just 2.5 percent of all water on earth is fresh water, 97.5 percent is salt water. In the words of historian and water law expert Robert Glennon, "With the earth mostly covered in water, it seems painfully obvious that the ultimate solution to our water crisis is to remove the salts."[12] Already, desalination plants turn salt water into fresh water in places like southern California, Israel, Saudi Arabia, and Qatar. Most experts agree that desalination will be an important response to growing populations and fresh water scarcity in the twenty-first century, especially in arid and semi-arid areas. Desalination will continue to be an important way to expand fresh water supply and thereby mitigate fresh water scarcity, especially as technological advances (such as nano-membranes for reverse osmosis) augur a future in which the cost of desalination becomes much more manageable for societies. But even desalination is not a full solution. Like many hydraulic technologies, it has drawbacks and unintended consequences. In addition to the current costs, for example, there are some negative outcomes, including leftover toxic brine salts. What is to be done with them?

This gives rise to the second objection to viewing technology as a solution to fresh water crises: The lure of a technological panacea is psychologically appealing, but it should not replace consideration of the goals toward which the technology is oriented and how it is implemented in particular contexts. As Glennon observes, "Many proposed 'solutions' to our water crisis involve quick fixes" that deploy emerging technologies. But they are not a "magical solution to the problem of water scarcity."[13]

Instead, the success of any technological intervention depends on myriad factors. For these reasons, it can be misleading to speak about "technology" in general. Ideas and technical improvements are always borne out in particular contexts and generate their own set of technical, environmental, and social issues to deal with, as desalination makes clear. A given technology is only as effective as the particular context, long-term goals, and management framework within which it is applied. Its potential costs are not only economic. So we have to ask: What kinds of technology are under discussion? In what contexts will they be used, and for what kinds of objectives? What are the potential downstream consequences? What is the projected life span of this technological "fix"? Who funds it? Who is responsible for implementation and maintenance? Who bears the burdens, and who benefits? In other words, technology is and will continue to be an important component of global fresh water supply, but it must be deployed within a more general ethical framework that involves clarity on objectives, rigorous social and environmental impact assessments, effective paradigms for implementation, and clear channels of accountability.

What Regions Will Be Most Affected by Fresh Water Scarcity?

Fresh water scarcity in the twenty-first century will affect the entire planet but not in a uniform way. Context matters. Still, some general statements are relatively uncontroversial: for example, climate change will amplify regional patterns of aridity or deluge, which in turn will have impacts on all manner of human activities, from subsistence economies to agribusiness and manufacturing. Arid and semi-arid regions are at greatest risk for physical fresh water scarcity and related social unrest. Areas that are already hot and dry—such as the southwest United States, sub-Saharan Africa, Australia, parts of Asia, and regions of India—will get hotter, receive less precipitation, and therefore experience more frequent, lengthier droughts. Diminished water content in soils will affect agriculture in negative ways. Environmental journalist and essayist William deBuys, for example, reports the "grim idea: that not just in the Southwest alone, but in regions throughout the world, the areas most likely to experience a decline in available water are those least able to withstand it."[14] The impacts will likely be severe. According to a recent UN estimate, "By 2025, 180 million people will be living in countries or regions with absolute water scarcity, and two-thirds of the world population could be under stress conditions."[15]

Absolute water scarcity refers to a dire lack of available fresh water, which is numerically represented as an annual supply of less than a thousand cubic meters per person. Experts and international governing bodies refer to communities, nations, and regions as "water stressed" when there is an imbalance between the available water supply and its use—in numerical terms, annual levels of less than seventeen hundred cubic meters of fresh water per person.

Who Will Be Most Affected by Fresh Water Scarcity?

Watersheds, ecosystems, and societies will all be affected by the complex dynamics of fresh water scarcity in the twenty-first century, but in terms of human impact, water stress and water scarcity most profoundly affect people living in poverty and other situations of vulnerability. And it is not just fresh water that matters: it is the combination of clean, fresh water and sanitation. Children are especially susceptible to negative impacts: more than 90 percent of deaths due to diarrhea in the developing world are in children younger than five years old and are largely caused by contaminated water. In fact, approximately fifteen hundred children die every day from preventable waterborne diseases. That is to say, one child dies from these causes roughly every twenty seconds.[16]

Women and girls bear a significant brunt of the burdens of fresh water scarcity. According to the UN, the collection and transportation of water "typically falls on women and children in developing countries—a task that can take many hours each day in drought-prone areas." This has enormous social consequences. When "it takes more time to gather water and fuel, the available time for education or other economic and political activities decreases. Already, the majority of children worldwide who do not attend school are girls."[17] This is an injustice unduly borne by the half of the population that is female. It enshrines patterns of male privilege. It also stagnates societal well-being, since the education of women and girls is strongly correlated to increased economic development.[18] For these sorts of reasons, fresh water and its counterpart, sanitation, are the cornerstones of public health, education, and economic growth. The absence of fresh water, by contrast, diminishes profoundly the possibilities for human life. In light of such factors, the Millennium Development Goals established by the United Nations have sought to reduce the number of people without access to fresh water and sanitation services.[19] Some benchmarks have been achieved in recent years, but reactions were rightly cautious when in 2012 the UN announced the "partial achievement" of Millennium Development Goal 7c, which pertains to access to clean water and sanitation. Global institutions were concerned that such news should not be interpreted as the completion of the goal. Indeed, even the Catholic Church chimed into the conversation. A Vatican press release timed to coincide with the MDG announcement as well as the March 2012 World Water Forum pointed out: "It should be kept in mind that the figures regarding such access usually put forth in international venues do not reflect the complexity of this phenomenon. The geographic distribution of the people still in need of adequate access to water makes the solution to the problems even more difficult."[20] Since 2015, the UN's Sustainable Development Goals have also identified access to fresh water and sanitation as a major initiative, but the question remains: How will this be achieved?

Water Sustainability, the Hydrosocial Cycle, and Water Justice

One of the goals that orients the work of many water experts is the pursuit of "water sustainability." According to Peter Gleick, water sustainability is the aspiration to achieve "the use of water that supports the ability of human society to endure and flourish into the indefinite future without undermining the integrity of the hydrological cycle or the ecological systems that depend on it."[21] Although this is a clearly an important goal, it says little about human social ethics or patterns of access within human societies. Yet throughout history, factors of geography and class privilege have shaped which groups of human beings have access to water, and these patterns matter for social ethics into the present day.

The stratification of access to clean, fresh water is not necessarily a new problem, but it is a problem with twenty-first century textures. This type of stratification has become especially apparent since the beginning of the industrial era. As environmental historian J. R. McNeill reports:

> The uneven history of the provision and treatment of urban water after 1880 was a case of escalating distinctions between the haves and have nots. Those who had clean water and good sewerage got it because they were comparatively rich, and getting it made them healthier and richer still. Those who lacked it, lacked it mainly because they could not afford it, and lacking it made them sicker and poorer still. . . . The increasing returns generated by investment in clean water helped to create, and widen, the cleavages in wealth and health that characterize the world today.[22]

Water scarcity in the present day continues to affect the world's poor (who are affected directly and deeply) more than the world's wealthy (who are usually affected indirectly and, by virtue of their expendable resources, can shield themselves from the most severe material consequences). In the twenty-first century, population growth, climate change, and economic globalization will further exacerbate both fresh water scarcity and the growing schism between rich and poor. In general, people with economic resources or political power will continue to have access to fresh water while the poor will spend their lives trying to get it. Thus, the issue of fresh water scarcity is also a problem of justice; that is to say, it is not merely *hydrological* realities that affect the flows of water or the bodies who are burdened by lack of clean, fresh water.

Fresh water is both hydrological and hydrosocial. It is a naturally occurring physical-material substance that is almost always mediated (that is, sourced and distributed) by human beings, political economies, and cultural practices—including legacies of colonialism, racism, and other forms of marginalization and exclusion. Geographers have named this insight the "hydrosocial cycle." In the words of one 2014 article on the topic:

> The hydrosocial cycle is based on the concept of the hydrologic cycle, but modifies it in important ways. While the hydrologic cycle has the effect of separating water from its social context, the hydrosocial cycle deliberately attends to water's social and political nature. . . . [It is] a socio-natural process by which water and society make and remake each other over space and time.[23]

Residents of water-scarce regions have intuitively known this for some time. In the United States, hydrosocial realities became nationally evident with the racialized patterns of cutoffs of water supply, as in Detroit in 2014, or the again racialized patterns of distribution of lead-contaminated water to already marginalized populations in Flint, Michigan, and elsewhere in the United States. Another crucial component of the hydrosocial cycle—especially globally—is sanitation, since the availability of sanitation shapes the ability (or inability) of women and girls, especially those who are menstruating, to participate in educational or economic activities outside of the home. Sanitation is thus a major site for thinking about water infrastructure and gender equity (see chapter 9).

The *hydrosocial cycle* is a useful concept for illuminating how access to water is shaped by power dynamics and cultural assumptions. It is a descriptive term, not a prescriptive (or normative) one: it tells us how things are but does not necessarily comment on how they *should* be. The "should," or normative aspect, is the domain of ethics. It takes description (hydrosocial cycle) and makes a judgment about what should be the case. The language usually used in this inflection is *water justice*—a normative idea prescribing what *ought* to be the case—specifically, the importance of seeking and achieving equality or equity in access to fresh water. Water justice usually means distributive justice: that is, the pursuit of a situation in which inequalities of outcome in terms of access to fresh water do not arise, regardless of a person's or family's ability to pay, or location of residence or race or class or gender. Justice as a regulative idea tends to have the features described above. But justice as enacted in a specific context does not have a uniform look, as Margreet Zwarteveen and Rutgerd Boelens point out: "Water justice is embedded and specific to historical and socio-cultural contexts. Water justice includes but transcends questions of distribution to include those of cultural recognition and political participation, and is intimately linked to the integrity of ecosystems. Justice requires the creative building of bridges and alliances across differences."[24]

Justice is an important virtue to pursue with regard to fresh water on all levels of scale, precisely because it is sui generis and sine qua non. What people can do, and who they can become, is shaped by where and how they have access to clean, fresh water. In anthropocentric perspective, our lives are, at core, radically dependent on this finite resource. But the reality of fresh water also transcends humanity. It is a crucial substance for ecosystems, species, climate, and the possibility of all life on this planet. Many factors determine fresh water's availability—including, but not limited to, geography and hydrography, hydraulic technology and infrastructure, social status, culture, gender, and political economy. Amid this mosaic of factors, finding ways to address fresh water scarcity and redress injustices is a slippery task.

Conclusion:
Facts, Frameworks, and Fatigue
in Pursuit of Just Water

The conceptual tools offered in this chapter are intended as reference points for subsequent discussions. But even in a compact primer on fresh water, the deluge of factual and statistical information regarding fresh water scarcity can be daunting—perhaps overwhelming. (As a quote from the BBC aptly aphorizes, "If you want to ensure mental meltdown, the statistics of the growing fresh water crisis are a surefire winner.") How does one navigate this factual, hydrological, and ethical morass in a sustainable way? It helps to remember that what we're talking about is, at core, quite tactile. If the impersonal statistics and scale of global fresh water crises seem to be a "surefire" way to flatten your sense of hope or the relevance of individual action, I encourage you to meditate particularly on *your* experiences of fresh water. What are your strongest associations of fresh water, in your memory and in the present day? How does water flow to your home? What are the features of the land and climate that shape your water supply? How does the hydrosocial cycle function in your community? Are there issues of justice that deserve attention? It is important to ground reflection in these ways because working with water is an ongoing task, the deluge of information can be overwhelming, and there is no single solution to the fresh water crisis. Fresh water challenges and crises are dynamic and shape-shifting depending on the hydrology of the region and the social systems and norms that dictate how water flows, to whom, and in what ways.

What is required is a sense of humility and adventure—a willingness to observe, to listen, to learn. You must pay attention to what you are seeing, as well as to what is hidden from your sight by virtue of your professional training, your socioeconomic background, your cultural or religious frameworks. You must cultivate a sense of nonattachment to any single approach or one-size-fits-all solution. Context matters, so you must begin where you are, exploring the significance of water for your community, your ecosystem, your society, your polity. You can and should seek the most up-to-date information about fresh water scarcity in your location and worldwide. Over time, you will begin to get a sense of how the many aspects of twenty-first-century water overlap. But you must begin somewhere, and for most people, that place is precisely where you are.

Three points are especially important to reiterate by way of conclusion. First, water crises must be addressed collectively, through political and collaborative efforts toward sustainable and just solutions. This means that fresh water is above all a problem of "we," not just "me"—or, as chapter 4 explains, it is a problem of what Catholic social teaching calls "the common good." Second, while there is a universal need for fresh water, there is no such thing as a universal solution to fresh water scarcity: the hydrological situation facing the Sahara Desert or the Tibetan plateau is simply not the same as that in Vancouver, and neither are the hydrosocial realities that shape patterns of water access and distribution. Responses to fresh water scarcity will be appropriate only insofar as they take this wide variety of physical and social realities into account. Third, especially in an era of climate change and population growth, solutions will also be dynamic and provisional. They will be about adaptation and situation-specific, long-term management oriented toward water sustainability and justice.

CHAPTER 3

Water

Human Right or Economic Commodity?

No small part of the value of fresh water lies in human beings' radical dependence on it. Water circumscribes the possibilities of becoming—as individuals, communities, and societies. As a result, the question *What is water worth?* admits of many possible answers. Yet in an era of economic globalization, terms such as "value" are often taken to be synonymous with "price." The reduction of value to economic exchange is troubling because it can threaten to elide other robust, noneconomic ways of valuing water. The question of water's value can be engaged through the register of economics. but that is only one conceptual framework among many, and it is by no means clear that exchange value and price are sufficient approximations of the complex, multifaceted reality that is fresh water. As political philosopher Michael Sandel has observed, "Markets leave their mark. Sometimes, market values crowd out nonmarket values worth caring about."[1] The values that individuals, corporations, and societies assign to water will affect not just humanity and civilizations but also ecosystems and most forms of life on this planet in the coming century and beyond. The challenge is to speak cogently and ethically about fresh water across cultural, philosophical, and geographical divides, and to do so in ways that prevent the profit-oriented logic of economic globalization from saturating and commandeering discourses on water sustainability and water justice.

In order to assess some of the ways by which capitalist political economies have shaped global perception of fresh water, two case studies are illuminating. This chapter first considers the birth of a fetishized commodity, bottled water, and focuses especially but not exclusively on the FIJI Water brand. Next, it turns to the privatization of the municipal water supply in Cochabamba, Bolivia, where multinational corporate motivation intersected virulently with situated community needs. Critical analyses of these cases help explain why access to fresh water is increasingly viewed as an issue of justice and rights for concerned communities, individuals, and governments around the world.

Message in a Bottle

Bottled water in its contemporary form was born, sparkling and still, in the crystalline waters of the French Alps, to the proud parents of Perrier and Evian.[2] It steadily grew into a luxury commodity for European elites. In glass and plastic, gallons and liters, bottles of water streamed across the Atlantic, found new niches in big-box grocery stores and corner markets, dazzled diners on the menus of elite restaurants, and quenched the thirst of high-spending guests at fine hotels. By the late 1990s, a fetishized commodity had come of age in the industrialized world. The transatlantic market viability of bottled water unleashed a corporate stampede to conquer the potentially enormous consumer market. Multinational corporations realized that bottled water promised major profits not just as a luxury good but also as a mainstream commodity. Thus, from Nestlé was born Poland Spring; from Coca-Cola, Dasani; and from PepsiCo, Aquafina. In some cases, the progeny is drawn from pristine mountain sources; in other cases, it is taken from municipal faucets, filtered, irradiated, and bottled for resale at an extraordinary markup. To this lucrative domain, therefore, "the biggest enemy" to profit—as articulated by a PepsiCo corporate executive in 2000—"is tap water."[3]

In the first decade of the twenty-first century, bottled water sales constituted a nearly 30 percent share of the global bottled beverage industry. Global sales of bottled water remain in the tens of billions of dollars—upward of $50 billion and perhaps as much as $100 billion. In the production of this consumable beverage, ordinarily disposable plastic bottles are pumped with spring, artesian, or filtered tap water; hermetically sealed; and shipped all over the world via plane, train, ship, or truck. The industry generates up to 1.5 million pounds of nonbiodegradable plastic bottles per year.[4] Nearly 17 million barrels of crude oil are used annually to manufacture the plastic bottles that are used once and then discarded (an amount of oil that would "keep 1 million vehicles on the road for 12 months"[5]). And only 13 percent of those bottles are actually recycled after being discarded. The rest go to landfills, where they leach toxic chemicals into the land.

Of course, in some parts of the world, bottled water is a key aspect of survival—where clean, fresh water is contaminated or extremely scarce, for example. In the United States, bottled water is recommended in places like Flint, Michigan, where lead contamination is rampant; or on many Native American reservations, where sufficient water infrastructure is nonexistent; or in areas undergoing major hydraulic fracturing, where concern about contamination of groundwater wells has led various companies to supply certain landowners with lifetime supplies of bottled water. In these places, and many others worldwide, bottled water is an important means of survival and disease prevention. By and large, however, the most prodigious consumers of bottled water in the United States and Europe have clean tap water at their fingertips twenty-four hours a day and are not in danger of drinking disease-ridden water. And despite growing concern about environmental effects from plastic bottle waste, bottled water remains a hot commodity. Many investors and corporations seem to wager that, in the words of Arthur Van Weisenberger, a consultant to the beverage industry, "People don't go backwards ... once they've developed a taste for bottled water, they won't give it up."[6] There is a proliferation of smaller brands, too. Some players in this market have been around longer than others, but all manner of bottled water products continue to emerge on the shelves of US grocery stores, including some from companies that tout themselves as environmentally friendly or socially conscious. One brand worth examining is FIJI Water, which has high market saturation in the United States.

FIJI Water was founded in 1996. Its first exports to the United States occurred in 1997, and it has remained a steady market presence. Plastic bottles travel from China to Fiji, and once filled with artesian water from the island, the product is transported from Fiji to countries including the United States, Australia, France, and Mexico. The water is described by FIJI corporation as "untouched by man" ("just as nature intended," adds the motto on some bottles), such that "until you unscrew the cap, FIJI Water never meets the compromised air of the twenty-first century, nor is it touched by another human being."[7] (Other bottled water companies have veered even toward eugenic rhetoric: "Born Better" is now a trademarked catch phrase of Poland Spring, suggesting perhaps that pure, clean and unsullied water can be birthed by market incentives.) Valuing the logic of purity, FIJI Water maintains that "no human hands are allowed to touch" the water from its proprietary aquifer. The company describes how the production facility "was built directly on top of the FIJI Water aquifer, where a completely sealed delivery system draws the water up from the protected chamber and places it directly into our iconic square bottles, which are made from the highest-grade terephthalate (PET) plastic resin."[8] As a matter of fact, FIJI Water is untouched by human hands in two ways: through the mechanization of the bottling process described above and also because the local community is not entitled to access this water. Surely the water, thus protected from the vagaries of contact with the twenty-first century, is crystalline. But purity is a slippery concept when it comes to bottled water. For while bottled water is, of course, partly about the water, it cannot be separated from the bottles, the shipping, the branding, the profits—all the collateral that trundles along with the cycle of production of this fetishized commodity. Potential and actual costs of bottled water are assessed in ways that usually fail to encompass environmental concerns, issues of local rights of access, or the long-term interests of the community, ecosystem, and water sources from which the water is drawn.

To call bottled water an environmentally friendly product is absurd. Yet in an age of persuasive marketing, this is precisely what a number of corporations do. FIJI Water launched a "green" campaign in 2008 (following the establishment of a community outreach foundation in 2007); in 2012, the company described its bottling plant as "carbon-negative" and aired advertisements asserting, "Every drop is green."[9] Water expert Peter Gleick retorts that this product isn't so much "green" as "greenwashed"—that is, "an attempt to do ethically or environmentally what shouldn't be done at all":[10]

> Fiji Water's efforts to position themselves as the most environmentally responsible bottled water prompted the American Public Media's Greenwash Brigade to award them a top 2008 Greenwash prize, noting the massive energy cost required to transport Fiji water to market, the evils of producing and disposing of plastics, and problems with the company's claim of "carbon neutrality."[11]

Much of the criticism aimed at the bottled water industry is entirely warranted.

A major ethical problem is that profits for most bottled water companies benefit corporate shareholders far more than community stakeholders. Granted, as journalist Elizabeth Royte acknowledges, multinational corporations do contribute to the local economy—even if only in the form of a few jobs in the short term. And there is something to be said for job creation: FIJI Water is reportedly a major employer on the islands that pays employees "twice the informal minimum wage."[12] But still, corporate responsibility in such situations is almost always entirely voluntary. And when the profit-driven interests of multinational corporations conflict with the interests of a local community or ecosystem, it is rarely the latter that benefit. Instead, it is local communities and watersheds that tend to bear the realized costs of any negative externalities. This is a problem of accountability, responsibility, and sustainability. As Gleick puts it,

> If everyone on the planet had access to affordable safe tap water, bottled water would be seen as unnecessary. If government regulatory agencies actually worked to protect the public from poor-quality water, false advertising, misleading marketing, and blatant hucksterism, sales of magic water elixirs would be halted. If public sources of drinking water were more accessible, arguments about the convenience of bottled water would seem silly. And if bottled water companies had to incorporate the true economic and environmental costs of the production and disposal of plastic bottles, as well as the extraction and use of sensitive groundwater, into the price of their product, sales would plummet.[13]

But sales have not plummeted. The continued demand for bottled water, coupled with prognostications of fresh water scarcity in many regions worldwide, suggests that bottled water will continue to be a lucrative commodity for the foreseeable future.

Bottled water has also become something of a fetishized commodity in a culture of conspicuous consumption—desired by many, ubiquitously available in the United States, and even viewed as a marker of status.[14] In this sense, bottled water is the single greatest marketing achievement in the history of civilization. Of course, trends are fickle, and in some cities the rejection of bottled water has now become a marker of lifestyle choice. Some high-end restaurants serve only tap water, and

Aveda and the city of New York's Department of Environmental Protection partnered in 2010 to promote tap water over bottled water during Fashion Week, and the company then teamed up with Clean Ocean Action to promulgate guidelines for "Protecting Clean Water."[15] A widespread "Take Back the Tap" campaign facilitated by Food and Water Watch has resulted in a pushback against bottled water on college campuses and in other institutions.[16] In 2007, an executive order from the mayor of San Francisco forbade city monies to be spent on bottled water, a move that was followed by legislation to this effect. Several national parks have endeavored to ban bottled water sales within their perimeters, citing the problem of plastic waste, while industry representatives have characteristically responded that they would prefer to amplify opportunities for recycling.

What kinds of issues are debated publicly when it comes to bottled water? Waste from plastic bottles, fossil fuel emissions required for transport, or the variable contaminant levels found in bottled water are among those that get public attention. In response to public pressure, bottled water companies have adopted a range of responses. Some have sought to reduce the amount of plastic used in their bottles: Dasani, for example, averred that its "Twist" half-liter bottle design "can be twisted down to half its original size. That means an end to overflowing recycle bins and the beginning of a fun new way to remember to recycle your empty bottles. So Twist loud and proud!"[17] Nestlé subsidiaries like Poland Spring and Arrowhead have also trumpeted plastic reduction efforts, brandishing the somewhat obvious claim that "smaller cap = less plastic." Meanwhile, bottled water companies have taken a range of other approaches to the image problem: FIJI Water, as noted above, started a community foundation and rendered its production plant carbon neutral, and other companies have likewise tried to offset carbon emissions. Still other bottled water companies attempt to couple sales of bottled water with charitable giving (Ethos Water, now owned by Starbucks, is the most obvious example of the latter, though others have proliferated in recent years).[18] The idea seems to be that, on balance, a consumer's potential discomfort over contributing to environmental degradation can be offset by the vague sense that this purchase is doing some kind of good, somewhere in the world—absolution by consumption, perhaps.

But problems with bottled water cannot be so easily assuaged. All bottled water floats upon an ocean of plastic and fossil fuels that even a charitable donation cannot ameliorate. Moreover, there are fundamental assumptions built into the availability of bottled water that pertain to property regimes and especially the privatization of (and profit from) a resource such as fresh water. As Royte puts it, the question of "privatization of a public resource, is too *outré* for most mainstream news outlets to pick up on, perhaps because it raises sticky questions of ownership and control, and it offends many Americans' ideas about the primacy of capitalism."[19] It is easier to salute incremental progress in plastic reduction or try to frame bottled water as a social good product than it is to engage in a discussion about what kind of thing water is. Is fresh water properly understood as a natural good, a common-pool resource, an ecosystem service? Is it amenable to private property regimes and management by private corporations, public-private partnerships, or public entities? Who or what should be able to profit from it, and by what means? As Peter Gleick explains in the conclusion to *Bottled and Sold:*

> In the end, the debate about bottled water is really a debate about the value of water, human rights versus responsibilities, environmental priorities and protection, economic markets versus public goods, government intervention versus government reform, and more. If we are thoughtful, however, we will see bottled water for what it is—the result of a failure to provide satisfactory public water systems and services for everyone—and realize that our obsession with bottled water can be overcome if we address the reasons people seek it out.[20]

Whether fresh water is a commodity or something else entirely—a moral entitlement, a human right, a public good—is a crucial debate that crested into global forums several decades ago.

What Kind of Thing Is Water?

For the past several decades, a debate has been raging—often out of sight—about whether water should be viewed primarily as an economic commodity or as a human right. A commodity is something that can be owned, traded, and sold for profit. To define water as a commodity is to assume that water can and should be owned, that it can and should be sold and traded in the market economy, and that the profit motive is a reasonable component of this process. Bottled water is an obvious example. Another type of privatization has to do with management of fresh water supply, in which private governance of municipal water is treated as a means to profit (usually by multinational corporations).

A human right, by contrast, is something due to all people, regardless of their ability to pay. The language of rights suggests that equity is far more important than profit; that the commodification of fresh water leads to inequities in distribution; and, therefore, that fresh water should not be valued primarily as an economic commodity. Further, many people insist that fresh water should be considered a public good or a part of the "global commons," meaning that fresh water is the kind of thing that should never be owned by any individual or corporation—nor bought, sold, or used to generate profit. To advocates of water justice, ownership of water is unacceptable, because access to clean, fresh water is a basic requirement for the most basic forms of survival. And when water is treated as a commodity, it is people living in poverty who are least able to afford it, and who therefore suffer most from its absence; women and children are especially affected in negative ways. In such cases, the "cost" or "price" of water is not written in bank accounts or bills. It is inscribed in the lives of those who must procure fresh water: on their bodies, which are literally burdened by the heavy liquid; in the forgone opportunities for education and economic improvement. These factors shape the horizon of people's lives. For these kinds of reasons, many advocates—including the Catholic Church (see chapter 4)—increasingly view access to fresh water as a fundamental human right.

Juxtaposing the logic of commodity with the logic of rights reveals that these designations are oriented toward fundamentally different goals, as well as means of achieving those goals. To call fresh water a commodity is to emphasize the goal of profit. People who think that fresh water should be identified primarily as an economic good place a very strong faith in the free market: they trust that the market is the best means of achieving efficiency and equity in distribution. By contrast, to call fresh water a human right is to emphasize the goal of justice. People who defend this view are deeply skeptical about the reliability of the free market to provide sufficient, equitable access to fresh water in ways that are accountable to stakeholders over shareholders. They are concerned about justice, aware of pernicious tendencies built into the profit motive, and therefore they insist that access to clean, fresh water is a basic human right.

In January 1992, the "Dublin Statement on Water and Sustainable Development" was signed by representatives from major, multinational corporations (largely the members of the corporate-run World Water Council, which sponsors the triennial World Water Forum) and selected government officials. It was issued six months before the 1992 United Nations Conference on Environment and Development in Rio de Janeiro. The Dublin Statement accurately described fresh water "as a finite and vulnerable resource, essential to sustain life, development and the environment," for which "effective management . . . demands a holistic approach, linking social and economic development with protection of natural ecosystems." That was a good start. Three principles later, things got dubious: "*Water has an economic value in all its competing uses and should be recognized as an economic good.*"[21] The document concludes that, as a result of water's "economic value in all its competing uses, it is vital to recognize first the basic right of all human beings to have access to clean water and sanitation *at an affordable price.*"[22] Objections from global activists and nongovernmental organizations were immediate, for it seemed fundamentally unjust that fresh water for survival should be linked to price. At worst, would access to fresh water be enshrined on the basis of ability to pay? Concern flared about the potential consequences of remanding the question of fresh water's value to the market. As this chapter later describes, since 2010 access to fresh water has been incorporated by the UN General Convention as a fundamental human right, so now debates abound about whether and how that right should be delivered—through the private sector and markets, or public entities, or some combination of these?

These wars of definition remain heated, but they come into public consciousness annually on World Water Day (March 22), when news outlets publish op-eds on fresh water and government officials invoke the significance of fresh water for development and peace around the world. Every third year, the corporate-sponsored World Water Forum invokes water as a "commodity," thereby valorizing its economic significance and suggesting that the global market can sufficiently address the problems of fresh water contamination and scarcity that plague much of the world. The World Water Forum gets significant press coverage—after all, money talks—but it is not the only show in town. For example, the Alternative World Water Forum 2012, which was held in the same city but at an alternate location, had as its motto: "L'eau, source de vie, pas de profit!" And as it has done every third year since 2003, in 2012 the Catholic Church again sent an official memorandum to the World Water Forum that emphasized the fundamental human right to fresh water, over and against its status as an economic commodity.

What kind of thing is water? By whom is it owned or managed? To whom is it made available, by what means, and on what terms? One potent case study for such debates revolves around the events that unfolded in Cochabamba, Bolivia, at the turn of the millennium. At odds over the fate of the region's fresh water supply were the local community, the government dictatorship, the conditions of an international development loan, and a subsidiary of a major multinational corporation.

Bolivian Water War?

The resource-rich but financially impoverished South American country of Bolivia received a development loan from the World Bank in the mid-1990s. One loan condition entailed the privatization of water supply in several municipalities. "Privatization" meant allowing a multinational corporation to assume the reins of water management, including distribution and pricing of fresh water supply as well as infrastructure repairs and development. Aguas del Tunari, which turned out to be a subsidiary of the global giant Bechtel, won the contract and—with the blessing and military enforcement of the Bolivian dictatorship—took the reins of the faltering, publicly administered water supply of Cochabamba, a town nestled in the mountains several hundred miles away from the capital of La Paz. It seemed an unlikely spot for conflict, but a series of management and economic decisions implemented by Aguas del Tunari—including but not limited to cutting off farmers' access to water—prompted the formation of a community group called La Coordinadora, which advocated fairer and more extensive distribution of water supplies as well as participation in the water management process. Several ethical questions underlay the Coordinadora's efforts: Who controlled Cochabamba's municipal water supply? Who had access to the water, and at what cost? Bolivian officials and Bechtel executives rebuffed efforts at transparency or reform. After days of peaceful protests, the standoff turned violent and a seventeen-year-old protester, Victor Hugo Daza, was killed by gunfire.[23]

The "water war" in Cochabamba occurred just as the Internet became a viable mechanism for global communications. As a result, the story and images relayed in that medium threw fresh water into global public consciousness in an entirely new way. Overnight and around the world, the names of Cochabamba and Victor Hugo Daza became rallying cries for critics of economic globalization, advocates of water justice, and human rights watchdog organizations. News outlets and popular nonfiction books debated the merits and problems of privatization, while trumpeting the idea that "water wars" would shape the political and economic landscape of the twenty-first century. The conflict was a feature story in erudite cultural journals, including the *New Yorker*. After protracted struggle and devastation to its public image, Aguas del Tunari withdrew from Cochabamba. The Bolivian government negated its contract and was promptly sued by the parent company, the multinational corporation Bechtel, for $50 million for breach of contract and lost profits. An Internet-mobilized international outcry eventually led Bechtel to drop the lawsuit and, in a symbolic but extremely belated gesture, to accept a token $1 payment instead.

Shortly thereafter, in 2002, the United Nations Educational, Scientific and Cultural Organization promulgated a nonbinding General Comment that "affirmed that access to adequate amounts of clean water for personal and domestic uses is a fundamental human right of all people," noting that "the human right to water is indispensable for leading a life in human dignity. It is a prerequisite for the realization of other human rights."[24] The nonbinding document further stipulates that the adequacy of water "should not be interpreted narrowly, by mere reference to the volume of water and technologies. Water should be treated as a social and cultural good, and not primarily as an economic commodity."[25] This nonbinding comment suggested that "parties to the International Covenant have the duty to progressively realize, without discrimination, the right to water, which entitles everyone to sufficient, affordable, physically accessible, safe, and acceptable water for personal and domestic uses"—in explicit contrast to "decisions taken at several international water forums in the 1990s, in which water was judged to be an economic commodity."[26] It is worth noting that up to that point, the only place the United Nations had yet recognized a binding right to water was in the Convention on the Rights of the Child (a document to which, it must be added, the United States is not a signatory). To be sure, there remain substantial obstacles to the global enforcement of the Universal Declaration of Human Rights and subsequent UN conventions, and the language of individual rights surely reflects a set of Western, liberal democratic preoccupations. Still, the language of human rights is as close to an internationally accessible, ethical vocabulary as has yet been found in an era of global pluralism.

Then, in 2006, Evo Morales became the first indigenous president of Bolivia, having run on a platform that included resource nationalism—that is, the conviction that Bolivia's natural resources are for Bolivians, not for transnational corporate profit. The case of Cochabamba is widely understood to have been a major aspect of his campaign's success. Disillusioned with international failures to articulate a climate treaty, in early 2010 Morales convened in Cochabamba the "People's Conference on Climate Change and the Rights of Mother Earth." During this time, participants crafted the "Declaration of the Rights of Mother Earth"—with thirty-five thousand signatories and several million rural supporters. Included in the declaration is an explicit requirement that "Mother Earth and the beings of which she is composed have the following inherent rights," including "the right to water as a source of life."[27] A Bolivian representative presented the declaration to the UN General Assembly for consideration, and although it seems unlikely that it will ratify this declaration as written, the UN did hold an interdisciplinary hearing on the topic in 2011. (In another gesture of affirmation if not practical support, the UN General Assembly named Morales the "World Hero of Mother Earth" and identified April 22 as "International Mother Earth Day.")

Thus in the span of a decade, Bolivia became a symbolic epicenter of global environmental advocacy regarding fresh water management and access, and Evo Morales became a symbol of indigenous leadership against the encroaching economic interests of multinational corporations. Also during this same time period—on July 28, 2010—the UN passed a General Convention that identified access to water and sanitation as a universal human right. Two months later, the UN Human Rights Council affirmed that the human right to clean water and sanitation is "inextricably related to the right to the highest attainable standard of physical and mental health as well as the right to life and human dignity."[28] Many questions remain about the scope, implementation, and implications of this newly articulated human right. The most basic question is: Why was water not stipulated as a right much earlier? One answer is that it was simply assumed to be self-evidently vital. The document quoted above, for example, suggests that "the exclusion of water as an explicit right" in the 1948 Universal Declaration of Human Rights "was due more to its nature; like air, it was considered so fundamental that its explicit inclusion was thought unnecessary." Global public consciousness over this issue is also epitomized in the appointment of Maude Barlow, a world expert and water justice advocate, as senior adviser on water issues to the UN during 2008–9. Barlow, Vandana Shiva, and many other activists and nongovernmental organizations offer a variety of formulations of the principles behind an assertion of a human right to water.[29] As the next chapter explains in detail, the Catholic Church also holds this view.

Words in themselves do not constitute a solution to the problem of access to fresh water. Scarcity, tensions, and conflicts continue in many parts of the world. Practical and political uncertainties also surround the idea of a human right to fresh water. But even while recognizing its drawbacks, rights discourse is vitally important, as are the insights propounded by water justice advocates. The language of water as a human right is an important corrective to any stance that would view water primarily or exclusively as a commodity. The sphere of value discourse must be widened, because commodity or exchange value is insufficient when water is the subject. Granted, fresh water is an extremely profitable substance in the twenty-first century. In some markets, it is more expensive than oil. But the pursuit of profit is rarely the means toward justice, sustainability, or the common good. Whether fresh water should be privatized—in the sense of being owned, allocated, or distributed in whole or in part by private, for-profit corporations—remains a topic of much debate. Corporations and business leaders are now arguing that the right to water is best achieved through the private sector, a claim that again raises persistent philosophical questions: What constitutes legitimate ownership or governance for a resource like fresh water? Should multinational corporations have exclusive access to, or control over, a common pool resource like fresh water? In this way, charged debates over privatization are also symptomatic of deep and enduring questions about ethics, politics, governance, and economics.[30]

In the early twenty-first century, widespread concern about the linkage between economic globalization and environmental degradation has led to several different attempts to articulate noneconomic bases for valuing fresh water. The Declaration of the Rights of Mother Earth, noted previously, has gained a committed following, while the discourse of fresh water as a universal human right has been formally affirmed by the United Nations. Principled guidelines about fresh water have been promulgated by prominent water justice activists: Maude Barlow has issued a "Treaty Initiative to Share and Protect the Global Water Commons," while Vandana Shiva has articulated "Six Principles of Water Democracy."[31] And a major judicial decision in Aoteaoroa/New Zealand in 2017 found the Whanganui River to be viably regarded as a living entity, akin to a legal person, in light of traditional Maori understandings of the river, which suggests that the values assigned to bodies of water are, in fact, amenable not just to traditionally Western forms of political economic valuation but also potential repositories of cultural and religious values in ways that bear lasting implications for governance.

Conclusion:
Valuing Water

Water requires creative economic, political, philosophical, and ethical attention. Science journalist Fred Pearce has suggested that "we need a new ethos for water—an ethos based . . . on managing the water cycle for maximum social benefit rather than narrow self-interest."[32] Such work must proceed from the basic insight that the values of water far exceed the designation of fresh water as a commodity or source of exchange value. Such designations matter because an assessment of value is, at core, a way of interpreting meaning; and value, like water, resists easy containment. How then can fresh water's values be understood apart from the viral logic of economic globalization? What resources from philosophical, religious, and cultural traditions— past and present—might help us think through and articulate alternative frameworks of value and courses of action regarding global fresh water scarcity in the twenty-first century? The task is crucial, because in the absence of dedicated conversation and action about the value of water, the default value mechanism seems rather likely to be the exchange-value-oriented assumptions of the late capitalist global marketplace. In fact, based on these sorts of concerns, fresh water has rapidly become a central environmental and social concern for the magisterium of the Roman Catholic Church. Chapter 4 explains the development of these claims in Catholic Social Teaching and explicates the Catholic Church's moral conviction that fresh water is a fundamental human right, even a right-to-life issue.

CHAPTER 4

A Right-to-Life Issue
for the Twenty-First Century

At his very first press conference in March 2013, the newly elected Pope Francis mused, "These days we do not have a very good relationship with creation, do we?" That is a question worthy of the pope's saintly namesake, Francis of Assisi, who since 1979 has officially been the patron saint of ecologists. Yet despite his avowed environmental charism, including his wide-ranging ecological encyclical *Laudato Si'*, Pope Francis is by no means the first Catholic pontiff to articulate the significance of the environment. Since the late twentieth century, Catholic environmentalism has pivoted on two key points, one theological and the other ethical. The theological insight is that the created world is good and is a sign of the creator: Creation reveals something of the creator and is imbued with meaning. The second pivot point of Catholic environmentalism is ethical: How does environmental degradation affect the most vulnerable people and groups in society? Catholic teaching—in line with all manner of historical and demographic evidence—understands that people living in poverty or other forms of vulnerability are most profoundly affected by resource scarcity or environmental degradation.

Moreover, Catholic ethical teaching sees much of contemporary environmental degradation as a problematic by-product of economic globalization. Pope Francis, for example, is no Marxist, but he would have strong words for the likes of neoclassical economist Milton Friedman, who thought that the social responsibility of business was to increase its profits. Instead, Pope Francis inherits a legacy of Catholic social teaching (CST) that links economic globalization, environmental degradation, and poverty. These social and economic teachings have taken shape since the 1960s and have found authoritative expression in papal encyclicals. The existence of this social, economic, and ethical critique of economic globalization and its negative outcomes has not been familiar to many Catholics in the United States, where the ethical issues that get airtime tend to have a distinctly reproductive flair. But the promulgation of *Laudato Si'* (*LS*) has demonstrated that although the Catholic Church has by no means shifted its positions on matters of sexuality, reproduction, or end-of-life ethics, the emphasis of CST is squarely on patterns of power and privilege that disenfranchise the poor and the earth. The range of moral, anchoring concepts and modes of analyses in CST are also increasingly seen as useful ways to reflect on individual and collective responsibility in an era of structural complexity and complicity. Drawing on the body of magisterial CST, this chapter explains how fresh water occupies a special focus for the Catholic Church and suggests that it is high time for the issue of access to fresh water to top the list of global right-to-life advocacy efforts. Conveniently, magisterial documents have for several decades explicitly addressed this topic, and Pope Francis has continued the trend.

Catholic Social Teaching: The Church's "Best-Kept Secret"

Like many secular and religious institutions, the Catholic Church is patriarchal. It encompasses a stunning diversity of Christian ways of life, spiritualities, religious orders, cultural traditions, liturgies, and communities, such that the 1.2 billion diverse Catholics around the world today could hardly be described as homogeneous. As chapter 1 indicated, Catholic theology engages with today's world through the mechanism of CST. Especially since Vatican II in the mid-twentieth century, theologians and church officials have sought to situate theological and moral wisdom within the context of global issues and advances in scientific and humanistic knowledge—on topics from evolutionary biology to labor relations, from corporate social responsibility to the ideals of democratic governance, from trafficking of women and girls to assisted reproductive therapies, from food scarcity to environmental degradation. In the words of Kenneth Himes, CST is where the Catholic Church seeks "to enlighten, inspire, and guide moral reform on social matters." Throughout, CST strives to promote the dignity and integrity of all human beings and increasingly attends to the fundamental conditions for the possibility of life.[1]

Since 1891, CST has become a body of official church teachings linking matters of faith with matters of justice in the world—social, political, economic, and (most recently) environmental. Beginning with Leo XIII's *Rerum Novarum* (known in English as "On the Condition of Labor"), early encyclicals dealt with social and economic issues. In 1967, Paul VI promulgated the encyclical *Populorum Progressio* ("On the Development of Peoples") and introduced the extraordinary insight that "development" is more than an economic phenomenon; rather, its aim should be the well-being of whole persons, in all of their embodied and spiritual needs and appropriate to their context. He called this "integral development," and it is an insight that John Paul II and Benedict XVI endorsed in their own encyclicals, where they observe that despite many technological advances and an increase in absolute global wealth, the achievement of integral development has been elusive. Properly understood, they insist, development is not just a matter of bank accounts and national economic growth; it is a matter of the well-being of bodies, families, communities, and societies. CST is appealing in no small part because, in the words of theologians David O'Brien and Thomas Shannon, CST "is precisely the effort to be *both* prophetic and responsible," and this makes it relevant to and "significant in the modern world."[2]

Through CST, the Catholic Church is increasingly focused on the global issue of fresh water. But most people in the United States, at least, have no idea that the Catholic Church stands for clean, fresh water for all people. Where, then, is Catholic advocacy for fresh water to be found? Theological and ethical reflection on fresh water appears in magisterial Catholic teaching in a variety of genres, including papal statements, addresses, and encyclicals (notably, including Benedict XVI's 2009 encyclical, *Caritas in Veritate*, and Pope Francis's encyclical, *Laudato Si'*). It is invoked multiple times in the authoritative 2004 Vatican publication of the *Compendium of the Social Doctrine of the Church*. And every three years since 2003, the Holy See and the Pontifical Council for Justice and Peace (PCJP) have issued important letters to the World Water Forum that outline the church's position on matters of fresh water and human and environmental well-being.

Like ecological reflection more generally, Catholic attention to fresh water is by no means limited to statements and publications from the hierarchical magisterium. Well-established, forward-thinking organizations—like Catholic Relief Services (CRS) and the National Catholic Rural Life Conference (NCRLC) in the United States or the Catholic Agency for Overseas Development (CAFOD) in England and Wales, as well as others worldwide—are steadily engaged in efforts to protect watersheds and support life through improving access to clean, fresh water. In different ways, a variety of religious orders—especially orders of women religious—have made fresh water part of their social justice ministries and charisms. Recognizing these diverse contributions is vital, and examples percolate throughout subsequent chapters. Nonetheless, this chapter focuses on teachings about fresh water from the hierarchical magisterium, where major interlocking themes recur.

From the many documents that constitute CST, eight ethical insights and imperatives can be identified with regard to fresh water. These insights are attested throughout a range of authoritative, magisterial sources, including papal encyclicals, especially *Caritas in Veritate* and *Laudato Si'*; the *Compendium of the Social Doctrine of the Church*; Vatican messages, speeches, and documents promulgated by the Holy See and the PCJP; and national or regional bishops' statements. Granted, not all documents are considered equally authoritative within CST, so it is important to note that papal encyclicals and the *Compendium* are at the top of the magisterial authority chain. These documents usually serve a heuristic function by raising important issues and establishing key ideas; at the same time, they are wide-ranging and so mention fresh water in relatively succinct ways. As a result, additional documents that directly and exclusively address fresh water are included here.[3] I read the frequency and content of various explorations of fresh water from the hierarchical magisterium as indicators that the church is engaging with the "signs of the times" on matters of fundamental moral concern.

Fresh Water in Catholic Social Teaching —Eight Insights

1.   The "Book of Nature" can be understood through embodied experience, intellectual reflection, and scientific inquiry. Human beings can discern how fresh water occupies a distinct and important role on earth.

Catholic theology has long maintained that there are discernible features of a natural order to creation. This insight is most frequently developed in relation to natural law theory, but it is present throughout the tradition and can be found in CST as well. CST invokes the idea of natural order to cosmic, earthly, and human existence. It emphasizes the importance of rightly ordered relationships within and among these realms. (In a slightly different way, Catholic theologians and ethicists have found deep connections among material, earthly realities, liturgy, and the transcendent—embodied, for example, in the sacramental substances and symbols of bread, wine, water, and oil.)

The "book of nature" is theological shorthand for humans' ability to discern important features of order and value in the world. And it is an idea that is significant for CST's treatment of fresh water in several ways. The 2003 and 2006 letters of the Holy See to the World Water Forums (in Kyoto and Mexico City, respectively) describe many different dimensions of water's essential, life-sustaining relationships in biological, social, religious, aesthetic, and ethical realms: "Water is a primary building block of life. Without water there is no life." The letters maintain that humankind is "called to live in harmony with creation and to respect its integrity," claiming that only when we do so "will we reach a true appreciation of the significance of water in creation and for humankind."[4]

Water is integral to biotic communities, ecosystems, and cultures. The bishops of the Columbia River Watershed (in the United States and Canada) nicely draw out this idea in their 2000 letter, *The Columbia River Watershed: Caring for Creation and Our Common Good.*

> As we study watershed land, air and water, we become aware of other members of the biotic community and the traditions and insights of regional peoples of the land. We come to recognize more fully the interrelatedness of life and the relationship of different lives to the environment in which we dwell. We come to know more than before and we recognize that we have much more to learn.[5]

The interplay of humility and epistemic confidence is an important mark of Catholic theology and ethics. Human beings are finite, limited creatures, but perceptual powers of sensation and intellect also help us discern the difference of order from disorder, of reality from illusion, and of truth from duplicity. To be sure, much rigorous work remains at the intersection of epistemology, natural science, and theological ethics. But CST regards the book of nature and scientific data as trustworthy sources of knowledge.

Initial formulations on fresh water in CST therefore indicated that "water is much more than just a basic human need. It is an essential, irreplaceable element to ensuring the continuance of life,"[6] and, as such, disorder in the book of nature can be manifest as the pollution and depletion of vital resources. *Renewing the Earth,* the 1994 pastoral letter of the US Conference of Catholic Bishops, treated water pollution as one of the problematic signs of the times. A decade later, the *Compendium of the Social Doctrine of the Church* depicted some of the "risky consequences" posed to fresh water reserves in the face of rampant deforestation and rapid desertification.[7] Thus the challenge—stated presciently by Pope Paul VI in 1972—is to prevent "disorderly exploitation of the physical reserves of the planet, even for the purpose of producing something useful."[8] And the problem is not just theoretical—it is immediate, for "today common agreement exists that the survival of humanity and all species on earth depends to a great degree on the fate of water."[9]

2.   *Human beings are stewards of creation, including fresh water.*

The term "creation" abounds with meaning. It refers to the natural world, but not only in an empirical, scientific way; the language is theologically significant, since it refers to God's creation as attested in scripture, liturgy, and tradition. CST depicts creation as a sign of the creator that must be respected and used wisely—not abused or viewed as a set of raw materials to be used for the short-term benefit of a few people. The proper stance is stewardship of the natural world, not domination or exploitation.

Unfortunately, humanity stands in danger of misusing the gifts of creation. CST of the past several decades makes clear how disordered values and ethically dubious decisions have led to environmental degradation (pollution, deforestation), the demise of nonhuman species, and human suffering. The Vatican has consistently expressed that fresh water is part of global ecological and human relationships, order, and harmony (as noted above). In *Laudato Si',* Pope Francis claims that fresh water "is an issue of primary importance, since it is indispensable for human life and for supporting terrestrial and aquatic ecosystems."[10] This moral aspect is threatened by human-caused water scarcity: "Water supplies used to be relatively constant, but now in many places demand exceeds the sustainable supply, with dramatic consequences in the short and long term."[11]

In this context, humans must adopt a stance of stewardship (or protection and wise use) of fresh water resources, rather than exploitation. The bishops of the Columbia River watershed insisted that "our unique role in creation as God's stewards carries with it a serious responsibility for service to God and to creation."[12] In practical terms, this amounts to treating fresh water not as an expendable entitlement, but rather as a good that requires judicious treatment. The bishops of the Murray-Darling Basin in Australia emphasize how, "As bishops, we would like to add our voices in support of the rivers and all those working to save them. . . . We see human beings as responsible before God for the well-being of the river system."[13] Of what does such responsibility consist? CST elaborates the requirements of stewardship through the idea of the universal destination of created goods.

3. Fresh water is one of the "goods of creation" meant for everyone, now and in the future.

Fresh water is a unique and vital "good of creation" that is meant for the benefit of all people across time and space—that is, around the world and for future generations. The concept of "created goods" being intended for the benefit of all people and not just a privileged few has an important twentieth-century history in the Catholic Church. The Vatican II constitution *Gaudium et Spes* held that "God intended the earth with everything contained in it for the use of all human beings and peoples. Thus, under the leadership of justice and in the company of charity, created goods should be in abundance for all in like manner." It added that the "universal destination of earthly goods" supersedes even legitimate, societal forms of property. This amounts to a radical statement of distributive justice: "everything contained in" the earth is intended by God "for the use of all human beings and peoples . . . for all in like manner."[14] Notably, this principle has not been actualized and, with regard to fresh water, it has arguably been hindered within today's neoliberal global market economy. The Synod of Bishops' 1971 document, *Justice in the World,* identified water as an explicit example of the universal destination of created goods: "air and water—without which there cannot be life—and the small delicate biosphere of the whole complex of all life on earth, are not infinite, but on the contrary must be saved and preserved as a unique patrimony belonging to all human beings."[15]

Emphasis on the universal destination of the goods of creation is prominent in the encyclicals of John Paul II, Benedict XVI, and Francis. With regard to water as a particular "good of creation" intended for all, a 2003 Address to the Diplomatic Corps by John Paul II described how "the problem of water resources" must be considered within the entitlement of "all peoples . . . to receive a fair share of the goods of this world and of the know-how of the more advanced countries."[16] So too has the PCJP emphasized that fresh water is a natural good meant for the benefit of all. It is, in their words, a "universal common good . . . its benefits are meant for all and not only for those who live in countries where water is abundant, well managed and well distributed. This natural resource must be equitably at the disposal of the entire human family."[17] More pithily, the *Compendium* insists: "The principle of the universal destination of goods also applies naturally to water."[18] The obligations extend across space (the entire world and human community) and time (for future generations as well as our own). As Benedict XVI stated in his 2010 Address for the World Day of Peace, "Natural resources should be used in such a way that immediate benefits do not have a negative impact on living creatures, human and not, present and future; . . . [and] that human activity does not compromise the fruitfulness of the earth, for the benefit of people now and in the future."[19]

4. Fresh water is an essential part of integral development.

"Authentic" or "integral" development is the powerful notion that well-being cannot be measured simply by economic growth or gross domestic product: development should be oriented toward the dignity of the whole person, and every person. This formulation encompasses fundamental needs that are not part of standard indices of economic development. Such a notion, according to Paul VI's 1967 encyclical *Populorum Progressio* and subsequent CST, should be understood to encompass the whole person—bodily, spiritual, social, educational, political, and economic. So too in his social encyclical *Caritas in Veritate* (which commemorated *Populorum Progressio*), Benedict XVI suggested that integral development cannot proceed without access to sufficient fresh water. In *Laudato Si'*, Pope Francis argues that fresh water is a prerequisite for the achievement of all other human rights. As the centrality of fresh water to well-being has become increasingly evident worldwide, the UN and other organizations well beyond the Vatican have put forward development agendas that take natural resources into account. Thus water was the focus of the UN Millennium Development Goal 7c, which sought to halve by 2015 the proportion of people without access to clean, fresh water or basic sanitation; and the current Sustainable Development Goals likewise foreground access to water and sanitation in Goal 6.[20]

5. Fresh water is a fundamental human right and a right-to-life issue.

Human beings have a responsibility to steward fresh water resources for the benefit of all, around the world and into the future. It is a primary resource that has a "universal destination." It is a fundamental component of integral development. The convergence of these insights translates into the Catholic Church's stipulation that fresh water is a human right. Especially since the papacy of Benedict XVI, the Vatican has regularly endorsed the right to water, especially safe drinking water: "Without water, life is threatened. Therefore, the right to safe drinking water is an inalienable right."[21] Pope Francis adds, in *Laudato Si'*:

Access to safe drinkable water is a basic and universal human right, since it is essential to human survival and, as such, is a condition for the exercise of other human rights. Our world has a grave social debt towards the poor who lack access to drinking water, because they are denied the right to a life consistent with their inalienable dignity.[22]

This is powerful language in an era of global pluralism, economic globalization, and environmental degradation. The idea of human rights enshrined by the UN is one of the few mechanisms for addressing international ethical issues. Given the past few decades' high-intensity global debate over whether water is a human right or an economic commodity (described in chapter 3), the Catholic Church's moral clarion call on the human right to water is extremely important. In the words of the PCJP: "Water is intrinsically linked to fundamental human rights such as the right to life, to food and to health." Since "access to safe water is a basic human right," it "should be interpreted in a manner fully consistent with human dignity and not in a narrow way, by mere reference to volumetric quantities and technologies or by viewing water primarily as an economic good."[23] The *Compendium* likewise underscores that "any merely quantitative assessment that considers water as a merely economic good" is inadmissible, and Benedict XVI echoed these observations in *Caritas in Veritate* as did Francis in *LS*.[24]

But the sharpest contemporary theological and ethical refrain proffered by the church is the idea that fresh water is not only a human rights issue; access to fresh water is described by the Vatican as "truly a right-to-life issue."[25] This is profound rhetoric, especially in the United States where the language of "right to life" is usually reserved for abortion, or possibly birth control. And while some people would hear "right to life" and think about Catholic opposition to the death penalty or euthanasia, and a smaller proportion still would associate immigration, universal access to health care, or ministry to homeless persons, very few would think about faucets, waterborne disease, sanitation infrastructure, or aquifer depletion. Fresh water is not viewed as a right-to-life issue for many Catholics in the United States but, in this regard, it is US Catholics who are out of line with official magisterial teaching.

6. *Water justice requires a preferential option for the poor.*

Many people in industrialized nations are accustomed to clean water that is available twenty-four hours a day from household faucets. On the other end of the spectrum, 663 million people lack access to clean, fresh water; 2.4 billion do not have access to sanitation.[26] In places where fresh water is unavailable or unsafe, water can be very expensive to procure. The results are wrought economically, or through bodily energy that is spent seeking and transporting the liquid itself, or through lost opportunities for education. People living in poverty who cannot afford to pay market price for fresh water are those who suffer most when fresh water becomes scarce. By contrast, those who have the ability to pay are most likely to obtain fresh water. But it is not the case that a person's need for water correlates to the ability to pay for it. Instead, fresh water is a fundamental condition for the survival of all human beings; in the language of CST, the goods of creation are meant for the benefit of everyone regardless of ability to pay, and societies must take special care to protect the fresh water access of people living in poverty and at the margins of society. This principled way of thinking about justice is known in CST as the preferential option for the poor. It has strong roots in Latin American liberation theology and is linked to the notion expounded by Pope Francis, in the first few days of his papacy, that he wants to serve "a poor church, a church for the poor." The *Compendium* succinctly summarizes the ethical impetus of the preferential option for the poor: "Satisfying the needs of all, especially those who live in poverty, must guide the use of water and the services connected with it."[27] Likewise, the PCJP's 2006

Letter to the World Water Forum indicates that "the primary objective of all efforts must be the well-being of those people—men, women, children, families, communities—who live in the poorest parts of the world and suffer most from any scarcity or misuse of water resources."[28] *LS* notes explicitly that fresh water is a core concern in the current era, and that its pollution or absence disproportionately affects people living in poverty.

7. *Technology is useful, but it is not a panacea.*

Fresh water is unevenly distributed across the world due to factors both natural and human-made. This is a challenge for distributive justice that is made more acute by the fact that this century will see increased fresh water scarcity due to patterns of population growth, climate change, agriculture, and industrial uses. So (as noted in chapter 2) it is entirely reasonable to wonder whether technology can solve the range of fresh water problems that are on the horizon. Indeed, technology can address fresh water problems in several general ways. First, technology can increase the efficiency of fresh water distribution and use; it can reduce waste or loss of water from municipal systems. Second, technology might be able to "create" additional supplies of fresh water—for example, with water-gathering techniques or desalination. However, although technology is useful and necessary, it is a tool rather than a solution to complex social and environmental problems. It is a means to ethical ends, not an ultimate end in itself. Moreover, technology brings with it the problem of unintended consequences. For these reasons, technology is not a panacea.

In the view of Catholic theology and ethics, the human capacity for creativity and innovation are proper expressions of human nature. But CST aptly warns that human uses of technology are ambiguous, yielding both good and bad outcomes. As such, technology is not a replacement for careful, ongoing, ethical reflection. Technology must always be used prudently, in the service of an ethical vision of justice and the preferential option for the poor. Technological innovation must go hand in hand with an ethical vision of the proper relationship of environmental impacts, eco-logical well-being, and human flourishing. The suggestion that technological innovation and application need to be conducted within a framework of prudence and downstream effects gives rise to something known as the precautionary principle, which is well known in risk assessment circles and stipulates that, when there are unresolved doubts regarding the safety or efficacy of a technology, more information must be gathered regarding those potential outcomes. This approach is fully endorsed by CST. The *Compendium* states in no uncertain terms that "in the realm of technological-scientific interventions that have forceful and widespread impact on living organisms, with the possibility of significant long-term repercussions, it is unacceptable to act lightly or irresponsibly."[29] As Francis extrapolated in *LS*:

> This precautionary principle makes it possible to pro-tect those who are most vulnerable and whose ability to defend their interests and to assemble incontrovert-ible evidence is limited. If objective information suggests that serious and irreversible damage may result, a proj-ect should be halted or modified, even in the absence of indisputable proof. Here the burden of proof is effectively reversed, since in such cases objective and conclusive demonstrations will have to be brought forward to dem-onstrate that the proposed activity will not cause serious harm to the environment or to those who inhabit it.
>
> This does not mean being opposed to any techno-logical innovations which can bring about an improve-ment in the quality of life. But it does mean that profit cannot be the sole criterion to be taken into account, and that, when significant new information comes to light, a reassessment should be made, with the involvement of all interested parties. The outcome may be a decision not to proceed with a given project, to modify it or to consider alternative proposals.[30]

Thus, the challenge and opportunity regarding technology, in the view of CST, is to direct human ingenuity (and techniques) to wise use in ways that honor the vulnerability of the poor and strive for justice over profit. What does this mean for fresh water? Magisterial documents have invoked several examples of the ambiguous potential of technological intervention in matters of water, including, for example, hydroelectric energy and irrigation. Dams and irrigation provide benefits but also entail significant noneconomic costs, including the loss of land (behind dams), the pollution of rivers (from pesticides and other agricultural runoff), and the over-extraction of nonrenewable fresh water from aquifers.

Methodologically, CST also insists on the principle of subsidiarity, which values the perspectives and decisions of people and groups who live downstream, or whose lives may be negatively affected by the proposed technology. These "stakeholders" are distinct from "shareholders," because while shareholders stand to profit from the successful corporate application of new technologies, stakeholders are the ones who are most likely to bear any negative (even if unintended and unforeseen) consequences. Thus, stakeholders need to have significant roles in the decision-making process. As Benedict wrote in *Caritas in Veritate,* decision making must include "the involvement of local communities in choices and decisions that affect [them and their land]."[31] Pope Francis, in *Laudato Si',* echoes his predecessor:

A number of questions need to be asked in order to discern whether or not [a given project] will contribute to genuine integral development. What will it accomplish? Why? Where? When? How? For whom? What are the risks? What are the costs? Who will pay those costs and how? In this discernment, some questions must have higher priority. For example, we know that water is a scarce and indispensable resource and a fundamental right which conditions the exercise of other human rights. This indisputable fact overrides any other assessment of environmental impact on a region.[32]

Likewise, the PCJP insists "that decisions and management responsibilities pertaining to water should take place at the lowest appropriate level," since while the "water issue is global in scope, it is at the local level where decisive action can best be taken."[33] This kind of accountability helps ensure that the benefits and burdens of a given technology are broadly considered and equitably shared.

8. *A culture of water is part of a culture of life.*

Since the absence of sufficient fresh, clean water carves a jagged edge through a person's ability to survive, the magisterium of the Catholic Church has come to view fresh water as a fundamental human right, indeed, a right-to-life issue. Special care must be taken to ensure that people living in poverty have sufficient access to this vital resource. The realization of these principled insights will require nothing short of a "culture of water"—a term coined by the PCJP and Benedict XVI in their messages to World Water Forums. This is both an invitation and a challenge to today's Catholics, particularly those in the United States.

What would it mean for the "culture of life" to encompass, always and everywhere, a "culture of water"? How different would the discourse surrounding "right-to-life" issues in the United States appear if these dimensions were to be taken to heart by all who have ears to hear? It is time to expand the conversation, as part of Pope Francis's assessment in *LS* that "we are faced not with two separate crises, one environmental and the other social, but rather with one complex crisis which is both social and environmental. Strategies for a solution demand an integrated approach to combating poverty, restoring dignity to the excluded, and at the same time protecting nature."[34] If longtime Vatican commentator John Allen Jr. is right that a Vatican Ecological Task Force could be a crucial component for furthering the church's theological and social mission in the twenty-first century and could draw together theological, ethical, liturgical, and spiritual resources for complex environmental issues, then why not delve into fresh, living water as a first subject?[35] In fact, the Vatican has arguably already begun to inculcate an ecclesial "culture of water" that explores environmental and social realities. In addition to advocating for a human right to water, Pope Francis has also established showers at the Vatican for Rome's homeless population and, in a scholarly vein, the Vatican has convened several summits on the topic of fresh water, including on topics both scientific and ethical—most recently, in a "Dialogue on Water" held in February 2017 in conjunction with the Pontifical Academy of Sciences.[36]

Conclusion:
A Right-to-Life Issue for the Twenty-First Century

In the first decades of the twenty-first century, it is abundantly clear that the institutional church is fallible. New data, perspectives, and forms of analysis can and should be integrated into magisterial reflections on topics like fresh water. Even so, the framework offered in this chapter has significant conceptual power. At best, it can be regarded as a mosaic that casts the question of fresh water's value into visible, principled, many-hued form. The resulting picture is evocative, though unfinished. What is sensible, illuminating, and resonant should be taken up in the broader discourses of fresh water ethics, for refinement and augmentation, for challenging and nuancing, for robust debate and critique. A fundamental criterion is whether it helps illuminate important moral insights that conduce toward the achievement of water justice amid a complex, dynamic set of hydrosocial realities.

The official documents cited in this chapter are relatively recent developments for the 2,000-year-old Catholic Church. They represent a steady and fruitful development of CST with attention to "the signs of the times," as called for by Vatican II, and they point toward normative commitments regarding the value and significance of fresh water, in light of social and environmental problems that have come to the fore in an era of economic globalization. A variety of organizations have adopted and adapted these principled teachings, such that the water-related projects of organizations like CRS, NCRLC, and CAFOD engage in ethical action that is linked to, but neither dependent solely on nor ultimately beholden to, magisterial teachings about fresh water. But these efforts, like the interpretive keys delineated above, are not intended as thinly veiled religious apologetics. Finding wisdom in CST does not require assent to Catholic dogma or teachings on other issues. One does not need to be a practicing Catholic, a Christian, or a theist of some stripe to perceive wisdom in the church's ideas on fresh water, or to support on-the-ground organizations like CRS or the NCRLC. Papal social encyclicals have often been addressed, after all, to "all people of good will." Pope Francis, in his first ecumenical meeting, referred to atheists as allies in "the careful protection of creation," and *Laudato Si'* is addressed to "everyone living on this planet."[37] If some insights from CST resonate with people who consider themselves atheist, unaffiliated, humanist, Jewish, Wiccan, or any other designation, then that is good news: in an era of economic globalization, collaboration on matters of ethical concern can and should extend beyond identity politics and metaphysical disagreement. Ethical alliances should not be coercive, nor ought they require creedal affirmations. Wisdom can be found in many places, and any compelling, persuasive, and helpful fresh water ethic will necessarily be the result of philosophical and ethical bricolage.

Fresh water ethics is very much a discourse in formation. Water relief organizations, scholarly institutions, think tanks, researchers, and concerned citizens are at work on this issue around the world, and they represent all manner of motivating insights and frameworks of knowledge. There is no one-size-fits-all vessel in which to contain and display truths about fresh water, which always exceeds the parameters of any single mode of analysis. In some ways, it is precisely this slippery ubiquity of fresh water that lends it to theological and spiritual imagination.

CHAPTER 5

The Agriculture/Water Nexus

The projected global population in 2030 is 8.5 billion people, and for 2050 the projection is 9.7 billion.[1] Everyone, present and future, will need food to eat, and agriculture currently accounts for approximately 70 percent of the world's fresh water withdrawals and over 90 percent of consumptive water use. Agriculture is the process by which arable land and crops are cultivated, receive water, and are harvested and used by human beings. Agricultural crops need not be intended directly for human consumption (corn for biofuels, alfalfa for animal feed, and cotton for textiles are all examples). Still, a significant proportion of agriculture is food related, and for the purposes of this chapter I treat agriculture and food production more or less interchangeably. Where does the water for agriculture come from? What are the impacts of industrial agriculture on water supply and quality? How watery are food products? How do food consumption preferences play out with regard to water and agriculture? How might religious values figure into conversations about agriculture, water sustainability, and justice?

Making Water Visible from Seed to Supper:
Virtual Water and Water Footprints

The wateriness of food is tantalizingly clear in the names of some produce, such as watermelon or watercress, or when sensing the liquid juices in a ripe cantaloupe or cluster of grapes.

The water content of food is much harder to perceive in grains of rice, sprouts of cruciferous vegetables, or racks of ribs. In fact, approximately 95 percent of water consumed during the life cycle of food is hidden: it is not visible in the final product, because it is water that was bestowed on fields during growing seasons or used for milling, cleaning, or otherwise producing the food we eat. Still, with every food substance, there is a history of water inputs. How can the wateriness of food be made visible?

Scholars have generated several ways to track inputs of water into food. The idea of *virtual water* was coined in the early 1990s by J. Anthony Allan, now an emeritus professor in the UK. Virtual water is a form of measurement that helps to conceptualize and track net flows of water. The concept refers to the amount of water consumed—or "embedded"—from start to finish in the production of various industrial and agricultural goods that are then traded among nations and regions. Tracking virtual water can reveal how societies direct water that originates in their territories, is consumed by agricultural (and industrial) processes, and is then traded or sold. In fact, Allan developed the concept of virtual water while puzzling over how water-poor countries in the Middle East managed to maintain a growing population under conditions of fresh water scarcity (one answer: such countries as Israel import water-intensive crops, deploying available surface or groundwater for other productive purposes). Economists, political strategists, and environmentalists use the measure of "virtual water" to assess patterns of water import and export on national and international levels.

Closely related to virtual water is the idea of a *water footprint*, which is a term that was coined by Arjen Hoekstra, a professor of water management in the Netherlands. The water footprint is analogous to the similar-sounding carbon footprint but, like virtual water, a water footprint reflects the amount of water consumed in the production of various goods or services. A water footprint incorporates direct and indirect uses of water and can be scaled to a range of levels. As the centralized Water Footprint Network explains:

People use lots of water for drinking, cooking and washing, but even more for producing things such as food, paper, cotton clothes, etc. The water footprint is an indicator of water use that looks at both direct and indirect water use of a consumer or producer. The water footprint of an individual, community or business is defined as the total volume of freshwater that is used to produce the goods and services consumed by the individual or community or produced by the business.[2]

For example, although one cup of coffee contains roughly eight ounces of hot water, the forty or so coffee beans brewed into that cup represent approximately 36.5 gallons of water from seed to bean. If you'd like to nibble on chocolate with your coffee, consider that a quarter pound of chocolate—just four ounces—requires 750 gallons of water to produce. Even more staggering is the water footprint of beef: roughly 1,800 gallons of water are required to produce just one pound of beef (more will be said about meat later).[3] Totaling up all of these goods and services over a set amount of time and scale can yield the water footprint of a person, family, institution, community, or nation. The water footprint is often a useful way for individuals to begin to understand how much of modern life relies on water inputs that are, more often than not, invisible in taken-for-granted daily habits and food products.

To make water visible in agriculture is to open a certain kind of aperture, from which still other factors come into view: the shape and scale of food systems; the socially constructed preferences that increase demand for certain crops over others; governmental subsidies and the political clout of agribusiness; the role of hydraulic technologies, such as irrigation and groundwater extraction; mechanized planting and sowing and their impacts on water retention capabilities of soil; the use of petrochemical fertilizers, pesticides, and herbicides and the downstream effects of these compounds; genetically modified seeds and monocultures. To be sure, contemporary agriculture is multifaceted, not monolithic. It is a complex social and economic reality that is shaped by geography, technology, hydrology, history, sociocultural habits, economics, and policy. Still, distinct values and practices have characterized agricultural production and related water use in the era of globalization and population growth that mark the late twentieth and early twenty-first centuries. A brief history of agriculture will help situate how the values and patterns of the last one hundred years matter for considering future patterns of consumptive water use.

A Brief History of Agriculture, from Prehistory to the Produce Aisle

Archaeological discoveries, pictorial representations, and written records point toward the advent of settled agriculture in several different areas of the world, all approximately ten thousand years ago. From that point into the present day, agriculture has persisted as a primary mode of human work and a form of productive relationship among human beings, land, and biotic life. Early agriculture involved cultivation of wild plants, followed by domestication of those plants in sedentary human settlements. The invention of the plow—around 6000 BCE—provided additional advances, followed by the eventual domestication of animal species such as the ox. Over time, settled agriculture facilitated an increase in the carrying capacity of the land—that is, it increased the quantity of food produced in a given area and thereby decreased the amount of land required to sustain a given population. For millennia, though, agricultural practices changed in only minor ways. The historian of antiquity Lukas Thommen notes that "ancient agriculture demonstrated great continuity: there was neither any revolutionary technological innovation in agriculture nor any mechanization, only some improvements in the tools and the methods of cultivation. No large-scale enterprises came into being"; instead, "forms of property and means of production" varied according to location.[4] Examples of regional differences include Egyptian agricultural systems of irrigation, or, in the Mediterranean regions of ancient Greece and Rome, the temperate climate proved hospitable to a diversity of crops such as olives, legumes, and fruits that were watered largely through precipitation.

Of course, agriculture was not static. Trade patterns among Europe, the Middle East, and Asia—and after colonization, Africa as well as North and South America—yielded exchange of new crops and products, from spices to maize. New technologies amplified agricultural productivity: during the medieval period, windmills gradually proliferated across parts of Europe and Asia and contributed to the processing of grains and other agricultural functions, including extraction of water. Still, as Thommen indicates, these improvements did not reshape the practice or character of agriculture on a large scale. Crop yield was determined by relatively stable factors such as microclimate, soil quality, and water supply. Eventually, the scientific and industrial revolutions ushered in a series of innovations in technology and economics that enabled societies to corral natural resources and put them to certain forms of productive use in new ways. The mechanical innovation and fuller realization of those developments in the nineteenth and especially twentieth centuries enabled human beings to revolutionize the character, outcomes, and scale of agricultural production. One of the most visible forms of that revolution is in hydraulic technologies, which amplified the kind of control farmers could have over water for their crops.

For most of recorded history, much of the water used in agriculture came from seasonal cycles of precipitation (a practice known now as "dry farming"). In semi-arid and arid regions, this often meant that water had to be drawn from wells or natural water sources and then transported to fields by manual or animal labor or rudimentary irrigation canals. Until the early twentieth century, large-scale storage and distribution of water for agriculture simply did not exist. The twentieth century, by contrast, saw an unprecedented and rapid proliferation of large-scale dams, irrigation canals, and deep wells. The scale of these hydraulic developments helped to establish global, industrial agriculture under the banner of the "Green Revolution," which enabled human communities to reach new levels of crop production in areas as diverse as the American West, Israel, and India. The industrial shape of agriculture that now characterizes much of the world is the direct result of hydraulic and other developments spawned from the Industrial Revolution, which has viewed water and land as resources to be directed toward economically productive ends.

Industrialization, Land, and Water in Nineteenth-Century US Agriculture

In the nineteenth century, Karl Marx noted that factory-based urban economies were altering the nature of agriculture in England. Rapidly growing urban centers such as London increasingly relied on food supply from rural areas, leading to shifts in agricultural production. Where local agriculture had once been prevalent, new regional and national networks were geared toward sating the hunger of urban populations, which then consumed the fruits of the countryside and created a trail of pollution through newly necessary mechanisms such as transportation and waste management. Marx observed how this shift amounted to a "metabolic rift" between human beings and the land. As John Bellamy Foster, Brett Clark, and Richard York have explained, "This rupture in the soil nutrient cycle undermined the regenerative capacity of the ecosystem. Marx argued that it was necessary to 'restore' the soil metabolism to ensure environmental sustainability for the generations to come."[5]

Marx's early observation about the "metabolic rift" of nineteenth-century agriculture was prescient. Across the Atlantic Ocean, foundations were being laid for a dramatic increase in agricultural efficiency and productivity in the United States. By the 1830s, a blacksmith named John Deere had grown frustrated with the insufficiency of wooden plows for Midwestern soils. He developed the first steel plow, which proved highly durable and led eventually to mechanized plows, which in turn facilitated fossil fuel–based, mechanized agriculture (replacing the human and animal energy that had borne agricultural labor for millennia). At the same time, the US federal government offered western land grants under the ideal of democratic expansion to settlers who were willing to explore and cultivate the wild frontier. The rhetoric was, at times, downright religious: the work of settlers would help to render a "New Eden" out of arid lands in places like California.[6] Some of these areas proved more hospitable to agriculture than others. In the American West, the semi-arid and arid climates defied expectations of settler-colonists from the loamy east coast: fresh water, in particular, was hard to come by. Indigenous societies that had long inhabited these regions had developed a range of ways of orienting food production to climate realities—but their presence was ignored, their societies relocated or diminished, and their claims to land ripped out from under them by the inexorable and government-sponsored march of US westward expansion under the banner of democratic progress.[7]

Climatic and hydrological difficulties did little to quell the ideology of agriculturalism endorsed by powerful engineers, businessmen, and regional planners. Those groups lobbied effectively for federal support for irrigation and hydraulic infrastructure in the American West—a vision that they presented as necessary for achieving democratic values, agricultural abundance, and economic productivity. Their clamor led to the 1902 National Reclamation (Newlands) Act, which enabled monies from the sale of public lands to be placed in a fund for the construction of irrigation projects. Because it amounted to the "federalizing of irrigation," historian David Worster refers to the Newlands Act as "the most important single piece of legislation in the history of the West."[8] Thereafter, a generation of national leaders viewed rivers as engines of economic productivity. In the words of engineer, mining magnate, and eventual president Herbert

Hoover, "Every drop of water that runs to the sea without yielding its full commercial returns to the nation is an economic waste."[9] Federal legislation during and after the Great Depression funded large dams and irrigation programs in the American West, for hydropower as well as agricultural development. And despite the Edenic, democratic rhetoric deployed to advocate these projects, it turns out that the primary beneficiaries were not small, family farms, but rather private corporations. This "conquest of arid America" was, as historians Jessica Teisch and Donald Pisani have independently expressed, part and parcel of a "climate of post-gold-rush technological change," optimism about scientific progress, and the consolidation of natural resources toward economically productive uses.[10]

These attitudes of technological prowess and economic viability rested, in part, on the assumption that natural resources were abundant on the new frontier. In the mid-nineteenth century, Alexis de Tocqueville had observed that "one must go to America to understand what power material well-being exerts on political actions and even on opinions themselves, which ought to be subject only to reason."[11] As the gold rush and Manifest Destiny encouraged settlers to explore and use the natural resources in the American West, the attitude of abundance became semi-official US policy. To that end, Donald Pisani reports how, in light of the seemingly endless nineteenth-century frontier, "American agriculture had always been characterized by the exchange of poor, exhausted land for virgin soil."[12] And as ideals of an economically productive agriculture took firmer root, American farmers in the West (followed eventually by the rest of the country)

> gradually became slaves of market agriculture and the new consumer culture. . . . The western farmers who watered their land after 1900 could not practice subsistence agriculture even if they wanted to; irrigation required substantial capital just to meet expenses. . . . The forces of capitalism were relentless and inexorable. . . . By the 1930s

much of the countryside had become tributary to the factory and the city, not the realm of autonomous family farms envisioned by proponents of the Reclamation Act in 1902.[13]

Agriculture was becoming agribusiness—thanks in part to hydraulic technologies, government subsidies, and the view that land and water should be used for short-term economic gain.

Hydraulic prowess was certainly visible in dams and irrigation canals. By the turn of the twentieth century, it also began to reach deep into the earth—far deeper than ever before. Innovations in drilling and pumping mechanisms facilitated extraction of water that had previously been inaccessible to human beings. "In the 1890s," writes water history and law expert Robert Glennon, "the development of rotary or centrifugal pumps gave High Plains farmers access to deeper groundwater aquifers." When coupled with the power of the internal combustion engine, "this development profoundly changed the face of western agriculture."[14] Access to never-before-used groundwater sources was a convenient and timely boon for twentieth-century agriculture: it amounted to the discovery of vast new supplies of fresh water and "enabled farmers to overcome the limitations imposed by Mother Nature."[15] As Glennon remarks, "Groundwater was . . . thought to be as inexhaustible as the air we breathe."[16] Such is not the case, but the assumption of abundance dies hard.

Cumulative advances in hydraulic technology facilitated a revolution in the scale of agricultural production, which was no longer at the mercy of seasonal rainfall or laborious transportation of fresh water. Arid and semi-arid regions, which had been only paltry producers of crops for most of human history, were now transformed by the influx of fresh water from dams, irrigation canals, and groundwater. Thus in 1960, Gilbert White, a professor of geography at the University of Chicago, opined that

in a strict sense, water can be brought wherever man wishes if he is willing to take the trouble to pay the cost of carrying out elaborate engineering works or of effecting other changes in the natural cycle of water. . . . Canals, aqueducts, pumps, diversion dams, storage dams are common devices for changing the place and time of water.[17]

Guiding economic philosophies of the time portrayed these technological, industrial, and agricultural developments as feasible, desirable, exportable—and profitable.[18] Many engineers and geographers such as White were optimistic about the transferability of scientific and hydraulic expertise to contexts worldwide. Historian Lynton Keith Caldwell observes that "with the development of hydraulic technologies even the initial absence of water has not precluded human settlement and economic development. Water transport technologies, exemplified by dams, canals, irrigation, aqueducts, and waste disposal systems, were an absolute prerequisite to the expansion of agriculture."[19] Then, in the mid-twentieth century, these hydraulic developments combined with fossil fuel extraction, petrochemical processing, mechanized sowing and harvesting, seed manipulation, and large-scale monoculture to facilitate an exponential increase in agricultural production in the United States and around the world.

Population, Petrochemicals, and Pollution:
High-Yield Agriculture in the Green Revolution

In 1798 the Reverend Robert Thomas Malthus published his monograph, *An Essay on the Principles of Population,* which put forward the idea that a struggle for survival results when population growth (which increases geometrically) eventually exceeds food supply (which does not compound in the same way). This idea has been wildly influential—it was, for example, a linchpin of Charles Darwin's theorizing—and in recent history it is perhaps most famously enshrined in Paul Ehrlich's fervor-inducing 1968 bestseller, *The Population Bomb.*[20] Ehrlich wrote that the rate of human population growth was disproportionate to agricultural production, such that the earth's carrying capacity would be out-paced by the growing human population. As Ehrlich presented the issue in the first edition, the "population bomb" is a problem of "too many people" and "too little food," and he predicted an imminent population crash due to resource scarcity.[21] This text and core thesis has remained wildly influential in environmental thought, despite heavily Orientalist and racist biases.

Devastating famines and food scarcity have certainly occurred in many regions worldwide. Yet, somehow, in the twentieth century world population tripled and more overall food crops were produced than ever before, even as vast numbers of people moved to urban areas. The primary reason that food production increased in the twentieth century was the Green Revolution. As journalist Wil S. Hylton framed it, during the Green Revolution, "Land that had been marginal became dependable; land that was dependable became bountiful."[22] The Green Revolution loosely refers to several decades, beginning around the time of World War II, which gave rise to unprecedented agricultural productivity around the world. During this time, scientific, technological, and economic developments contributed to massive increases in agricultural efficiency and productivity through the development and application of synthetic fertilizers and pesticides, herbicides, and fungicides; genetic manipulation and hybridization of seeds; innovations in the production of industrial machinery for agri-cultural planting, tilling, and harvesting; hydraulic feats such as large-scale dams, irrigation, and extraction of water from ground-water sources, especially aquifers; furrow-to-furrow planting of monocultures (one crop per field) and the decline of crop species diversity; and the consolidation of farmland and farm operations by corporate-run agribusiness. For several decades, these fac-tors have combined to render highly productive crop yields and agricultural profits. The trend is quite likely finite, however. The amount of arable land has decreased in the past few decades, the result of industrial agriculture's litany of discontents: soil exhaus-tion, salinization, depletion of water sources, and desertification.

The tale of the Green Revolution must also be told as a tale of hydraulic technologies, petrochemicals, and economic incentive. As agriculture expanded to arid and semi-arid lands under the auspices of government subsidies and global trade markets, ever more water was required to grow economically desirable but thirsty crops, like cotton. Dams, irrigation canals, and groundwater extraction brought the water to thirsty farms. Government subsidies (along with sales of hydroelectric power) underwrote the costs of long-distance water transportation.[23] These hydraulic technologies facilitated the twentieth century's sixfold increase in the amount of water withdrawn and used.

Another key development in the amplified productivity of agriculture was the fossil fuel–based, synthetic production of nitrogen fertilizer. In the mid-twentieth century, the surfeit of ammonium nitrates "used for explosives in World War II, were redeployed towards synthetic fertilizers and placed on American farms."[24] The results have been staggering. As Michael Pollan explains the origin of industrial agriculture in *The Omnivore's Dilemma,*

> Liberated from the old biological constraints, the farm could now be managed on industrial principles, as a factory transforming inputs of raw material—chemical fertilizer—into outputs of corn. Since the farm no longer needs to generate and conserve its own fertility by maintaining a diversity of species, synthetic fertilizer opens the way to monoculture, allowing the farmer to bring the factory's economies of scale and mechanical efficiency to nature. . . . Fixing nitrogen allowed the food chain to turn from the logic of biology and embrace the logic of industry.[25]

This synthetic nitrogen-based conquest of soils has replaced the prior process of multilayered, organic, cyclical vegetative decomposition and generation. Award-winning author and journalist Katherine Gustafson has aptly summarized the ambiguous petrochemical pervasiveness of industrial agriculture:

The massive use of nitrogen fertilizers created out of fossil fuels . . . allows for large-scale, mechanized production by fewer and fewer farmers but also pollutes groundwater, acidifies soil, and threatens biodiversity. These fertilizers are used in excess, as crops only absorb about one-half of the nitrogen in fertilizers that are applied to fields, leaving tons to run off into waterways and wreak havoc on marine ecosystems. Chemical pesticides, of which 1.1 billion pounds were used in the United States in 2007, also pollute our soil and water and are associated with cancer and endocrine disruption in farmworkers.[26]

Harnessing the expressive power of both images and words, the book *Petrochemical America* (a collaboration between photographer Richard Misrach and landscape architect Kate Orff) depicts the results: crop yield has increased but much pollution and degradation has also occurred, "adversely affecting the biology of our soils and . . . leading to the collapse of downstream marine ecosystems due to the combined effects of erosion, hypoxia, and eutrophication."[27] Toxicologists, hydrologists, and urban planners bear witness to the declining health of rivers, estuaries, and even regions of the ocean as a result of the effluent from petrochemical fertilizers, herbicides, fungicides, and pesticides. A pungent example can be found in the Mississippi River watershed, which begins in Minnesota and bisects the United States through its outlet into the Gulf of Mexico. Petrochemicals flow into the Mississippi River watershed from Midwestern agribusinesses, generating runoff that has created a "nearly 8,500-square-mile 'dead zone,' so called because its lack of oxygen kills aquatic life," including the Gulf's formerly "high-value seafood" and local economies.[28]

The cycle is pernicious: Midwestern agribusinesses produce monocultures—primarily corn, secondarily soybeans—that are susceptible to disease and so require ever more petrochemical cocktails of pesticides, herbicides, and fungicides. Many of these chemical compounds are endocrine disruptors or carcinogens and have been linked to public health disasters such as cancer and fetal deformities. For such reasons, in 2004 the European Union banned the herbicide atrazine from use in its territories.[29] Despite the EU ban, atrazine is still used prolifically in the United States and many other countries around the world. In the US Midwest, atrazine is deployed for many reasons, including modest (but often rhetorically inflated) agribusiness attempts to slow soil degradation through no-till agriculture. After application, atrazine is absorbed into the land and flows as runoff into the Mississippi and other rivers, where it permeates the water supply. It is also unwittingly absorbed, inhaled, and consumed by farmworkers and suburban consumers on a regular basis.[30] The Natural Resources Defense Council (NRDC) in 2009 conducted a meta-analysis of water monitoring data for atrazine "and found pervasive contamination of watersheds and drinking water systems across the Midwest and Southern United States." Moreover, NRDC presents US monitoring mechanisms as "inadequate" and "weak," thereby effectively "compounding the problem, allowing levels of atrazine in watersheds and drinking water to peak at extremely high concentrations."[31] Numerous other chemical compounds used in agriculture have dubious toxicological outcomes. Although crop yields have increased as a result of petrochemical applications, so too downstream bodies of water have become increasingly suffused with atrazine and other synthetic, agricultural petrochemicals. Ingestion of these compounds is not a choice for most individuals; rather, it is a reality of bioaccumulation, such that most of the bodies of the planet's people—including the unborn—carry chemical composites ingested through food consumption, water supply, and even the air we breathe.[32]

In many nations, industrial agriculture depends on hydraulic infrastructure that supports a model of food production that creates massive profits for agricultural, petrochemical, and seed-development corporations. And indeed, it has facilitated a fabulously productive agricultural economy, at least from the view of short-term crop yield and economic profit. There are other consequences. In the United States, the overlap between federal subsidies and industrial food production tends artificially to suppress food prices at grocery stores and discourage innovation toward ecologically informed agricultural practices. Small to mid-size individual and family farms struggle to break even financially in a complicated food economy. Bodies of farmworkers bear the brunt of toxic overload from working in pesticide-laden fields.

And although industrial agriculture has increased the quantity of food produced and facilitated population growth, it has not necessarily remedied ongoing problems of human hunger. Of course, global hunger is a complex problem, but many experts agree that a major problem is access and distribution, not mere scarcity: the world's food is not necessarily in the right distribution channels at the right time.[33] Even within the United States there are vast differentials in access to fresh, healthy food depending on one's socioeconomic status and geographic location, with many lower-income urban areas now being referred to as "food deserts."

Ecological Consequences: Depleted Groundwater and Soils

High-yield, petrochemical-intensive industrial agriculture is unhinged from key ecological factors, most notably water supply and soil health. Increased demand for fresh water has been answered in the short term by dams, irrigation, and groundwater extraction. But withdrawal and consumption of water at current rates is unsustainable. The ongoing development and application of chemical fertilizers, herbicides, and pesticides present major toxic consequences; in addition to polluting rivers and soils, some petrochemicals contribute to global warming (ammonium nitrate, for example, degrades to nitrous oxide, which is a potent greenhouse gas). Industrial monoculture is also devastating to soil health as chemicals saturate soils and the practice of furrow-to-furrow monoculture, which utilizes every available inch of property, has exhausted soils worldwide. Thus, while the Green Revolution has promoted high-yield, resource-intensive, industrial agriculture around the world in the twentieth and now twenty-first centuries, it has also come with real ecological and social costs.[34] As Wes Jackson of the Land Institute explicated the situation in 1980,

> Consider these paradoxes of our time. There is less soil on our fields each year, but there is more total production from the fields. The soil becomes increasingly poisoned from farm chemicals and salts from irrigation, and still there is more production. A million acres a year are lost to urbanization, and production climbs. There is a continual decline in the variety of germ plasm, and therefore our major crops are increasingly vulnerable to pests and diseases, yet crop production climbs. There is less water for irrigation in our aquifers, and yet more total water is being pumped, contributing to an increase in production.[35]

The short-term focus of industrial agriculture has depleted topsoil, drawn down aquifers, and saturated land and water with synthetic chemicals. Sadly, most of these ecological costs are invisible within the short-term calculus of quarterly or annual reports.

Degraded soils and depleted aquifers are often intangible abstractions—indeed, perhaps even distractions—to consumers at big-box grocery stores who are distanced from the sources and methods of production. As Charles Bowden observed in 1977,

> Industrialized societies have decided that the important criterion in measuring farming productivity is the yield of energy and not the investment. Progress is determined by raising a field from 40 bushels of something to 80 bushels of something. . . . Thus, Americans in general seem unaware that behind the glories of their agriculture lie a standing army of plant scientists and extension agents, a gluttonous appetite for fossil fuels, and legions of machines. Crop varieties are lauded if they prove lusty

consumers of fertilizer and water. This way of thinking
makes perfect sense in a world where coal, oil, natural gas,
and groundwater are limitless, renewable resources.[36]

Thus, more than thirty years later, the system of industrial agriculture continues apace, often out of sight and thus out of mind.
Green Revolution–inspired industrial agriculture is a significant
system of food production in the present day, but it is not a sustainable long-term approach. Yes, the world needs to be fed, but
it needs to be fed in perpetuity, not just in the short term, and
it needs to be nourished, not just provided with empty calories.
The challenge for governments, societies, and farmers is to facilitate a series of peaceful agricultural revolutions geared toward
crop resilience and the protection of vital natural resources—most
fundamentally, soil and water—so that agricultural production
can be maintained for current and future generations. A threefold
glimpse of industrial agriculture's visible and invisible impacts on
fresh water supply can demonstrate how the current paradigm is
unsustainable. We begin with the Aral Sea before turning to large
dams and concluding with the problem of aquifer depletion.

The Devastation of the Aral Sea

Once upon a time, the Aral Sea was a vacation destination,
"renowned in the Soviet Union for its blue waters, plentiful fish,
stunning beaches, and bustling fishing ports."[37] No longer. Now,
NASA satellite maps reveal the Aral Sea as three small pools cow-
ering at the far edges of what was formerly the northern shoreline of the sea. A line indicating the approximate shoreline in 1960
bears witness to the profound decimation of a sea that formerly
covered "an area the size of Belgium and the Netherlands combined."[38] Science writer Fred Pearce recounts his visit to the region:

About three miles out to sea, I spotted a fox. It wasn't
swimming. The sea as marked on the map is no longer a

sea. The fox was jogging through endless tamarisk on the bed of what was once the world's fourth largest inland body of water. In the past forty years, most of the Aral Sea in Central Asia has turned into a huge uncharted desert. For the most part, no human has ever set foot there. This new desert is adding dry land twenty times the size of Manhattan every year. . . . The United Nations calls the disappearance of the Aral Sea the greatest environmental disaster of the twentieth century.[39]

What happened?

The sea, of course, did not dry up of its own accord. In keeping with hydraulic principles of the Green Revolution and in pursuit of short-term economic gain from cotton production, during the latter half of the twentieth century the former USSR diverted the two major tributaries that flowed into the Aral Sea and rerouted those waters to whet the enormous thirst of cotton farms in a dry climate. More and more water was taken until the tributaries no longer reached their terminus in the sea. The once-bustling fishing and shipping industries of the area collapsed. The soil became—and remains—highly saline and full of toxic chemicals. Dust storms abound, and regional weather extremes have intensified.[40] The regional economy is decimated. The human communities that remain are plagued by chronic anemia and birth defects. And the once-sparkling, vast Aral Sea is now a paltry series of three hypersaline pools, simmering on a concave basin of toxic dust. The desert landscape is punctuated only by the occasional fox or the rusted hulls of ships beached far from shore.

As with many ecological tragedies, the chain of causality in the desiccation of the Aral Sea is painfully clear in retrospect. But this turn of events was not a matter of apparent concern to the engineers, businessmen, and politicians who plotted and orchestrated the diversion of the Amu and Syr Darya. Experts like Gilbert White, for example, in 1960 described the Amu Darya as among "the great and perennial streams . . . which rise in well-watered mountains and flow out across dry plateau and plains to the sea." He stressed that while such "streams" have "huge seasonal variations, they do carry water throughout the year."[41] Yet in the twenty-first century, the Amu Darya (like many rivers worldwide) always stops short of the sea. The withering of such rivers is a bleak symbol of industrial agriculture's thirst. At the very least, it affirms the conjecture of maverick hydrological theorist Karl Wittfogel, who observed in 1957 how "the pioneers of hydraulic agriculture, like the pioneers of rainfall farming, were unaware of the ultimate consequences of their choice. Pursuing recognized advantage, they initiated an institutional development which led far beyond the starting point."[42] Hydraulic optimism has led to hydrological overreach.

The decline of the Aral Sea is tragic. It is also a relatively straightforward case. We can point to the specific policy decisions made by the former USSR—to grow cotton; to divert the rivers for irrigation—and the direct, disastrous downstream consequences. The causal chain is fairly straightforward. But what of cases with more complex chains of causality?

Dam It All?

Large dams are a visible example of twentieth-century enthusiasm about hydraulic technology. Fred Pearce suggests that "dams became symbols of modernism, of economic development, and of mankind's control over nature. Russia wanted its own Hoover Dam; so did Egypt and Japan and China and India. Hoovers sprouted across Latin America; Britain built replicas for its colonies as parting gifts before independence. No nation-state, it seemed, was complete without one."[43] The twentieth century was indeed the era of large dams. Yet in recent decades, a crescendo of resistance to large dams has emerged from many different parts of the world. Activists, scholars, scientists, and policy makers have published scathing critiques of the social and ecological devastation that accompanies these massive structures and have challenged the economic ideologies and accounting practices that undergird state support for large dams, as well as the terms of transnational development loans that require hydropower and irrigation projects.[44] Partly in response to those critiques, the World Commission on Dams was formed in 1998 to evaluate the costs and benefits of large dams worldwide. The commission issued its final report, *Dams and Development: A Framework for Decision-Making,* in 2000. It concluded that while "dams have made an important and significant contribution to development," in "too many cases an unacceptable and often unnecessary price has been paid to secure those benefits, especially in social and environmental terms, by people displaced, by communities downstream, by taxpayers and the natural environment."[45]

In the United States, large dams are increasingly viewed as things of the past. But in many parts of the world, massive dam projects continue unabated—the result of long-term hydrological and geopolitical strategies, agricultural policies, and residual conditions of development loans. For example, the Three Gorges Dam, begun in 2006, is part of China's long-term energy, hydrological, and economic strategies, but it has also been the subject of intense scrutiny and international critique. Three Gorges is, according to the International Rivers Network advocacy group, "the world's largest hydropower project and most notorious dam," setting records for "number of people displaced, number of cities and towns flooded, and length of reservoir."[46] Still the Chinese government continues its stoic defense of the project. Indeed, from Africa to South America and Southeast Asia, the fervor of dam building is ongoing, and concern about control of the headwaters—as in the damming of the Blue Nile in Ethiopia—amplify international tensions. Corporations and governments continue to propose and implement new massive dam structures for hydropower, irrigation, and manufacturing (examples include Belo Monte in Brazil and the Sarawak Dam in Malaysia). In the twenty-first century, dams are considered by some to be relics of hydraulic modernity, yet they also continue to serve practical and strategic functions especially for industrializing nation-states.

Groundwater Depletion: Mining Ancient Aquifers

Concrete structures like dams, reservoirs, sluice gates, and canals that snake through a landscape are visible manifestations of large-scale hydraulic technologies. But there is much more to twentieth- and twenty-first-century hydraulic technologies and water consumption than meets the eye. In fact, some of the most significant fresh water sources are hidden deep underground, well out of sight. The groundwater thus hidden from view amounts to roughly 30 percent of all the fresh water on this planet.

Humans have long dug wells and sought deeper sources of water, but for most of human history large-scale groundwater extraction simply wasn't feasible: the water was too deep, too diffuse, required too much energy to draw up—basically, it was just too hard to get. But then, during the twentieth century, new hydraulic technologies effectively increased the available fresh water supply for agriculture, manufacturing, and domestic uses. The hydraulic "discovery"—and exploitation—of deep groundwater has had cascading effects: massive agricultural expansion, significant population growth, amplified industrialization. Not all groundwater resides in aquifers, and groundwater is usually linked in substantial ways to surface water. Still, the water in aquifers has often accrued over centuries, millennia, and in some cases millions of years such that the most ancient, finite water supplies are colloquialized among water experts as "fossil water."

The fossil water in cavernous, underground formations has underwritten the construction of cities, farms, and civilizations. Water from deep aquifers, accessed only since the twentieth century, has allowed the amplification of food production and population growth in the twentieth and now twenty-first centuries.

But some of this groundwater is not renewable on any humanly meaningful time scale. Analysts at Circle of Blue, a nonprofit water think tank and journalism center, predict a sustained

> economic and social reckoning that some of the world's agricultural hotspots will face in the coming decades. California's Central Valley, India's Gangetic Plain, the North China Plain, and the Arabian Peninsula—all are key farming regions, all are sucking out groundwater at unsustainable rates. Some 1.7 billion people, roughly a quarter of the world's population, live in areas where aquifers are under stress.[47]

In those areas cited above—and a great many others, like the Ogallala Aquifer that supplies water for Midwestern agriculture in the United States—these trends show no sign of abating. On the contrary, the expectation is that continued population growth, augmented in various ways by the effects of climate change and industrial agriculture, will render the water/agriculture nexus ever more visible and its stakes ever higher. Robert Glennon, who first brought the full implications of groundwater depletion to American audiences in his 2002 book *Water Follies,* explains that "excessive groundwater pumping has caused the ground to collapse; rivers, lakes, and springs to dry up; and riparian habitat to die. If we continue to exploit our groundwater resources in this way, we will eventually run out."[48] This is not hyperbole.

Effects of aquifer depletion are already beginning to be felt as farmers from India to China, from South Dakota to Kansas and Texas, are digging ever-deeper wells to access ever-diminishing amounts of groundwater. The Ogallala Aquifer has declined, on average, five to six feet per year; since 1990 the water in that aquifer has diminished by approximately one hundred feet. Such numbers might sound amorphous, perhaps even unimportant to those distanced from hydrological reality—until one considers the Ogallala's subterranean magnitude beneath the topsoil of the US Midwest. In journalist Hylton's words:

Sprawling beneath eight states and more than 100 million acres, the Ogallala Aquifer is the kind of hydrological behemoth that lends itself to rhapsody and hubris. Ancient, epic, apparently endless, it is the largest subterranean water supply in the country, with an estimated capacity of a million-billion gallons, providing nearly a third of all American groundwater irrigation. If the aquifer were somehow raised to the surface, it would cover a larger area than any freshwater lake on Earth—by a factor of five.[49]

The problem of groundwater depletion is global. According to Ismail Serageldin, former World Bank economist and director of the Library of Alexandria, in 2009:

There are a host of technical problems—water tables are dropping, for instance—that have created the need for a new agricultural revolution. It's clear, however, that proper management of all the inputs of agriculture (water, land, labor, and energy) is the key to producing enough food for everybody, as well as making sure that it's adequately distributed and produced in a sustainable fashion. . . . For years and years, we've taken for granted the availability of water.[50]

In the twenty-first century, where will the water for agriculture come from? What forms of agriculture will be prioritized and incentivized given changing climates and water supplies? These key questions for the coming century challenge the model of industrial agriculture so widely proselytized during the Green Revolution. There must be better ways.

Rethinking Industrial Agriculture in the Face of Hydrological Reality

It is good news that farmers, activists, scholars, experts, and governments around the world are beginning to reassess the water-intensive, short-term, high-yield practices encouraged by the Green Revolution in light of ecological devastation. Yet the challenge of the agriculture/water nexus is not merely a localized problem that can be fixed with a technical or technological intervention, that is, by tinkering with an aspect of the current system but leaving the overarching system of value and practice in place. Granted, localized water challenges are real and important; they are what Wes Jackson would describe as "problems *in* agriculture," which tend to be viewed as isolatable, technical issues.[51] A variety of technological developments will be important for grappling with these types of water-related issues *in* agriculture in the coming decades. But the holding efficiency of the irrigation canal in Texas or Nebraska, for example, won't matter much when the Ogallala Aquifer runs out of water. What the water/agriculture nexus reveals at larger scale is, in the terminology of Wes Jackson, less a problem *in* agriculture than a problem *of* agriculture—namely, "the threat *of* agriculture to the biosphere itself."[52]

The challenge is to reconceptualize, and then implement, a different kind of agriculture altogether. This amounts to, as Ismael Serageldin put it, "a new agricultural revolution" that is attuned to fresh water supply and soil health. To that end, an increasing number of farmers and citizens, scholars and activists, think tanks, governments, and transnational organizations, are exploring how the future of farming lies in the plausibility of discovering forms of regionally sustainable, adaptive agriculture. This would entail forms of food production that ensure the integrity of watersheds and water sources; that establish diverse crops in climate-appropriate regions; and that are guided by principles of long-term sustainability and the resilience of crops as well as natural resources like soil and water. Important work in this vein occurs in many places, including but not limited to The Land Institute in Kansas; the Stone Barns Center for Food and Agriculture in New York, which partners with researchers at Cornell University; Food and Water Watch; FoodTank; and many others.

To view agriculture through the aperture of hydrological reality requires a focus on several concrete practices and insights. As aquifers are depleted and climate change intensifies regional patterns of drought or deluge, crops will need to align with the realities of water and climate: planting thirsty crops like cotton in semi-arid and arid regions will simply not be hydrologically sensible or sustainable. Hydrological realism in agriculture will also be characterized by attempts to improve the efficiency of water delivery and diminish water waste—by technical interventions to diminish the evaporation of water from reservoirs, irrigation canals, and pivot irrigators, or by an increase in drip irrigation. In places where it is feasible in terms of both climate and crops, the practice of dry farming could be resurrected. And no small number of farmers will need to opt to let some fields lie fallow in order to concentrate their water supply on key crops that are planted in other fields (or, as is happening in the dry southwest of the United States, farmers may opt to lease their water rights to thirsty municipalities simply because it generates a more reliable income).

One of the biggest challenges for twenty-first-century agriculture is the incentive structure of the industrial agricultural economy, which is a particularly short-term, yield-focused form of valuing agricultural products, for which government subsidizes the cost of water either directly or through historic, legal entitlements owned by agricultural interests. So long as this structure remains in place, industrial agriculture is not just unlikely to incorporate long-term externalities like aquifer depletion, soil salinization, or widespread pollution; it is fundamentally unable to do so. Far less can industrial agriculture provide a reliable platform for constructively valuing the long-term health of the soil, the ongoing renewal of groundwater, or the quality of surface water. In the current system, ecological inputs ensnared in the vortices of the industrial economy are of little consequence. What matters instead is short-term productivity and profit over and against any other considerations, including water quality and soil health.

At present, agriculture is characterized by extremely thirsty, mechanical, and petrochemically intensive farming practices that are geared toward hyperproductivity of monocultures and, ultimately, economic profit. Even in 1945, years before the full force of the Green Revolution had spread worldwide, Aldo Leopold saw with characteristic prescience how it

> was inevitable and no doubt desirable that the tremendous momentum of industrialization should have spread to farm life. It is clear to me, however, that it has overshot the mark, in the sense that it is generating new insecurities, economic and ecological, in place of those it was meant to abolish. In its extreme form, [industrial agriculture] is humanly desolate and economically unstable. These extremes will someday die of their own too-much, not because they are bad for wildlife, but because they are bad for farmers.[53]

Wendell Berry and subsequent generations of agrarian thinkers have made clear that industrial agriculture poses big-picture questions of values that are not mere matters for small farms, agricultural economists, or residents of the Midwestern "fly-over" states. These are also philosophical and ethical issues that pertain to anyone for whom seeds eventually become suppers, and certainly for people and regions where agriculture is a major part of subsistence or exchange economies. For Berry,

> Critical questions are being asked of our whole society: Are we, or are we not, going to take proper care of our land, our country? . . . At present, these questions are being answered in the negative. Our soil erosion rates are worse now than during the years of the Dust Bowl. In the arid lands of the West, we are overusing and wasting the supplies of water. Toxic pollution from agricultural chemicals is a growing problem.[54]

What is entailed in reconfiguring and revaluing agriculture with regard to long-term sustainability and health of humans, soil, and water supply? Theological and social ethicists suggest some directions—drawing on the resources of religious imaginations—to envision and then incarnate forms of ecological agriculture.

Water, Agriculture, and Theological Ethics

Berry and others have made clear that agriculture is not just another mode of productive labor or an engine of economic growth; it is also, more fundamentally, a way of ordering relationships among human beings, land, and other forms of life. So it makes sense that modern agriculture has begun to receive sustained attention in theology, as environmental and ecological realities are filtered through historical, ethical, and theological modes of analysis.

For example, the work of scripture scholar Ellen Davis makes use of the Hebrew Bible's many references to land, agriculture, famine, farming, aridity, drought, and deluge, observing that "the Hebrew Scriptures are land-centered in their theological perspective."[55] Although the Hebrew Bible is not just an agrarian tractate, for Davis it is an illuminating conversation partner with contemporary agricultural practices and philosophies. In a related but distinct way, Protestant theologian Norman Wirzba combines analysis of modern food systems with a Christian sacramental stance toward food as "a holy and humbling mystery, . . . precious because it is a fundamental means through which God's nurture and love for the whole creation are expressed."[56]

Proponents of "Sabbath ecology" employ scriptural practices and metaphors in conjunction with prescriptive recommendations for sustainable agriculture. Mark Graham, in *Sustainable Agriculture: A Christian Ethic of Gratitude*,[57] critiques industrial farming practices while proposing virtue-based remedies for contemporary food systems. And farmer, philosopher, and theologian Fred Kirschenmann explicitly finds God on his farm. His essay, "Theological Reflections while Castrating Calves," invokes theological doctrine as well as his lived experience as a farmer. "I have been extremely fortunate in my life—and grateful—," he writes, "that I have so often been humiliated by all that I have not known as I encounter the divine in the flesh-and-blood experiences of daily life on a farm, including the simple act of castrating calves."[58] His incarnational sensibility suggests that Christian theology has "too often reduced the doctrine of the incarnation to a one-time event" that happened millennia ago, on one evening when a poor woman gave birth in a stable because there was no room at the inn. Like recent generations of Catholic theologians and ethicists, this Protestant farmer-philosopher suggests that the experience of the divine is also mediated through the idea of love of neighbor and, in particular, "through flesh and blood *relationships,* even relationships with those who may happen to be our enemies."[59] As such, human beings must develop what Kirschenmann calls an "ecological conscience," an "awareness that *all* members of the biotic community of which we are a part are our 'neighbors' and that eternal qualities of life await us in those relationships."[60]

Catholic Social Teaching and Agriculture: Contributions and Omissions

Agriculture has increasingly become a topic of frequent reflection within official Catholic social teaching (CST) as well as broader discourses of Catholic thought. For several decades, popes have offered formal, annual reflections on agriculture and development on the occasion of World Food Day. Matthew Whelan has observed that these statements tend to include ethical and theological analyses about the negative effects of global economic development and industrial agriculture.[61] Likewise, the *Compendium of the Social Doctrine of the Church* maintains that "radical and urgent changes" are necessary "in order to restore to agriculture—and to rural people—their just value as the basis for a healthy economy, within the social community's development as a whole."[62] In the realm of Catholic social thought and practice, the National Catholic Rural Life Conference (NCRLC) in the United States has steadfastly and with great nuance articulated the importance of "an agricultural ethic for a global generation" and sustainable agriculture within a framework of human beings as stewards of creation. The NCRLC also actively advocates for land, farmers, and healthy agricultural and economic systems, as does the global humanitarian agency Catholic Relief Services. Both are explicit about the importance of water.

More sustained magisterial consideration of the water/agriculture nexus can be found in the US Bishops' 1985 pastoral letter, *Economic Justice for All,* which noted "the increasing damage to natural resources resulting from many modern agricultural practices: the overconsumption of water, the depletion of topsoil, and the pollution of land and water."[63] The bishops also noted that that "although the United States has set a world standard for food production, it has not done so without cost to our natural resource base."[64] In addition to concern for ecological viability and preservation of natural resources into the future, John Paul II described in 2002 how "water is a basic factor in food security" and insisted that technical solutions as well as international interventions need to be oriented toward "the well-being of those people—men, women, children, families, communities—who live in the poorest parts of the world and therefore suffer most from any scarcity or misuse of water resources."[65] In 2003, the Pontifical Council for Justice and Peace recommended that, since the primary use of water worldwide is for agriculture, "new irrigation development needs to be carried out with proper environmental impact assessment."[66] More recently, bishops in the persistently dry continent of Australia have affirmed that "the success of agriculture in the Murray-Darling Basin has come at largely unforeseen cost. We can now see that there are physical and ecological constraints to agriculture in Australia."[67]

What, then, might a Catholic vision of the agriculture/water nexus look like? The bishops of the Columbia River Watershed proposed one ideal vision:

> In agricultural operations, we envision that farms are carefully integrated into, and respectful of, their environment. Where feasible, farmers produce organic crops that safeguard water quality and the health of their families, consumers, livestock and local wildlife. Water is carefully conserved through innovative irrigation techniques.[68]

The bishops of the Murray-Darling Basin stipulate a complementary vision of "strong rural communities, deeply in touch with the land and the rivers, working in a variety of agricultural enterprises, producing the food that feeds our nation and other nations in ecologically sustainable ways."[69] The realm of policy and practice is messy, but it is worth noting that the moral vision articulated by representatives of the magisterial Catholic Church increasingly sounds strikingly similar to visions of ecological, socially just agriculture proposed by farmers and thinkers like Wes Jackson, Fred Kirschenmann, and Wendell Berry. One need not defend Catholic dogma in order to value the long-term health of soil and water in the practice of agriculture, although theological and ethical analyses are increasingly bringing important perspectives to global conversations about industrial agriculture, ecological resilience, and human health. These kinds of convergences are important sources for individual and collective discernment about values surrounding land, soil, water, and food systems.

One glaring omission in mainstream CST is the topic of how individual food choices can function to demonstrate religious-moral commitment with dominant food systems. Most notably, while CST has been fairly consistent in structural analysis of agricultural trends worldwide, it has also been relatively silent on issues of meat production. This seems a glaring omission from several moral angles. First, the production of meat is water intensive, and meat has high virtual water content: plant-centric vegetarian or vegan diets represent net conservation of water resources. Second, the production of meat and the conditions of animal farming—especially but not exclusively in the United States—raise major ethical questions about the welfare of the animals as well as the treatment of workers. Third, the Catholic Church has a long history of endorsing fasting from meat for spiritual or moral purposes. Given the ethical issues linked to meat consumption, it seems particularly odd that Pope Francis did not suggest reducing reliance on meat as a direction for individual or collective action in his encyclical *Laudato Si'*. Instead, it is Protestant, Jewish, and Islamic ethicists and scholars who have made the case for ethical vegetarianism (though not, standardly, for hydrological reasons). For example, Laura Hartman ably considers the significance and complexity of contemporary patterns of resource consumption in an industrial economy, including the question of whether it is theologically and ethically viable to eat meat. "On balance," she says, "the arguments seem to indicate that I should make a habit of avoiding meat consumption, or at least being quite selective about the meat I do eat."[70]

Conclusion:
Radicalism and Incrementalism

I hope that Wes Jackson is right to suggest that "if we solve the problem *of* agriculture"—that is, the values around which its practices are oriented—then "we can solve most of the problems *in* agriculture."[71] Granted, problems *of* the agriculture/water nexus are deeply entrenched in industrial agriculture, which is highly profitable to a small number of powerful corporations, significantly subsidized by the federal government in the United States, and linked in profound ways to the fossil-fuel economy. In light of these realities, revolutionizing agriculture in the twenty-first century will be no small feat. It will require both incrementalism and radical change. The necessary first step for rethinking the agriculture/water nexus is to adopt an unflinching hydrological realism. The good news is that this work has begun in various contexts—by concerned citizens, parents, activists, scholars, farmers, journalists, and policy makers. There is a growing awareness that modern industrial agriculture is unsustainable from the perspective of the twenty-first-century water supply. This awareness can be transformed into a peaceful revolution toward ecological agriculture that is attentive to soil health and crop rotation as well as the fostering of food economies that support life within bioregions, watersheds, and "foodsheds."

With clarity of vision comes responsibility. The past few decades have provided ample evidence of a litany of industrial agriculture's detrimental effects—from atrazine to depleted aquifers; from degraded soils to nutrient-poor monocultures; from amplified short-term crop yield to polluted waters brimming with carcinogenic chemicals; from profligate irrigation projects to marine dead zones. The bounty of industrial agriculture must be understood not only by its productive legacy but by its persistent counterweights, these pervasive negative effects. Many such negative consequences were (presumably) neither directly intended nor even foreseen. But they are evident now, on the molecular scale of endocrine disruptions and on the global scale of ongoing petrochemical pollution, soil degradation, and depletion of fresh water supplies. Because these effects are now clear, to ignore them or rationalize away these negative aspects is to engage in a form of "culpable ignorance"—an immoral decision to look away from the stark realities that suggest that change is necessary. There are real challenges in re-envisioning agriculture to promote differently robust versions of growth and flourishing. These challenges are of course political, economic, cultural, and technical. But they are also *moral* challenges that require nuanced and interdisciplinary data, wide frames of analysis, a move away from the solipsistic value of economic profit, and attention to context. It remains an open question whether and how a tentative equilibrium may be found for the planet's vital trinity of hydrological realities, ecological sustainabilities, and agricultural sufficiencies.

CHAPTER 6

Climate Change and Water in the Anthropocene

"Climate change is all about water," says Zafar Adeel, who, from 2010 to 2012, chaired the UN interagency coordination platform for all issues related to fresh water. He adds that "water is the medium" through which climate change will most profoundly affect all societies and ecosystems.[1] Since interactions among climate change, hydrology, and society will be significant factors in water scarcity and social crises going forward, this chapter charts what climate change has to do with water.

Geology, the Anthropocene, and Climate Change

Scientists know that planet Earth formed approximately 4.5 billion years ago. Eventually, surface temperature hovered at a level amenable to liquid water and then aquatic life. The earliest fossils indicating the presence of cells date back to 3.5 billion years ago. Eukaryotic cells and an oxygenated atmosphere came into the world approximately 2 billion years ago. Between 495 and 545 million years ago, multicellular organisms flourished and evolved during what is now known as the Cambrian Explosion.[2] *Homo sapiens* as our immediate ancestors emerged relatively recently—only about fifty thousand years ago. The human species is a relative newcomer to the history of this rocky, carboniferous planet, and it is only in the past several hundred years that our species has realized the vastness of deep geological time.

Put into geological perspective, the human species is a late-comer to this world, whose history and depth far exceeds our presence and also our comprehension. If the history of earth were to be envisaged as a twenty-four-hour day, as the quip goes, we humans would pop onto the scene at just before midnight—at 11:58:43 p.m., give or take a second. This sort of calculation is a recent invention, but it is rooted in nineteenth-century British geology, which demonstrated that the world was far older than previously accepted (often Bible-based) calculations had admitted. The awareness and mobilization of deep geological time has had revolutionary—and evolutionary—consequences in the past 200 years. In fact, Charles Darwin built his theory of evolution by natural selection in *The Origin of Species* (1859) on the idea of gradual changes to species' traits over vast periods of time.

At roughly the same time, much more was unfurling in England that was also predicated on the long geological scale of planetary development: the Industrial Revolution was powered by hydrocarbons—coal, in particular. (In general, coal is fossilized carbon from animal remains; petroleum—oil and gas—is fossilized carbon from plant detritus.) Since the mid- to late-nineteenth century, industrialized and industrializing civilizations have become mass consumers of these fossilized, sedimentary fuel sources. The twenty-first-century global economy has quite literally been built on the extraction and use of coal, oil, and gas—fossilized sediments that accrued over millions, even billions of years.[3] During the Industrial Revolution, a segment of humanity began to use coal and other fossilized hydrocarbons in ways that led to massive economic growth and patterns of resource exploitation that still shape the contemporary world. As societies have tapped into some of the oldest stuff on earth and then burned it to great productive effect, global carbon dioxide saturation has increased dramatically, intensifying background rates of climate change. This is why scholars refer to climate change as "anthropogenic"—etymologically, this means that climate change is caused by human beings, though the claim made by analysts is more specific: human societies' extraction and combustion of fossil fuels under capitalist economies has led to amplified dynamics in the climate system that render it not just a difference in degree but also a difference in kind. As Holmes Rolston III, a noted environmental philosopher and winner of the Templeton Prize in Science and Religion, has argued: we *Homo sapiens* are "the one species in the history of the planet that, now in this new millennium, has more power than ever for good or evil, or justice and injustice; indeed, the one species that puts both its own well-being and that of life on Earth in jeopardy."[4]

For these and related reasons, some scientists have proposed that the present geological epoch should no longer be called merely the "Holocene" but rather the "Anthropocene," or the epoch in which human beings became a force that alters the earth in permanent, geological, and irreparable ways. Nobel prize–winning atmospheric chemist Paul Crutzen and ecologist Eugene Stoermer coined the term "Anthropocene." The concept refers, in Crutzen's words, to the "geology of mankind"—by which he means a geological epoch shaped primarily by ongoing global, human activities. The conceptual point is that for the first time in the history of the earth—indeed, the universe—human beings are now a prominent, decisive force that co-determines the earth's environmental state. Furthermore, some of these changes to earth systems may be permanent. Thus the term "Anthropocene" links the human prefix—"anthropos"—with the standard geological suffix as a way of denoting large-scale, human-caused alterations in earth systems. Crutzen and others claim that "the Anthropocene represents a new phase in the history of both humankind and of the Earth, when natural forces and human forces became intertwined, so that the fate of one determines the fate of the other. Geologically, this is a remarkable episode in the history of this planet."[5]

In 2008, the Geological Society of London—a long-standing, august body whose historical membership list includes the likes of Charles Darwin—affirmed, "by a large majority, that there was merit in considering the possible formulation of this term [the Anthropocene]: that is, that it might eventually join the Cambrian, Jurassic, Pleistocene, and other such units on the Geological Time Scale (GTS)."[6] There are vibrant, sharp, and incisive internal debates among geologists and earth scientists about whether and how the Anthropocene is an apt scientific category; indeed, the International Commission on Stratigraphy—which governs such decisions—deployed an active Anthropocene Working Group to consider whether the term should be adopted formally in the GTS and make recommendations to the larger governing body on that matter.[7] Beyond geological debates, the notion of the Anthropocene has captured the imagination of scientists and scholars, journals and policy makers, ethicists and teachers—perhaps because it concisely conveys a massive shift in perspective about the forces that shape nature.[8] The idea of the Anthropocene revises the assumption that earth systems operate independently of human influence. In 2011, a special feature in the *Economist* summarized the significance of the Anthropocene neologism:

> It is one of those moments where a scientific realisation, like Copernicus grasping that the Earth goes round the sun, could fundamentally change people's view of things far beyond science. It means more than rewriting some textbooks. It means thinking afresh about the relationship between people and their world and acting accordingly.[9]

As theologian Michael Northcott frames it: "The idea of anthropogenic climate change challenges the relations of nature and culture in space and time in ways that are fundamental to the Newtonian schema."[10] A litany of experts and institutions argue that the Anthropocene idea functions not just scientifically but also culturally.

The dominance of a global, fossil fuel–driven, capitalist economy has led to economic and material improvements for many people—most especially those in Western industrialized nations.

At the same time, the now global capitalist fossil fuel economy has led to negative consequences, including environmental degradation, health problems caused by pollution, and vast differentials in wealth and privilege worldwide.

The historical origin of the fossil fuel–extractive trends that have created the conditions of possibility for modern economies (and hence the Anthropocene moniker) are the same dynamics that have amplified global climate change. Thus, paradigm-shifting though the notion of the Anthropocene may seem to be, critics rightly point out that the notion obfuscates something important: environmental degradations are not the result of all human beings qua human beings. Instead, contemporary depletions of earth systems are the results of certain historical, industrial decisions and the different structures of benefits and burdens that accrued to some people during the era of Western industrialization. By describing planetary degradation as a species-wide phenomenon, the idea of the Anthropocene may be erroneously taken to mean that all human beings are equally responsible for subsequent environmental and social degradations. This observation led scholars Andreas Malm and Alf Hornborg to remark astutely that the idea of the "Anthropocene" is a potential misnomer—because it casts massive earth systems destruction as a *species-wide* phenomenon when, really, the largest responsibility for anthropogenic climate change accrues to a very specific segment of humanity.

As Malm and Hornborg make clear, it was mostly a small, privileged, largely male, and white European portion of *Homo sapiens* working within the riches and exploits of imperialism and colonialism that catalyzed and benefited from the Industrial Revolution's technological innovation, extractive potency, and nascent economy. These legacies of power have been built into the structures of contemporary economic globalization, fossil fuel extraction, and consumption. In their words: "The fossil economy was not created nor is it upheld by humankind in general."[11] In reality, "the historical origins of anthropogenic climate change were predicated on highly inequitable global processes from the start."[12] This is true historically and remains so in the present day: the world's wealthiest countries (the United States among them) remain the most significant emitters of fossil fuel emissions per capita. The ethical problem, often felt acutely at the intersection of climate change and water, is that those who have caused the damage are not generally the ones who feel the most intense results.

While planetary environmental changes include consequences with which all of humanity must in some way grapple—as the term Anthropocene implies—it is also the case that not all members of humanity are equally responsible, either causally or morally. Malm and Hornborg conclude that "transhistorical—particularly species-wide—drivers cannot be invoked to explain a qualitatively novel order in history, such as mechanized, steam-power production of commodities for export to the world-market."[13] The specificity of the origin of anthropogenic climate change means that "attempts to attribute climate change to the nature of the human species appear doomed" to "vacuity," given the particular, historical, social, and economic conditions upon which fossil fuel extraction and global economies have been predicated, leveraged, and maintained.[14]

Climate Change, Scientific Uncertainty, and Matters of Faith

Global climate change is driven primarily by fossil fuel extraction, combustion, and the resulting proliferation of potent greenhouse gases—most notably, carbon dioxide and methane.[15] There are other sorts of feedback cycles that contribute to global climate change (including, for example, a decrease in the ability of frozen surfaces to reflect solar rays, so that ice caps and polar regions absorb more heat and melt even more quickly; the thawing of permafrost and peat bogs, which emit significant amounts of methane; the increased demand for cattle farming, since cattle belch methane;

and deforestation, which eliminates rainforests as carbon sinks). According to the US Environmental Protection Agency:

> Human activities are altering the carbon cycle—both by adding more CO_2 to the atmosphere and by influencing the ability of natural sinks, like forests, to remove CO_2 from the atmosphere. While CO_2 emissions come from a variety of natural sources, human-related emissions are responsible for the increase that has occurred in the atmosphere since the industrial revolution.[16]

Recent political pandering to climate change deniers, who refer to anthropogenic causes of climate change as one theory among several contenders, has streamlined with the disconcerting tendency of the Trump administration and its supporters to endorse the purported viability of "alternative facts." It is important to consider, then, how climate scientists know what they know and what we should make of the language of "theory."

Climate science is a robust accretion of many different types of scientific methodologies and data, generated over time and by numerous researchers around the world. Processes identified by Svante Arrhenius in the nineteenth century, along with data gathered from atmospheric chemistry since the 1950s, indicate that carbon dioxide saturation in the atmosphere is increasing; this correlates, generally, to rising temperatures. More recently, paleontologists have assessed climate trends from the geological past, indicating how fossil fuel extraction and combustion since the Industrial Revolution has amplified climate change beyond natural, background levels. Meanwhile, environmental scientists continue to assess measures and impacts of climate change on the earth's ecosystems, and social scientists assess the impacts on the world's human populations. Scientists therefore have data from the past and from the present. They do not have access to data from the future (yet). So, when it comes to climate projections, scientists can extrapolate from past and present data, but they can't predict with total accuracy how all aspects of that future will look, because the planet is a very complex set of systems within which global climate change manifests itself in different ways in different contexts. Human societies (especially through the vehicle of governmental policy) have enormous potential to amplify or diminish the degree to which the planet warms in the future through revision of energy policies and subsidies to fossil fuel companies.

What kinds of measures are used to track climate change? One standard measure is atmospheric carbon dioxide saturation. Since the Industrial Revolution, it has increased from roughly 280 parts per million (ppm) to over 410 ppm. Also during this time, the temperature of the planet has increased by approximately two degrees. A frequently cited range of temperature increase is four to ten degrees Celsius by the year 2100. We don't know for sure. Again: in science, uncertainty is not a proxy for fundamental error. This is true in climate science, as in other scientific disciplines. As neuroscientist Stuart Firestein has argued in his book *Ignorance: How It Drives Science*, some kinds of uncertainty are in fact endemic and properly central to the practice of responsible, reputable, data-driven scientific inquiry and discovery.[17] General predictions come to fruition in ways that cannot be known, down to every detail, in advance. Scientists do not (yet) inhabit the future. But with massive accretions of data and ever-more-specific mathematical models based on that longitudinal data, the range of predictive accuracy continues to improve. Climate science is therefore based on well-founded prediction and anticipation—not ungrounded speculation. Uncertainty, here, is endemic to the generation of scientific knowledge, not a whimsical preference for one sort of opinion over another.

Climate science deniers, however, view uncertainty as an epistemic failing. They take a simplistic view of the concept of uncertainty and imply that scientific uncertainty means that climate predictions are untrustworthy. This is false. The primary causes and feedback cycles of climate change amplification are known, and they are anthropogenic, linked to fossil fuel economies that emerged in Europe during the Industrial Revolution and to the global economic structures that have been passed down from that time. What limited "uncertainty" remains has to do with fine-tuned conjecture about exactly how hot it's going to get, in what places, and with what consequences, as a range of variable factors. As it turns out, the biggest wild card in climate change is political: specifically, what actions will be taken on fossil fuels.

Therefore, when lawmakers and public figures suggest that there is uncertainty in climate science, or that scientists are characterized by dubious data-gathering methods, there is a political upshot: it allows lawmakers to skirt the issue of how to take action on the effects of climate change and thus to draw attention away from the ethical question of *what should we, as a society, do?* This is an important and problematic category error, because although it is surely not the role of government to set the scientific method, it is assuredly the role of government to govern—that is, to decide what policies and programs will best protect the interests of citizens and the security of the nation, given what is demonstrated by the best of contemporary research in the sciences and social sciences. (It is telling, for example, that the World Bank and International Monetary Fund jumped on board with the imperative of addressing climate change in 2012 and 2013, and US military generals as well as former secretaries of state acknowledge that climate change is one of the biggest threats to international security in the twenty-first century.)

Unfortunately the United States continues to underwrite the fossil fuel economy in significant ways. An International Monetary Fund study indicated that in 2011, the United States subsidized fossil fuel use by $502 billion—nearly half of the total of global subsidies for that year.[18] The withdrawal of the United States in 2017 from the Paris Climate Accords signals the falsely isolationist hubris of the Trump political administration, which disdains inconvenient scientific truths in exchange for vacuous nationalist, ad hominem rhetoric. Unfortunately for humanity, the dynamics of the global climate system do not adhere to politicians' rhetorical posturing or other obfuscations; climate change proceeds despite (one might even say, because of) such tactics of avoidance. Methane, carbon dioxide, and other greenhouse gases care not a whit for legislative decrees about whether or not global warming is a hoax or how far the sea level is "allowed" to rise. Instead, carbon dioxide keeps accumulating in the atmosphere; the global temperature keeps rising; sea level creeps upward.

In the United States, inaction on matters of environmental, social, and economic policy related to climate change is the default stance at present. (Arguably, with the gutting of the Environmental Protection Agency under the Trump administration, "inaction" is not a strong enough term: there is a pronounced and alarming recidivism on environmental regulation and policy, or anti-environmentalism.) But as any ethicist will tell you, inaction is not a neutral position. Inaction is itself always choice—it is the choice *not* to act. In this case, it is a collective choice with massive economic and ethical consequences. Worldwide, the vast majority of nations and transnational institutions recognize that global climate change must be addressed. Many cities, states, and communities in the United States do, too, such that after the United States withdrew from the Paris Agreement under President Trump's direction, many mayors and some governors opted to adhere to its standards.

Historical memory is also a useful tool for demonstrating how much backsliding there has been on matters of political responsibility for ameliorating climate-related issues. Consider, for example, the following words, which were penned in 1990 by a prominent international leader:

> The gradual depletion of the ozone layer and the related "greenhouse effect" has now reached crisis proportions as a consequence of industrial growth, massive urban concentrations and vastly increased energy needs. Industrial

waste, the burning of fossil fuels, unrestricted deforestation, the use of certain types of herbicides, coolants, and
propellants: all of these are known to harm the atmosphere and environment. The resulting meteorological
and atmospheric changes range from damage to health to
the possible future submersion of low-lying lands.

While in some cases the damage already done may
well be irreversible, in many other cases it can still be
halted. It is necessary, however, that the entire human
community—individuals, States, and international bodies—take seriously the responsibility that is theirs.[19]

Or consider this quotation, from the same year but a different
international figure:

The threat to our world comes not only from tyrants and
their tanks. It can be more insidious though less visible. The
danger of global warming is as yet unseen, but real enough
for us to make changes and sacrifices, so that we do not
live at the expense of future generations. Our ability to
come together to stop or limit damage to the world's environment will be perhaps the greatest test of how far we can
act as a world community. No one should underestimate
the imagination that will be required, nor the scientific
effort, nor the unprecedented co-operation we shall have
to show. We shall need statesmanship of a rare order.[20]

The words belong to John Paul II and Margaret Thatcher, respectively, neither of whom was equated with liberal-leaning policies
nor known for environmental advocacy. That is the point: nearly
thirty years ago, these moral and political leaders advocated for
action in ways that are far stronger than the Trump administration
and much of the US political establishment. The forward-thinking,
frank assessments of the pope and prime minister in 1990 reveal
just how myopic and erroneously isolationist are the pronounce-

ments of current US politicians and their science-denying constituencies heading into the third decade of the twenty-first century. In stalled public discourse, what is to be done? The problem is real and immediate. While clean technologies can be deployed to minimize emissions, the true long-term necessity lies with weaning economies and societies off of fossil fuel extraction and combustion and toward sustainable energy options that bring far fewer negative externalities than do fossil fuels. The longer our fossil fuel–based economies continue to belch carbon dioxide and methane, the more significant and devastating will be the results—including inundation by ocean level rise, increased global temperatures, extreme weather events, and ongoing drought that destroys agricultural production. Past and present trends indicate that the burdens of climate change will be disproportionately carried by people living in poverty.[21] So it is no surprise that Paul Crutzen and colleagues anticipate that "the present and likely future course of environmental change seems set to create substantially more losers, globally, than winners."[22] The winners, one can safely assume, will not be the vast majority of the global population who live amid various kinds of economic, environmental, and social duress. As Vandana Shiva reports:

> It is the poorest people in the Third World who will be most severely affected by climate change, drought, melting glaciers, and rising sea levels. The peasants, pastoralists, and coastal communities will become environmental refugees as rains disappear, crops collapse, and rivers go dry. . . . Whether water is life-threatening or life-sustaining depends to a large extent on the ability of climate justice movements to end atmospheric pollution.[23]

In this way, the problem of climate change in the Anthropocene presents quandaries for consideration in moral and ethical theories. Whether direct or indirect, proximate or remote, intended or not, human agency and responsibility in the Anthropocene have decidedly different textures than in previous epochs. It is, as John Paul II framed it, a reality of "crisis proportions." The benefits of (and lion's share of responsibility for) the fossil fuel economy's offspring, anthropogenic climate change, are unevenly distributed. So too are the burdens—for, perversely, it is generally those who have consumed the least fossil fuels and who are least industrialized, who nonetheless are most dramatically affected by the ravages of a changing climate and the vagaries of water supply (as the next section demonstrates).

Even the Roman Catholic Church is well within the Anthropocene's conceptual and moral gambit: since 1996, Paul Crutzen has been among the elite scientists who constitute the Pontifical Academy of Sciences. Perhaps because the Catholic Church tends to think and move in millennia (as opposed to fiscal quarters or election cycles), it is additionally intriguing to note that the top levels of leadership of the Catholic Church, from Pope Francis in his encyclical *Laudato Si'* and tracing back to Benedict XVI and John Paul II, have pointed out climate change as a problem linked to exploitative global economic practices that bears negative impacts for vulnerable populations. These pontiffs have underscored a truth that US political leaders rather conveniently ignore: global systems of energy production, and in some instances basic assumptions of economics, must be reconfigured if climate change and its many effects are to be stopped or mitigated, because fossil fuel–enabled growth bears negative externalities that shroud the planet in heat, drought, and related forms of social disaster.

Where some politicians on national and global levels proclaim the value of inaction until the salvific potential of green technologies can be unleashed, the writer Amitav Ghosh, although not a Catholic, has rightly observed, "*Laudato Si',* by contrast, does not anywhere suggest that miraculous interventions may provide a solution for climate change. It strives instead to make sense of humanity's present predicament by mining the wisdom of a tradition that far predates the carbon economy."[24] He concludes: "Bleak though the terrain of climate change may be, there are a few features in it that stand out in relief as signs of hope," among them "the increasing involvement of religious groups and leaders in the politics of climate change."[25] Indeed, both Benedict XVI's *Caritas in Veritate* (2009) and Pope Francis's *Laudato Si'* (2015) took a firm stand against climate change and environmental degradation as a result of ill-considered economic processes and called on superdeveloped nations, such as the United States, to engage in technology transfer. In the realm of Catholic thought and practice, the Vatican has committed to going carbon neutral. The US National Catholic Rural Life Conference has developed faith-based study guides on climate change that incorporate scientific consensus, critical reflection on contemporary reality, and engagement with key aspects of Catholic faith. In a different but complementary way, the Catholic Coalition on Climate Change steadfastly amplifies and communicates significant Catholic perspectives on climate change to a network of members; in partnership with the US Conference of Catholic Bishops, it also facilitates education and action plans for parishes, schools, business leaders, and scholars. More people than ever are aware of ecological concern within the Catholic Church, due to the popularity of Pope Francis and the release of his encyclical *Laudato Si'*, with its explicit mention of climate change in the very first chapter.

Given the anthropogenic amplifications of global climate change, the particular forms of socially stratified privilege that have caused it, and the disproportionate burdens allocated to the world's poor as a result, what ought to be done—as individuals, as communities, as societies, as nations? That is the key question for Anthropocene ethics, and any sufficient responses will be written, at least in part, through the medium of water.

The Climate/Water Nexus

Water is the hammer with which climate change will hit the earth.
                                                            —Travis Huxman

Water is at the heart of contemporary climate realities. A 2012 report from the National Academy of Sciences to the Pentagon warned that "the security establishment is going to have to start planning for natural disasters, sea-level rise, drought, epidemics, and other consequences of climate change."[26] The National Resource Council (NRC, a part of the National Academies) in 2010 listed fresh water resources as a primary concern in a changing climate.[27] And according to the National Center for Atmospheric Research:

> Changing climate will directly affect the global hydrologic cycle. Many of these effects will be felt regionally, with, for example, potential for flooding or drought increasing. In addition, changes to water quality, quantity, and supply reliability may have effects on human health, aquatic ecosystems, and agricultural and energy production, among other ecosystems and economic sectors.[28]

A basic maxim about the climate/water nexus is that wet places will get wetter and dry places drier. The NRC's 2010 report on climate change spells out what that means:

- Water availability will decrease in many areas that are already drought-prone and in areas where rivers are fed by glaciers or snowpacks;
- A higher fraction of rainfall will fall in the form of heavy precipitation, increasing the risk of flooding and, in some regions, the spread of water-borne illness;
- People in ecosystems in coastal zones will be exposed to higher storm surges, intrusion of salt water into freshwater aquifers, and other risks as sea levels rise.[29]

These are primary effects. Additional downstream effects will also accrue. The remainder of this chapter depicts the most significant dimensions of the multifaceted climate/water nexus and, so far as possible, offers some principles to guide public policy and ethical decision making about climate and water in the Anthropocene.

Water Vapor and Climate Feedback Cycles

Water can exist in three phases: solid, liquid, or vapor. The first two forms of water—solid (ice) and liquid—are both visible and tangible. The form of water that we tend to think about less is vapor. As it turns out, atmospheric water vapor is extremely important and is a major part of climate change. In 2008, NASA satellite data confirmed the long-standing scientific hypothesis that "warming and water absorption increase in a spiraling cycle."[30] In other words, water vapor amplifies temperatures because it holds more heat. This, in turn, amplifies precipitation trends: A 2013 study by the National Oceanic and Atmospheric Administration demonstrated how societies can reasonably expect, by the year 2099, a 20 to 30 percent increase of precipitation in the Northern Hemisphere.[31] The 2008 NASA study stated that water vapor also amplifies "the warming effect of other greenhouse gases," such as CO_2. In all these ways, water vapor is an invisible but important aspect of the climate/water nexus.

Drought, Desertification, and Aquifer Depletion

Because of the atmospheric dynamics of water vapor and climate change, dry places will get drier. Thus the NRC report, quoted above, indicated that fresh water supply will decrease "in many areas that are already drought-prone and in areas where rivers are fed by glaciers and snowpack." In many regions of the world, increased aridity will contribute to desertification. As aridity increases, seasonal cycles of precipitation will become less reliable. Societies that have deep aquifers will continue to extract that fossil water at rates that are far from renewable. This is especially the case in dry regions where farming or industry form the backbone of the regional economy and also consume the majority of water resources. As seasonal runoff and rivers become less reliable, aquifers will also be primary sources for domestic water. The problem, of course, is that aquifers are finite.

In coastal regions, seawater intrusion will lead to the salinization of aquifers. Already this is a concern or a reality in places worldwide, for example, the Patasco Aquifer beneath much of Maryland, or the coastal aquifer beneath Gaza and Israel, or the salinity plume beneath Los Angeles.

Agricultural Changes

As chapter 5 made clear, agriculture will have to change in the twenty-first century. The characteristics of industrial agriculture—coupled with climate change and various related factors like drought, desertification, and aquifer depletion—point toward a continued trajectory of diminished agricultural productivity, degraded soils, petrochemical contamination of water supply, and overextraction of water from aquifers. Worldwide, established patterns of agriculture will cease to yield standard harvests. Especially in arid and semi-arid areas of the world, it will make little sense to continue to grow thirsty crops or to irrigate fields over long distances. Instead, "resilience" and "adaptation" will become key terms for agriculture at the climate/water nexus.

Already in the Americas, drought has led to crop declines. Vandana Shiva reports, for example, that "in 1996 the worst drought of the century in the United States hit Kansas and Oklahoma, destroying millions of acres of wheat. The United States' wheat reserves dropped to their lowest level in 50 years."[32] The summer of 2012 and subsequent months brought scalding temperatures and diminished rainfall to the Midwest. A consortium of scientists and Catholic Relief Services announced in mid-October 2012 that "higher temperatures and erratic rainfall will likely threaten beans and corn in Central American nations."[33] Worldwide, increased temperatures may result in large areas becoming untenable for planting key subsistence crops.[34] Floods will drown some crops in wetter regions of the world, while drought will desiccate others. In low-lying urban areas, floods pose a different kind of problem, as families are forced out of their homes and economic activity is stalled for weeks, months, or years—as was the case with Hurricane Katrina in New Orleans in 2005 and with Hurricane Maria in Puerto Rico in 2017. The impacts continue to be felt most dramatically by people living in situations of economic poverty, which in the United States often correlates to legacies of racism.

In dry regions, experts predict that agricultural demand for water will increase amid rising temperatures and evaporation. Zafar Adeel (of UN-Water) suspects that "demand for water to irrigate crops may rise as transpiration increases with higher temperatures." (Transpiration is the process by which water moves through a plant and is released into the atmosphere as vapor.) This sounds like basic supply-and-demand economics, until we realize the catch: water does not yield a new supply. Increased demand might bring higher prices, but it does not bring enough water to absolve us from responsibility for the preservation of dwindling surface and ground water supplies. (As chapter 2 pointed out, human technological innovations such as desalination have a role to play in mitigating water shortages, but they are not solutions in themselves.)

These dilemmas will have distinct regional and national textures, even while the overall trend will be global. The term bandied about by hydrologists is *megadrought:* drought conditions that persist for decades.[35] These are not seasonal changes; these are longer-term and therefore require different kinds of responses and mitigation measures. In an era of climate change, decades-long drought is not so much an aberration as a new kind of normal. Thus, there is concern about twenty-first-century food scarcity. In light of these changes to water supply and worries about food security, agricultural adaptation will be very important.

What are possible responses? First and foremost, societies need to explore—on a regional basis—what forms of agriculture are environmentally sustainable, economically appropriate, and resilient in a context of climate change. It seems likely that a decrease in industrial-scale agriculture, an increase in smaller- to mid-scale farms, the growth of regionally specific crops, and increased focus on regional food economies will be promising venues for adapting to the challenges that climate change poses to water and agriculture. Second, government subsidies to massive agricultural corporations need to be drastically reduced; instead, substantial energies and tangible resources need to be put into empowering small-scale farmers. In the United States, for example, we must ask: What forms of agriculture are incentivized by federal subsidies and maintained by powerful agricultural lobbies? Do these forms of agriculture make sense in the twenty-first century? As chapter 5 depicts, the resounding answer is "no." Researchers, farmers, and ethicists agree that our current practices of agriculture are unsustainable. It seems obvious to suggest the lopsidedness of large-scale industrial agriculture that produces monocultures while consuming massive quantities of water, injecting synthetic chemicals into the land and watersheds, and depleting the quality of the soil. Yet agribusiness on this model is precisely what is incentivized by current US policies and government subsidies. To that end, Danielle Nierenberg, a food and agriculture expert and co-founder of FoodTank.org, suggests that agricultural subsidies in the United States disproportionately support large-scale agribusinesses over the small-scale producers who are more likely to be engaged in sustainable food production and may be challenged by drought or commodity price fluctuations. Changes in government support services could reduce this deficit and improve food and water security.[36]

In sum, current models of agribusiness and global food production will need to change in a range of ways and for a multitude of reasons. Fresh water scarcity and the climate/water nexus raise enormous questions for agriculture in the twenty-first century. Those questions will be answered sufficiently only when decisions about agriculture are made according to awareness of local climate and water supply, climate-specific and resilient crops, and the pursuit of sustainability.

Environmental Migrants

Through drought, desertification, and aquifer depletion, global climate change wields major impacts on fresh water supply and agricultural production. But without fresh water and food, human beings cannot survive. People who live in situations of poverty, especially within a subsistence economy, are especially vulnerable to environmental degradation. Thus, when water disappears and crops fail, many people must seek sustenance in other places and by other means. The umbrella terms "environmental refugees" and "environmental migrants" refer to people who have been displaced because of environmental factors and related stressors. Technically, however, these are environmental migrants, since the term "refugee" is reserved by the United Nations for people who flee political or religious persecution. Environmental migrants are therefore not entitled to the rights and protections given to refugees.

To be sure, for most of human history, people have moved in search of better lives, seeking out regions rich in natural resources or more amenable to agriculture. What is different now is the scale of migration due to environmental factors—a difference so great as to be not merely a difference in degree but also a difference in kind. In the early years of the twenty-first century, one expert declaimed:

There is a new phenomenon in the global arena: environmental refugees. These are people who can no longer gain a secure livelihood in their homelands because of drought, soil erosion, desertification, deforestation and other environmental problems, together with the associated problems of population pressures and profound poverty. In their desperation, these people feel they have no alternative but to seek sanctuary somewhere, however hazardous the attempt. Not all of them have fled their countries, many being internally displaced. But all have abandoned their homelands on a semi-permanent if not permanent basis, with little hope of a foreseeable return.[37]

For example, 10 million people fled droughts in sub-Saharan Africa in the mid-1990s; only half eventually returned home. In China, "at least six million [people] deserve to be regarded as environmental refugees, having been obliged to abandon their farmlands due to shortages of agricultural plots in the wake of decades of population growth."[38] Many environmental migrants move to cities, thereby amplifying processes of urbanization.

At the climate/water nexus, drought is only one among several factors that create the phenomenon of environmental migrants. Deluge can lead to migration, for example when large-scale flooding damages subsistence economies (such as shrimp farming in coastal areas). Moreover, large-scale public works projects—especially large dams—lead to involuntary displacement of millions of people. In China and India in the past few decades "a cumulative total of 50 million" people have been displaced due to flooding of their homelands or other forms of co-optation, usually related to the construction of large dams.[39]

Water, Security, and Conflicts

Since the mid-1980s, politicians, pundits, and water wonks have wondered whether water might be the "new oil." As water becomes increasingly scarce, will it be a cause of conflict—even war? Experts disagree. The variety of opinions is due partly to the speculative nature of the question, which is hard to answer in the abstract. Still, scholarly tomes and public forum discussions continually invoke the topic of water wars, particularly with regard to regions that are frequently cited as places where water contributes to simmering political and social conflict, such as the Middle East and parts of Africa, or Asia and Southeast Asia, where countries' geopolitical strategies for the twenty-first century include building large dams to shore up surface water supply or orchestrating land grabs to ensure groundwater access.

Beyond politicians and pundits, many aid organizations and scholars also identify water scarcity—especially its relationship to food insecurity—as a contributing factor to a range of conflicts, including genocide in Sudan or the Arab Spring of Northern Africa.[40] In the Middle East, control of fresh water was essential to the formation of the modern State of Israel, both politically and nationalistically. Israeli scholar Alon Tal observes:

> Within the twentieth-century context of Jewish nationalism, water was the key to creating a vibrant agrarian economy and a fulfilled rural citizenry. . . . Not simply a commodity, it belongs to the realm of ideology. Hydrological considerations influenced foreign and defense policies. . . . Water development had political backing at the highest levels.[41]

Author Diane Raines Ward further elaborates on water's role in conflicts in the Middle East:

> Water has already been a factor in igniting at least one full-scale conflict—the Six Day War of 1967, when the Arab League, angered at Israel's construction of its National Water Carrier, which had appropriated much of the water of [the] Jordan River for use in Israel, began to dig canals to divert two Jordan tributaries, the Hasbani and Wazzani Springs. Israelis immediately shelled and destroyed both projects. The attacks by Syria, Egypt, and Jordan that eventually followed had many causes, but water remained a priority for both sides.[42]

More recent social scientific research indicates that prolonged periods of climate-induced drought were a contributing factor in both the Egyptian spring uprising and in the Syrian crisis, which has led to millions of migrants seeking survival, shelter, and livelihoods. In the present day, fresh water remains a highly contentious issue between Jordan, Palestinians, and the Israeli government, which has put firm restrictions on the types of access that Palestinians can have to fresh water sources (including the Jordan River and aquifers).[43] This trend seems unlikely to abate anytime soon, though, as chapter 8 suggests, any lasting peace in the Middle East is unlikely to emerge without stipulation and agreement on use and distribution of fresh water.

Water is a component of conflicts around the world in myriad and complex ways. (The Pacific Institute offers a compendium timeline of water conflicts and a podcast about the topic.)[44] This was true in the past, it is true at present, and it will likely remain so in the future. Zafar Adeel has remarked that because water is central to human life, it inherently contains the potential for discord. The intuition is that since we can't do without water, we will go to great lengths to access or retain it, even to the point of armed conflict. As Mark Twain memorably, if apocryphally, quipped in reference to the tumultuous history of conflict over water in the western United States, "Whiskey's for drinkin', and water's for fightin' over." But water is not always the direct or sole cause of armed conflict, and water shortages need not always result in community standoffs, political conflict, or full-scale war. Some experts are quick to note that in the history of the modern world, there have been more instances of cooperation over water resources than there have been cases of armed conflict. To this end, transboundary water negotiator Aaron Wolf emphasizes how fresh water can bring people together, not tear them apart.[45] Similarly, Kader Asmal, then chair of the World Commission on Dams, indicated that water "can be our catalyst for peace."[46]

It is crucial to recall that it is futile to ask the question of water wars in the abstract. Context matters. Thus to speak responsibly about water wars or water conflict, we have to ask: What types of conflicts? In what regions? Under what conditions? In relation to what other factors? Often overlooked in hype about water conflict is the fact that not all battles involve bodily aggression or weapons. In fact, some of the most important water conflicts of recent decades have been legal and economic—pertaining to the questions of who owns water, who can profit from it, who pays for its distribution, who oversees its management, and with what forms of accountability. Water justice advocates like Maude Barlow and Vandana Shiva see the economy, and especially the corporate ownership of fresh water supply and privatization of municipal waterworks, as the most important and insidious type of water conflict facing the twenty-first century. Since nations and corporations will survive the twenty-first century only if they have a water strategy, in recent years there has been a global scramble for water rights and purchase of water-rich land. In this global water grab, which is particularly evident in many parts of Africa, rich nations and multinational corporations are buying land and groundwater rights out from under the daily lives of individuals and communities. This is a problem of global proportions. It has to do with issues of sovereignty and sustainability of natural resources, as well as the values embedded in the global economy. In the atmosphere of contemporary economic globalization, the idea of a "public good" currently has limited political traction, but it is an important notion that can help expand notions of water's value beyond the economic. This sort of conflict of definition may not be armed, but it is ridden with peril and encumbered by privilege and privatization. In such ways will water in the twenty-first century assuredly be a site of conflict.

Energy Production

Fossil fuel combustion powers the global economy and sustains contemporary lifestyles while heating the planet at an alarming rate. Water is frequently an invisible but essential partner in fossil fuel extraction, since it is required to release, process, and refine petroleum products, generating toxic effluent. Contaminated water is therefore often an "output" of fossil fuel extraction in the form of flowback and produced water (that is, water that comes out of the earth after a well is drilled, containing chemical agents and therefore rarely fit for human consumption or reuse in agricultural or municipal contexts—although some progress is being made in reusing flowback water for horizontal hydraulic fracturing). In hydraulic fracturing, for example, contaminated water that has been belched forth from underground must be stored in industrially lined disposal ponds above ground; it should not re-enter the water supply, and if it does, public and environmental health crises (of large or small proportions) are likely to ensue.

Even when water is minimally used in the extraction process, there can be downstream consequences for surface and groundwater—for example, when pipelines leak or wells fail to contain toxic chemicals. The concern over leakage from the Dakota Access Pipeline, and its potential effects on water supply, was a major issue for advocates and self-proclaimed Water Protectors at Standing Rock, South Dakota, whose rallying cry was the Lakota phrase *mni wiconi,* "water is life" (see chapter 7). At worst, contamination of water sources can lead to effects on humans, ecosystems, and livestock. Pollution of rivers and streams and subsequent public health crises in downstream communities and economies are well attested worldwide. There must be better ways to generate the energy that powers the global economy. What about renewable energy sources such as wind, solar, ocean wave energy, or classical forms of hydropower?

The benefits of solar, wind, and wave technology revolve around the fact that these sources of energy are ongoing. The drawback is that the technology for harnessing these energy sources is not as developed as is fossil fuel technology, nor is the scale and reach of infrastructure attached to those means of energy production currently sufficient to power the lifestyles of many people in the industrialized world. These objections are real, but it is also important to recognize that they are by no means insurmountable with a dose of human technological innovation and investment in energy infrastructure. Solar, wind, and wave power would dramatically cut down on emissions of carbon dioxide and methane, compared to fossil fuel–based energy production. Thus, from our vantage point of the climate/water nexus, solar and wind power look very promising indeed. Can the same be said of hydropower?

The motive power of fresh water has been harnessed for many centuries through windmills and related technologies. But hydropower in the twentieth century is not of the windmill variety; rather, it raises the specter of large dams. For a system to convert water's kinetic energy into useful amounts of electricity for contemporary society, enormous quantities of water must be contained behind large dams, then released on command to run through sluices and turbines that generate electricity. Then the water has to be channeled somewhere after it has been released from the dam, while the electricity has to be distributed somewhere else. Some of these logistical challenges—like how to get the electricity to the faraway city—are by no means insurmountable. Technological innovation and investment in infrastructure can probably improve efficiency. And while classical hydropower is a source of energy for many cities worldwide, it comes with a range of vexing social and environmental problems.

Large dams, first developed in the United States and then exported worldwide, have allowed societies to corral surface water and direct it toward irrigation (see chapter 5) and energy production. In the mid- and late-twentieth century, the World Bank and International Monetary Fund made large-scale hydropower a condition of many development loans. Then, in response to rising global opposition to large dams, in 1997 the World Bank and the World Conservation Union established the Global Commission on Large Dams. The commission's final report, released in 2000, stated:

We believe that there can no longer be any justifiable doubt about the following: Dams have made an important and significant contribution to human development, and benefits derived from them have been considerable. In too many cases an unacceptable and often unnecessary price has been paid to secure those benefits, especially in social and environmental terms, by people displaced, by communities downstream, by taxpayers and by the natural environment. Lack of equity in the distribution of benefits has called into question the value of many dams in meeting water and energy development needs when compared with the alternatives.[47]

But large dams continue to be woven into the fabric of modernization and industrialization, especially in places like China, where the scale of manufacturing, agriculture, and population growth present real challenges for water supply in the twenty-first century. Dams come with major costs beyond the obvious capital expenditure. When large dams are built—such as Three Gorges in China, Belo Monte in Brazil, or the series of Narmada dams in India—vast areas of formerly inhabited and often arable land are submerged under water. People who live in those areas are displaced, usually without adequate (and sometimes without any) compensation. Large dams, in other words, create millions of environmental migrants around the world.

Large dams can also amplify the effects of climate change. Behind large dams that receive high concentrations of phosphates and nitrates from industrial agriculture, the water quality can be quite low, since those chemical compounds accelerate the eutrophication of reservoir water. (Eutrophication is the depletion of oxygen in the water, usually accompanied and exacerbated by the proliferation of algae.) In fact, the United Nations Environment Programme describes eutrophication as "one of the most widespread environmental problems of inland waters."[48] This is a problem for potability of water, to be sure, but it is also a climate problem, because large quantities of methane are released into the atmosphere. Moreover, in arid and semi-arid regions, large dams, such as the Hoover Dam in the US Southwest or the Aswan Dam in Egypt, lose a significant proportion of their fresh water to evaporation. Since both methane and water vapor intensify climate change patterns, it seems that large hydroelectric dams come saddled with a range of environmental costs.

Conclusion:
Anthropogenic Climate Change and Water

Climate change's disproportionate recent amplification above paleo-historical baselines is due primarily to the combustion of fossil fuels and current political attachment to fossil fuel economies. What societies decide to do (or not do) about energy sources and then about climate change adaptation or mitigation will have major consequences in the twenty-first century. The effects of climate change will be unevenly distributed and borne predominantly by people living in poverty who did little to create or benefit from the dynamics of the fossil fuel economy. This exacerbates an ethical problem that becomes even more dire when viewed through the lens of fresh water, that substance most vital for life on earth—because water is the primary mechanism by which climate change will affect societies and individuals in the twenty-first century. Fresh water must therefore be a key term in conversations about climate change, the Anthropocene, and fossil fuel economies from scientific, policy, and ethical perspectives. On all levels of scale, from the individual to the transnational, human action or inaction will reveal what it is that societies value. It behooves those who have benefited from the legacies of the fossil fuel economy—especially, though not exclusively, privileged populations in the United States—to act well, no longer ignorant of the historical, social, and economic structures that conduce to this privilege. The structures of climate injustice in the Anthropocene bear our imprints and require ethical remediation, even if incomplete.

CHAPTER 7

Water from Rock

Standing Rock and *Laudato Si'*

The problem of water is partly an educational and cultural issue.
—Pope Francis

Mni wiconi—water is life.

—Lakota saying

Scientific consensus is now clear: the intensification of twenty-first-century anthropogenic climate change is a direct result of human extraction and combustion of fossil fuels. Yet scientific clarity does not always lead to effective political action or societal consensus in the face of powerful economic and political interests that are vested in maintaining a fossil fuel–based industrial economy. Within this disheartening context for public discourse, debate about fossil fuels in the contemporary United States tends to follow two broad scripts.

The first script argues that US reliance on foreign fuel is a threat to national security and economic growth, so what we need is to achieve energy independence. Therefore, it is important to cultivate energy sources from within our borders or from proximate, irenic nation-states (such as Canada)—and so much the better if "bridge fuel" development efforts (to provide transition fuels that reduce carbon emissions) bring jobs and economic growth to the United States. Such efforts could include fossil fuel development within the continental United States and Alaska and would not necessarily preclude funding initiatives for renewable energy. The second script argues that fossil fuels are part of the problem, not the solution. Only with a move away from fossil fuel energy will societies—especially industrialized nations like the United States—ever achieve long-term economic growth and environmental sustainability, including mitigation of climate change. Fossil fuels are a necessary crutch for the time being, perhaps, but continued reliance on them is driven by special interests that do not serve the common good. The pursuit of corporate profit through fossil fuel extraction is particularly problematic, both because of the entrenched oil and gas lobby in the United States and because the economic status quo focuses on economic growth as the ultimate value, without sufficiently incorporating the negative externalities that accompany fossil fuel extraction, processing, and consumption. This second script worries about outcomes beyond economics that are caused by the incentive structure of profit-and-growth economic practices. It points out how it is always in the economic interests of fossil fuel companies to externalize costs—including nonmonetary costs that are often borne by local communities or ecosystems. As a result, the second script calls for governmental and public oversight of the fossil fuel industry, including strong regulations on fossil fuel extraction; the accountability of fossil fuel corporations to stakeholders (not just shareholders); the protection of watersheds; and the promotion of renewable energy sources. It argues that efforts to cultivate and incentivize clean, sustainable energy sources should be redoubled. In recent years, moral and legal actions over the Dakota Access Pipeline (DAPL) have illuminated some of what is at stake—in terms of fossil fuel pipelines, tribal sovereignty, watershed stewardship, and public activism.[1]

   In the twenty-first century, fresh water crises and conflicts result from complex intersections of hydrogeology, globalized political economies predicated on resource extraction, and diverse cultural understandings or social norms regarding the distribution and use of water. This chapter pairs awareness of global fresh water dynamics with Pope Francis's remarks in *Laudato Si'* (*LS*) about fresh water and indigenous cultural value; it places those remarks in conversation with rallying cries for the sacredness of water as articulated by indigenous activists at Standing Rock who protest the construction of a gas pipeline across their lands and under the Missouri River in the Dakotas.[2]

The first section of this chapter describes how water protectors at Standing Rock make significant moral claims about water- and sovereignty-based indigenous resistance to the pipeline and to the political economies of domination that support it. The second section turns to Pope Francis's developments of Catholic social teaching (CST), summarizing two topics put forward in *LS*: normative commitments about water and justice, and epistemic-ethical appeals to indigenous ecological knowledge. The third section integrates those claims with reference to Standing Rock and concludes that the DAPL project is a prime example of when environmental-ethical values of indigenous peoples should be honored, and the pipeline not constructed, even while recognizing the myriad knots of energy, environmental, and economic considerations at play.[3]

The Dakota Access Pipeline, Standing Rock, and *Mni Wiconi*

Following a half-century in which Army Corps of Engineers projects dammed and diverted various water sources, the Lakota Sioux of the Standing Rock reservation have for several decades advocated for sufficient access to clean, fresh water for their lands and people. In November 2004 a Senate hearing convened by the Committee on Indian Affairs was held on objections pertaining to Army Corps of Engineers' diversion of portions of Missouri River tributaries to facilitate barge commerce downstream. While the corps argued for the primacy of economic benefit resulting from increased barge traffic on the Missouri, Standing Rock Sioux chairman Charles Murphy presented evidence that the corps' actions had negatively affected the water supply of the reservation:

> We don't have the water to provide for our people. One year ago . . . we had approximately 10,000 people without water. These were Indian and non-Indian people within our reservation of 2.3 million acres [and 18,000 people]. . . . Senator, we have a major issue out there with the management of the Missouri River situation.[4]

Tim Johnson, Senator from North Dakota, added that the situation is "particularly disconcerting given the treaties that bind the Federal Government's responsibility to our tribes in North and South Dakota."[5]

The issue at that time had to do with distribution problems resulting from drought, the formation of Lake Oahe (itself a mid-twentieth-century invention of the Army Corps of Engineers), and incomplete infrastructure. But the pattern of disregard for the Standing Rock Sioux's concerns about water was at this point quite clear, and the effects on the bodies of the reservation's residents were dramatic. For example, the testimony notes that several dialysis centers had to be closed due to lack of water. Kent Conrad, US Senator from North Dakota, stressed that one problem lay in how "this is all overwhelmingly managed for the benefit of the barge industry downstream. . . . This dire situation . . . underscores the need for change in the management of the Missouri River. We can't afford this any longer. People's lives are at risk without water. What could be more clear?"[6] And North Dakota Senator Byron Dorgan put the moral and legal point firmly, interrogating the Army Corps of Engineers:

> Is the assured supply of water for citizens who receive that water from the river a higher priority than other priorities,

or is it simply equivalent to others? . . . In my judgment, the management of the river must understand that the first and most important priority is to make sure that we don't have people cut off from an adequate supply of water.[7]

The relevance of such questions and concerns over access to water as a *justice* issue, a structural problem, and a militaristic connection was clear to Senator Daniel Inouye, chair of the Committee on Indian Affairs. In his closing remarks, he noted the parallels between the Army Corps of Engineers' actions affecting the Standing Rock Sioux, on the one hand, and the US military's reception in Iraq:

When our troops entered Baghdad, the people there received us with cheers and with huzzahs. . . . But we noted that within a week these same faces became faces of anger. And in our hearts we knew that there were many causes for this. One of the major causes was that we did not have plans to repair the damaged water systems and the damaged sewer systems.[8]

Such an admission has profound implications regarding the militaristic–colonial complex that mediates access to water. Given these historical precursors and structural tendencies, it was perhaps not surprising that the Army Corps of Engineers fast-tracked the Dakota Access Pipeline through the Standing Rock reservation to transport fossil fuels from the Bakken oil shale, crossing and traveling under the Missouri River. Proponents of DAPL point out that transportation of shale oil through pipelines is safer than overland transit on highways or railways. Opponents respond that the dangers to water sources are unacceptable, and the continued societal reliance on fossil fuels should be phased out in pursuit of clean energy options.

Energy Transfer Partners, the operating company for DAPL, asserts that it has followed procedure in soliciting input from the

Sioux. Representatives from the reservation disagree and have filed a lawsuit claiming that due process was violated. Moreover, indigenous activists argue that the permitting process itself is fundamentally flawed in ways that reflect neocolonial mentalities of the US government and the extractive industrial-profit complex of contemporary multinational corporations. They further claim that water, as a source of life, is more important than extractive industries' desire for a pipeline in this particular place. As the website of the Standing Rock Sioux phrases it: "In honor of future generations, we fight this pipeline to protect our water, our sacred places, and all living beings."[9] Indigenous Environmental Network elaborates on the issue this way:

> In North Dakota, Indigenous leaders from the Standing Rock Nation are fighting the Dakota Access Pipeline (DAPL). This pipeline will carry over a half a million barrels of oil per day from the Bakken Oil Shale Fields. The route the pipeline will take, if approved, will be laid under multiple bodies of water, to include the Missouri River located a half mile upstream from the Standing Rock reservation. This river not only supplies drinking water to the tribe but is a major tributary to the Mississippi River where more than 10 million people depend on it for both human consumption and irrigation for the nation's "bread basket." This pipeline when it fails—and it will fail—will destroy land and water with little, if any, chance of remediation/cleanup. We only need to look at the devastating Yellowstone River, Kalamazoo, and many others. Protesters have continued to resist construction peacefully, despite surveillance and intimidation from the state.[10]

Consultation with tribes is expected, but how this requirement is to be fulfilled is quite vague. Thus, according to the *New York Times*,

The Corps says it reached out extensively to tribes before it gave approval for the Dakota Access pipeline to cross bodies of water, including the Missouri. The Standing Rock Sioux, it says, canceled a meeting to visit the pipeline's proposed crossing across Lake Oahe. The tribe says it was not properly consulted.[11]

The director of Indigenous Environmental Network, Tom Goldtooth, argues that "consultation" has not been sufficiently interpreted:

What the US calls consultation is not consultation but a statement telling people what they're doing after millions of dollars have been invested, painting Indigenous Peoples as spoilers. The right of free, prior and informed consent begins prior to the planning process, not when their bulldozers are at your doorstep.[12]

After many months of crescendoed peaceful protests by tribal citizens, allied tribal nations, and supporters, there was some optimism when in December 2016 then-President Obama did not grant a "last remaining easement" to "drill under the Missouri River at Lake Oahe and complete construction of the pipeline," and would require an environmental impact statement to consider alternate routes.[13] Such momentary optimism, however, must be understood in the context of a shifting political climate. Within the span of just two months after President Obama's intervention to require a thorough environmental impact statement, President Trump granted an easement allowing the pipeline to continue. That, in turn, drew an immediate legal challenge from the Sioux. The pipeline—and resistance to it—will continue to be mired in legal and political machinations.

Meanwhile, it must be said that the mechanisms of the state—North Dakota, the Army Corps of Engineers, or the federal government—have not primarily been geared toward protecting the protesters. Instead, physical and digital intimidations have

occurred: from the accusation of signal-jamming drones block-
ing wireless internet at the Oceti Sakowin base camp (obscuring
communication and online activism), to arrests of filmmakers, to
fire hoses of hot water being sprayed at protesters in the middle
of winter on a rural highway. As the American Civil Liberties
Union summarizes:

> More than 200 tribes and several thousand indigenous
> people from across the country have gathered in North
> Dakota to protest the Dakota Access Pipeline. The pro-
> testers are defending the land and water using little more
> than the right to assemble and speak freely—a protection
> afforded by the US Constitution. In response to the pro-
> tests, North Dakota's government suppressed free speech
> and militarized its policing by declaring a state of emer-
> gency, setting up a highway roadblock, and calling out the
> National Guard.[14]

Such litanies of structural, legal, and physical intimidations
forestall blithe optimism. But neither do these intimidations
occlude the strength of heart expressed by the water protectors, indigenous activists, and allies. The nonviolent approach
embraced by Standing Rock leaders is rendered visible by an
image from the night that the water hoses were sprayed on
peaceful protesters. For Louise Erdrich, writing in the *New
Yorker,* the enduring image is of a person, "covered in ice and
praying, [illustrating] the resolve that comes from a philosophy
based on generosity of spirit."[15] Brenda White Bull, a military
veteran and Lakota woman, stated simply: "The highest weapon
of them all is prayer. . . . The world is watching. Our ancestors
are watching. . . . We are fighting for the human race."[16]

The conflict at Standing Rock embodies a tangle of disenfranchisements over water, land, sovereignty, and economic benefit that obviously has unique features. But it is also simultaneously
emblematic of broader structural patterns of disenfranchisement

and settler colonialist legacies wrought upon the lives, cultures, and lands of Native peoples in the United States and worldwide. Roxanne Dunbar-Ortiz, in the award-winning book *An Indigenous People's History of the United States*, notes:

> Through economic penetration of Indigenous societies, the European and Euro-American colonial powers created economic dependency and imbalance of trade, then incorporated the Indigenous nations into spheres of influence and controlled them indirectly or as protectorates. . . . In the case of US settler colonialism, land was the primary commodity.[17]

David Archambault II, then chairman of the Standing Rock Sioux, specifies this as a "familiar story in Indian Country":

> This is the third time that the Sioux Nation's lands and resources have been taken without regard for tribal interests. . . . When the Army Corps of Engineers dammed the Missouri River in 1958, it took our riverfront forests, fruit orchards and most fertile farmland to create Lake Oahe. Now the Corps is taking our clean water and sacred places by approving this river crossing. . . . Protecting water and our sacred places has always been at the center of our cause. The Indian encampment on the Cannonball grows daily, with nearly 90 tribes now represented. Many of us have been here before, facing the destruction of homelands and waters, as time and time again tribes were ignored.[18]

Seasoned journalist and activist Bill McKibben likewise situates the conflict within this larger history of disenfranchisement:

> Native Americans live confined to bleak reservations in vast stretches of the country that no one thought were

good for much of anything else. But those areas—ironically enough—now turn out to be essential for the production or transportation of the last great stocks of hydrocarbons, the ones whose combustion scientists tell us will take us over the edge of global warming. And if former generations of the US Army made it possible to grab land from Native people, then this largely civilian era of the Army Corps is making it easy to pollute and spoil what little we left them. . . . A spill from this pipeline would pollute the Missouri River, just as spills in recent years have done irreparable damage to the Kalamazoo and Yellowstone rivers. And that river is both the spiritual and economic lifeblood of the Standing Rock Reservation, one of the poorest census tracts in the entire country.[19]

In other words, DAPL—like many extractive projects worldwide—is inextricably interwoven with legacies of racism, economic exploitation, and histories that make this particular case a familiar kind of story.

The embodied burdens are real, and they are unevenly distributed: The pipeline will disproportionately affect vulnerable Native American populations, as research by geographers Jennifer Veilleux and Candace Landry has indicated.[20] It is important to note that when US scholars attend to the Standing Rock protests as a site of water activism, we must also be willing to ask why similar kinds of attention may not be paid to the travesties and attempts at recovery of historically marginalized and racialized communities like Flint, Michigan, where water sources are not just hypothetically tainted but were truly and pervasively contaminated in ways that once again reveal the systemic racisms built into US infrastructure.[21]

Activists from the #NODAPL movement generally predicate their resistance to the pipeline on two major ethical claims: first, water is life; and second, indigenous sovereignty should outweigh for-profit, neocolonial, and government-backed expansion of extractive industry infrastructure. To these ethical claims are added twenty-first-century expressions of historical forms of resistance and solidarity: the online and in-person collaboration of more than two hundred Native groups in expressing solidarity over protecting water and opposing the pipeline, for example. Marion Grau observes some of the water protectors' hybrid identities and aptitudes:

> It is heartening to see many young indigenous women in particular lead and speak. They are quick to tell the gathered crowds that they are college-graduated and able to use tech-savvy information strategies through outlets such as Indigenous Environmental Network and many others. They are gloriously hybrid leaders—the "digital natives" nobody was thinking of when they coined that term—combining the best of subversive education and information technology, blending indigenous and post-industrialized ways of being.[22]

Where linkages among systemic disenfranchisements and violent actions of the state are particularly evident, powerfully symbolic solidarities have sprung up—as with the many military veterans who journeyed to North Dakota to protect the Native bodies who were in turn protecting the water. Some of these military veterans included Native Americans, who "serve in the US military at a higher rate than any other ethnic group."[23] Tribal chairman David Archambault II addressed veterans with gratitude: "What you are doing is precious to us. I can't describe the feelings that move over me. It is *wakan,* sacred. You are all sacred."[24] In these ways and more, #NODAPL is a crucial site and moment for collective consciousness about historical and contemporary forms of domination, which have been structurally, legally, and physically unrelenting on subaltern human bodies and bodies of water. The slogans "we are water," "water is sacred," and *Mni wiconi* are vital portals to twenty-first-century forms of justice.

Laudato Si':
The Value(s) of Water and
a Papal Turn to Indigenous Knowledge

Given the Catholic Church's historical vindications of European colonization in the Americas with its late-fifteenth-century papal bulls, it may seem surprising that the current pope has stressed the importance of indigenous knowledge and value systems.[25] As Bill McKibben put it in the *New York Review of Books*, such admiration for cultural diversity and indigenous knowledge is remarkable coming from the leader of an institution that "first set out to universalize the world."[26] Of course, Pope Francis is a man whose ministry and theological reflection has been shaped by the experience of serving and leading religious communities in South America. This experience forms some of the background to *Laudato Si'* (*LS*) and reflects a liberation theology orientation to praxis and social justice. Moreover, in *LS* and in numerous addresses, Pope Francis is clear that local and indigenous populations are repositories of cultural-moral values regarding the environment and should have central roles in any decisions affecting their land.[27]

This is potentially promising, as many indigenous leaders have noted. But in this beginning is a crucial caveat: it can be dangerous when the spur to recognition of pluralistic value systems comes from a centralized patriarchal authority that is historically associated with colonialism and universalism and normatively expounded by predominantly white scholars in the northern hemisphere, especially in the United States. What, then, are important ground rules to establish as (mostly white) scholars of Catholic social teaching such as myself engage the papal suggestion that indigenous cultures need to be respected and honored? Literature engaging this question is extensive and nuanced in several disciplines, including liberation theology, decolonial discourses, and indigenous activisms. This topic deserves much fuller treatment in CST. Several insights come to the fore.

First, "indigenous" is not a uniform category but instead reflects enormous diversities, even while there are consistent and recognizable historical patterns of colonialism, racism, disenfranchisement, and cultural obliteration. Second, "indigenous knowledges" (plural) or the input of these sovereign peoples is not a category to which lip service can be paid and then proceed with business-as-usual (as has generally been the case with "consultations" with Native peoples, with a case in point being DAPL, as indicated in preceding sections). Instead, these conversations have to be truly subject to an open range of possible courses of action, even economically undesirable ones, within which the more powerful parties do not get to determine ultimate outcomes but rather defer to the historically marginalized and vulnerable populations that will be most affected by various projects (as Pope Francis notes in *LS*). In a related way, third, there needs to be an explicit baseline ethical-procedural requirement that rejects any reinscription of historical or epistemic harms, and is wary of blithe appeals to "inclusion" without actual praxis. Fourth and finally, there is a profound difference between "standing with" and "speaking for," whether as researchers or activists. Nado Aveling, describing a process of discernment regarding research agendas and the vagaries of the scholarly gaze, suggests that even for well-intentioned and justice-oriented scholars,

> the journey from my hitherto "emancipatory" position grounded in a white western paradigm, to being a reasonably effective ally has taken time and necessitated an in-depth exploration of, not only the literature dealing with Indigenous methodologies, but also a return to the scholarship that critically deconstructs whiteness. My primary aim was to investigate what Indigenous scholars were saying about research and find out what a non-exploitative, culturally appropriate approach to research might look like and where I might "fit" in terms of doing research.[28]

If such caveats can be recognized, and the journey of discernment and self-critique within the research establishment can be heeded, then the pope's recognition of indigenous knowledge is timely.

Scholarly authority is not the same as lived cultural praxis on matters of ecological and social values, but it is a vehicle for communication, reflection, and perhaps (in this case) the galvanizing of Catholic communities. As John Thavis observed, the "struggle at Standing Rock has made allies among people of many faiths, and should resonate with Catholics who are listening to this pope's social teaching."[29] As many activists and scholars have noted, the twenty-first century is a time of rising awareness of indigenous knowledge and insights, consolidated activist alliances, and pluralistic values regarding the protection of land-people-water-culture. Scholars such as myself can amplify the firsthand experience of water warriors and explicate what resources or norms CST may offer to such struggles. In such ways we can seek to stand in epistemic and ethical solidarity, as long as we recognize that the perspectives we bring to the conversation are offerings, not answers.

Fresh Water in Catholic Social Teaching and Laudato Si'

Statements on fresh water in *Laudato Si'* represent a distilled and slightly expanded version of magisterial teaching on a topic that has been in development for over a decade.[30] Pope Francis suggests that water conveys something holy, something requiring attitudes and actions of respect and reverence, because it is a gift from God that is fundamental to human dignity and the sanctity of life. Since at least 2003 John Paul II, Benedict XVI, the Pontifical Academy for Justice and Peace, and now Pope Francis have articulated the importance of access to clean, fresh water. These concerns include the lack of access to fresh water in non-industrialized nations; the impacts on the poor and vulnerable; the ways in which commodification of water impedes access to this fundamental good; and the corrective conceptual mechanism of viewing fresh water as a fundamental human right.[31] Pope Francis expands the language, too, adding: "Our world has a grave social debt towards the poor who lack access to drinking water, because they are denied the right to a life consistent with their inalienable dignity."[32] In his address to the United Nations on September 25, 2015, he further explained that water is among the things that allow people "to be dignified agents of their own destiny." As explained in chapters 3 and 4, such ethical claims are noteworthy in themselves. They are also particularly suggestive when coupled with the pope's statements on indigenous cultural value and ecological knowledge, and then considered in the context of Standing Rock.

The Turn to Indigenous Communities and Cultures

In *Laudato Si'* Francis compares cultural elimination to species extinction: "The disappearance of a culture can be just as serious, or even more serious, than the disappearance of a species of plant or animal."[33] In addition, it is possible to discern in *LS* an emphasis on the importance of indigenous sovereignty and self-determination, including cultural frames for understanding, valuing, and managing ecological systems and relationships. What would it look like for the Catholic Church and other dominant institutions—including, for example, the US government or Army Corps of Engineers or Energy Transfer Partners—to truly consider pluralities of values based on the epistemic authority of colonized peoples? Granted, in *LS* Francis does not explicitly consider what indigenous cultures may offer to ethical discourse on water. But the epistemic point stands: the pope's recognition of indigenous traditions provides an opening to consider how multiple ways of being and understanding constitutive relationships can enrich, challenge, and construct countervailing accounts to the dominant historical, colonial-industrial, Western political economic forces that have shaped patterns of valuing and distributing water (and other entities of the natural world). Does the papal appeal to the value of indigenous cultures provide a glimpse of affirmation of humanity's essential plurality, perhaps even validating subaltern authority, with implications for governance? And are there any substantive, normative linkages that can be made between *Laudato Si'* and Standing Rock?

Water Justice and Indigenous Knowledge between *Laudato Si'* and Standing Rock

Mni wiconi (water is life) is a refrain and rallying cry for #NODAPL actions. It summons the idea of the sacredness of waters that sustain human and ecosystemic function, and it points toward the moral imperatives of tribal sovereignty and environmental justice. Along with "Water is Sacred" and "We are Water," *Mni wiconi* appears on posters both handmade and digital, on the front lines of protests and solidarity/fund-raising concerts, and on the home pages of the Indigenous Environmental Network and the Standing Rock Sioux. What has Catholic social teaching—especially *Laudato Si'*—to say to this contemporary situation? John Thavis suggests that even while Pope Francis hasn't directly addressed the Standing Rock situation, "he has been present" in the hearts and minds of water protectors. Chairman David Archambault II reportedly sent a letter to the pontiff, "thanking Francis for his statements, explaining the pipeline battle and asking for the pope's prayers."[34] Consider, then, what the following words from *Laudato Si'* mean for Standing Rock:

It is essential to show special care for indigenous communities and their cultural traditions. They are not merely one minority among others, but should be the principal dialogue partners, especially when large projects affecting their land are proposed. For them, land is not a commodity but rather a gift from God and from their ancestors who rest there, a sacred space with which they need to interact if they are to maintain their identity and values. When they remain on their land, they themselves care for it best.

> Nevertheless, in various parts of the world, pressure is being put on them to abandon their homelands to make room for agricultural or mining projects which are undertaken without regard for the degradation of nature and culture.[35]

This passage needs little translation to Standing Rock and DAPL: effective procedural collusion between the Energy Transfer Partners corporation, the government permitting process, and the Army Corps of Engineers has led to the construction of a major project linked to extractive energy economies that has not considered the Standing Rock Sioux to be "principal dialogue partners," not even when their lands are affected. The slogan of *Mni wiconi* and assertions of prayer as a form of protest clearly indicate that there are major spiritual values at work at Standing Rock, in ways that resonate with the papal observation that "land is not merely a commodity but a gift from God and their ancestors." And certainly, major pressures (structural, legal, and physical) are being placed on the Standing Rock water protectors.

But is verbal or written exhortation enough? Mark Silk of Religion News Service observed that despite the papal call to attention and action, "these issues cut no ice with the Catholic bishops of North and South Dakota, or with the US Conference of Catholic Bishops itself, whose silence on the Dakota Access pipeline was deafening."[36] Indeed, the silence is deafening when one notes the post-*LS* absence of diocesan Catholic involvement in, or advocacy for, Standing Rock's unique concatenation of environmental justice and religious liberty. Where are the local and regional dioceses or Catholic universities that could adroitly bring such values to religious discourse and ethical reflection? Finally, in February 2017—one day before Pope Francis hosted a "Dialogue on Water" at the Pontifical Academy of Sciences in Rome—US Jesuits, Red Cloud Indian School, and St. Francis Mission issued a joint statement decrying DAPL and calling it "morally unacceptable." Tim Kesicki, SJ, president of the US Jesuit Conference, noted that

Jesuits have been working beside and ministering to native peoples for centuries. We stand in solidarity with native peoples in Standing Rock and around the world who are advocating for environmental and human rights in the face of extractive industry projects. Like Pope Francis, we recognize that water is a fundamental human right.[37]

In some but not all senses, then, Silk's 2016 estimation rang true: "It was the usual liberal-left religious suspects who stepped up—mainline Protestant denominations, Reform Jews, Evangelicals for Social Action, the Franciscan Action Network, the Leadership Conference of Women Religious"[38]—followed in 2017 by Catholic priests and laity involved with education and service on the Pine Ridge and Rosebud Reservations. This is not to suggest that all Catholics are dispassionate, of course: many individuals who understand Catholicity to exist not in abstruse creeds but in embodied practices have found ways to support the efforts at Standing Rock, from online advocacy to physical presence. Consider the example of Eric Martin, one of many people drawn for spiritual, ethical, and civic reasons to support the water protectors, who wrote in the *New York Times*:

> I had come with a group of Catholic Workers for reasons anyone studying or teaching theology as I do might find obvious. The violation of basic dignity happening here defies the consistent refrain by the prophets and Jesus to do justice with an eye toward the exploited. We had been told white bodies could help by surrounding native ones, shielding them while they sought to protect their water.[39]

These are crucial actors and visible forms of solidarity, expressed by those who take the linkage between theology and praxis to be central to lives of faith.

Even so, the values of water justice and indigenous cultural knowledge that are embedded in *LS* seem not yet to have permeated the heavily frocked US Catholic establishment. This is tragic on numerous levels—for the bodily integrity risked daily by the water protectors, for the lost opportunity for Catholic social teaching to be expressed bravely and with much-needed mainline leadership by Catholic churches, for the lack of attention to the convergence of life-giving pluralistic values on the centrality of water to life and as a "right-to-life issue," and for what it reveals about the selective attention that some US Catholics pay to papal encyclicals and CST more generally. The lack of integration is also tragic given the hype that *LS* received both before and after its promulgation in 2015, and in light of the fact that—in the words of Marion Grau—the "vision of the movement gathered at Standing Rock is anything but secular, it is deeply religious and spiritual, but also defiant of those two overused categories."[40] Some of the most important religious liberty issues of the twenty-first century will be at precisely this nexus of environmental degradation, indigenous rights, and water justice. Whether the most profound implications of *Laudato Si'* will be deflected or embraced by dominant cultures and Catholic leadership in dioceses and universities remains to be seen. There may not be grounds for optimism, but as has been abundantly evident at Standing Rock, neither is it cause for loss of hope.

Conclusion:
Who Speaks for Water?

At stake in Standing Rock and other conflicts over fresh water worldwide in the twenty-first century is the question of who authoritatively narrates the story, substance, and value of water. Who accounts for the flows that determine distributive systems and ethical parameters by which communities in various parts of the world must live? These are crucial grounding questions for any sufficient ethic of water justice if the twenty-first century is going to avoid repeating the hubristic brutalities of the past. It is a positive turn that throughout the twentieth century and now the twenty-first, many nondominant cultures and indigenous action groups have challenged the values embedded in Western forms of development-incentivized resource management, especially pertaining to water, and have done so in ways that give rise to myriad expressions of solidarity and the formation of geographically disparate but ethically proximate digital communities.[41] It is also cause for hope that Pope Francis seems to be drawing attention to the moral insights and ecological-cultural claims of Native peoples, not merely a personal charism but as a series of principled claims built into some of the most authoritative types of teachings on Catholic faith and morality.

This chapter has suggested that *Laudato Si'* generates important normative anchors that connect with indigenous claims about sovereignty and integrity of waters made by #NODAPL water protectors at Standing Rock. Catholics who affirm papal authority, especially those in the Dakotas specifically and the United States more generally, should be attending to the ways in which Catholic teaching calls for express protection of vulnerable human beings, indigenous cultures, and water.

In the case of fresh water, the Catholic magisterial embrace of water as a human right and fundamental life issue aligns in profound and obvious ways with the Lakota Sioux claim, *Mni wiconi.* And the convergence of *LS* with water justice and indigenous knowledge at Standing Rock provides an opportunity to put faith into action: that is, to discern how variegated ways of life and knowledge traditions should be regarded with profound respect and humility. No longer the "other" of normative Western discourse, indigenous traditions must be conversation partners and sources of deep knowledge and critiques against dominant-extractive-industrial value systems, environmental–social subordination to short-term economic benefit, and colonialist legacies of domination. Dominant society's norms regarding valuation and allocation of water should not be blithely considered as best courses of action from an ethical perspective. The historical default is not always worthy of deference, for as Jeremy

Schmidt points out, the norms that condition the distribution and flow of waters in the United States are themselves historically contingent constructions that reflect certain configurations of power.[42]

Given how norms regarding use of water (not to mention decision making about water) are conditioned by legacies of colonialism and domination, it is time to recognize that water is a socio-natural liquid, and thus to attend to values of water that have been historically marginalized through patterns of colonialism and neocolonialism. First, any sufficient ethic of water justice will embody careful and historically informed value-epistemology. It will proceed by welcoming diverse cultural perspectives grounded in land and forgotten/occluded/colonized histories. It bounds past entrenched anxieties about moral relativism by refining how diverse cultural value systems mesh with ethical systems. Second, any stalwart and sufficient ethic of water justice will require that the people most affected by water decisions have a strong voice at the table of decision making, attuned to asking: Who benefits, in what ways? Who bears the burdens, for what duration? What is it that we are not yet seeing? As Pope Francis wrote in *LS*:

> A number of questions need to be asked in order to discern whether or not [a given project] will contribute to genuine integral development. What will it accomplish? Why? Where? When? How? For whom? What are the risks? What are the costs? Who will pay those costs and how? In this discernment, some questions must have higher priority. For example, we know that water is a scarce and indispensable resource and a fundamental right which conditions the exercise of other human rights. This indisputable fact overrides any other assessment of environmental impact on a region.[43]

Finally, any sufficient ethic of water justice will recognize that the discernment and implementations of norms and policies are hardly static. Water, both noun and verb, is a trickster: always in motion and context-specific, it takes the shape of any container—whether a vessel or a river, a political-economic system or a religious ritual. Yet amid that diversity, there is still a universal truth: *Mni wiconi*—water is life. Water justice requires honoring the water protectors who hold this truth against the structures, legal regimes, and physical oppressions that accompany our particular iterations of neocolonialism, at Standing Rock and beyond.

CHAPTER 8

The Jordan River

He said to me, "Mortal, have you seen this?" Then he led me back along the bank of the river.

—Ezekiel 47:6

What does theology have to do with hydrology? Theologian Denis Edwards has remarked that even when Christians "are deeply committed to ecology . . . they cannot see a connection with the story of Jesus . . . [and so] it is an urgent task for theology to show the interconnection between the living memory of Jesus and the issues that confront the global community."[1] So too, despite the increased attention that Catholic social teaching has given to fresh water as a human right, it is still the case that many Christians struggle to connect biblical stories to contemporary fresh water realities. This chapter and the next chapter therefore turn to well-known texts and locations from the Bible and Christian practice in order to examine connections among theology, ethics, and contemporary fresh water realities. What do hydrology and hydropolitics have to do with the natural history of the Bible, the interpretation of familiar religious stories, or contemporary Christian rituals? What could this mean for thinking about water ethics in the present day? One place to begin is on the banks of the River Jordan.

The Shape of the Jordan River Today

The Dead Sea is quietly heaving. Its predatory shores pursue the salty sea and press it inward, exposing sandy sinkholes the size of houses. Truth be told, this is not the fault of the sea: waters always hold an elusive agency toward their own persistence. Nor is this strictly the fault of the shores, which are merely accessory to the Dead Sea's decline. It might be said that the fault lies with the Jordan River, which for centuries has fed fresh water into its hypersaline terminus, but which now flows toward the sea as a pea-green, sluggish trickle of agricultural runoff. The meager flows of the Jordan are causing the decline of the Dead Sea, but what causes the decline of the Jordan River? Does it matter? Should it? In some ways the story of the Jordan River is a story that intersects with those of many rivers worldwide; in other ways, it is unique. The presence or absence of fresh water affects concerns about security, political power, economic viability, and more. In this way, sociopolitical and environmental realities resist clean separation; the Jordan River is resolutely hydrosocial, insofar as it involves aridity, irrigated agriculture, colonial legacies, economic incentive, engineering projects, population demand, political power, nationalist narratives, and religious resonances.

Environmental Aspects: Water, Demand, and Climate Change

Historically, the Jordan River flooded its banks with seasonal cycles of precipitation. Groups of resident agro-pastoralists inhabited the valley floor, and until the twentieth century environmental change was due mostly to overgrazing and agricultural clearing of forests. Polymath scientist and longtime resident of the region Daniel Hillel describes how, over time, "as the forests were cleared for fuel or timber, and as the slopes were cultivated and overgrazed, more and more of the exposed soil was scoured off the hillsides and was laid down in the valleys."[2] This is a classic synopsis of the effects of deforestation, a phenomenon that is common historically and in many other locations worldwide. Hillel depicts the hydrography—that is, the shape and journey—of the lower Jordan River in this way:

> After traversing the Sea of Galilee (known as Lake Kinneret in Israel), the river twists its way in an incredibly sinuous manner through the gray chalky marls of the lower valley. Squirming madly as if trying to escape its fate, the Jordan finally completes the journey from its cool crystal-clear origin to its literally bitter end, where it dies a tired death in the warm, murky brine of the Dead Sea.[3]

For all of recorded history, the Jordan River has terminated with "a tired death" in the Dead Sea. Yet it is in the past century that human impacts have most dramatically shaped the river and altered its flow. During the twentieth century, as in other arid regions worldwide, the waters of the Jordan were subjected to intensified demand, ranging from domestic use by growing populations to ongoing sociopolitical contestations and hydraulic engineering innovations (especially for extraction of water from aquifers and irrigation of crops), as well as extended periods of drought.[4] As a result, the flow of the lower Jordan River decreased by 90 percent between the mid-twentieth century and the beginning of the twenty-first century.[5] Hillel described in 1994 how Lake Kinneret (the Sea of Galilee) "serves as a natural reservoir, regulating the flow of the lower Jordan. In recent decades, the lake has also served Israel as an artificially regulated reservoir: a dam built at its southern end allows water managers to control the outflow."[6] A team of hydrologists affirmed in 2008 that,

> Lake Kinneret, Israel (the Biblical Sea of Galilee), the only major natural freshwater lake in the Middle East, has been transformed functionally into a reservoir over the course

of [approximately] 70 years of hydrological alterations aimed mostly at producing electrical power and increasing domestic and agricultural water supply.[7]

Just south of the lake, in the span of the lower Jordan River valley, at several points the river barely runs at all. At others, it seems a mere stream of slow-moving, pea-green sludge, a composite aqueous solution of industrial and domestic pollution and agricultural runoff.

To complicate matters further, in coming years the Jordan River valley is expected to feel major effects of climate change. A joint report by NASA and the University of California at Irvine in early 2013 presented striking evidence that the annual rate of water loss, especially from aquifers, is higher than expected in the region. Geophysicists report that "for people living in the Jordan River region of the Middle East, such changes can have immediate devastating impacts as water resources are already scarce and overexploited."[8] The hydrological stakes may well intensify in coming years, as continued demand on groundwater puts major pressure on the Mountain Aquifer (under the West Bank) and the Coastal Aquifer (under Gaza) that provide water to significant numbers of Palestinians, who are already under much tighter water restrictions than Israelis. (A July 2017 UN report decreed nearly all of Gaza's water to be unsafe and Gaza itself to be nearly "unlivable.")[9] These realities will bear social impacts in a location already known for its long-simmering tensions. Surface and groundwater sources in this arid region are vital and, when coupled with sociopolitical aspects, in the future may be increasingly tenuous.

Sociopolitical Aspects: Controlling and Distributing Water

In *Rivers of Eden,* Hillel indicated that "although the amount of water at issue is small, the rivalry over the Jordan is even more intense than that over the region's much larger rivers. . . . The relationships among the Jordan River's riparian states are exceedingly complex hydrologically as well as politically."[10] Or, as a pamphlet from the Jordan River Foundation delicately suggests, "The area of the River Jordan has a formidable history, and is well known both within and beyond the Middle East region."[11] Contestations over the waters of the Jordan River in modernity can be traced to nineteenth- and twentieth-century colonial enterprises and the lasting legacies bequeathed to the region by the colonial powers' demarcation of borders leading up to the creation of the State of Israel in 1948. The subsequent legacy of political negotiations—some diplomatic and others militarized—speaks, at least in part, to the problem of water and boundaries in the Jordan River Valley.[12]

While Israel has long been a people according to the Hebrew Bible, Israel the state is a recent invention. The Levant region was subject to European colonization, which led eventually to the creation of the State of Israel in 1948. While the atrocious legacy of Nazi Germany provided moral justification for the creation of the state of Israel in the eyes of many, it is also the case that these political demarcations did not occur in ways that made hydrological sense, nor were they well conceived with regard to the existing nations and peoples of the region, who also had strong historical and cultural ties to the land, and who were in too many cases evicted forcibly from their homes and lands.

Political agreements enshrined some parameters of water sharing in the region. For example, Annex II to the 1994 Israel–Jordan Peace Treaty identified the midpoint of the Jordan River as the international boundary between Israel and the Hashemite Kingdom of Jordan; it also specified the precise amount of seasonal flow to which each country is entitled. During an overlapping period, the 1995 Oslo Accords led to nascent governance agreements between Israel and the Palestinian Territories. Those accords created not just the Palestinian Authority but also the Palestinian Water Authority, which is responsible for water procurement and distribution in the Palestinian Territories. Despite this accord, it is fair to say that there are major, ongoing tensions between these political entities, and water is often a central concern. Issues include Israeli military presence and state support for settlements (including water extraction) in the West Bank, as well as Israel's control of most of the water and fragmented governance by the Palestinian Water Authority. These fundamental issues continue to generate significant mistrust and profound differences in water access and maintenance of infrastructure quality.[13]

In July 2017, Israel and Jordan signed a much-hyped water deal that was intended to increase water supply to several key locations in the region. The "Red-Dead" plan would pipe water from the Red Sea, desalinate it, and leave the brine in the already hypersaline Dead Sea; allow Israel to use that desalinated water for new farms in the desert; and in return, Israel would distribute other fresh water supply in greater quantities to Amman and the West Bank. It is difficult to know whether this intervention would sufficiently resolve the territorial, political, and hydrological squabbles that have long been part of the social geography of the Jordan River valley. Negotiations and paths to implementation were stalled in the simmering of political tensions when in an unrealated incident an Israeli officer shot two Jordanians in Amman. As longtime environmental writer and historian William deBuys phrased it, "One of the . . . portions of the planet most threatened by a decline in water supply stretches from Lebanon and Israel through Iraq and Iran to Afghanistan, lands beset by generations of intense conflict, where the stress of water shortage can inflame old grudges."[14] Even when not incendiary, water is not neutral. As Israeli scholar and environmentalist Alon Tal has noted, water for agriculture in this region is more than a functional liquid. "Within the twentieth-century context of Jewish nationalism," he writes, "water was the key to creating a vibrant agrarian economy and a fulfilled rural citizenry. It held the power to translate the pioneers' lush European aesthetic into a greener Middle Eastern landscape." Tal adds that water used for agricultural purposes in this way "became an integral part of the national identity" and actually "belonged to the realm of ideology."[15] Upon water was the nation of Israel built.

Israeli innovations in irrigation and water reuse are world-renowned: drip irrigation, for example, originated in Israel, and reuse of wastewater for agriculture is a common practice. Still, even with such focused efficiency, some of the crops grown are very thirsty and not naturally suited to arid regions, in both Israel and Jordan. With a growing population of over 15 million people and a sixfold increase in water use since the mid-twentieth century, the Middle East's precarious water balance has been tightly—if silently—tethered to the international political economy of water. In 2002, geographer J. Anthony Allan articulated the importance of international food systems for this region through his concept of virtual water, which reveals how Middle Eastern nations have imported vast amounts of virtual water in the form of grains and other crops. (See chapter 5 for a fuller account of virtual water.) Since those vital grain crops are grown and watered elsewhere, the region has largely avoided devastating levels of fresh water depletion. Thus, Allan elaborates that "the Jordan Basin is . . . a useful laboratory in which to observe the miraculous workings of economically invisible and politically silent 'virtual water,' accessible primarily through the international grain market."[16] He continues: "Throughout the past fifty years, Middle Eastern governments have leveraged the global political economy in order to implement otherwise unsustainable allocation policies," and "importing a ton of wheat therefore relieves a community from having to harness one thousand tons of its own water resources."[17]

Even with net imports of virtual water in the form of wheat, agriculture remains an influential sector in the Jordan River basin, and so agricultural water withdrawals and consumption contribute to the depletion of surface water and aquifers. In light of this fact, some efforts at cross-river conservation of fresh water supply could provide a model for transboundary collaboration in the future. The regional environmental organization Friends of the Earth Middle East (FoEME), for example—which has headquarters in Tel Aviv, Bethlehem, and Amman, and which was honored as one of *Time* magazine's "Environmental Heroes" for 2008—has established a program called "Good Water Neighbors," which promotes cooperation among villages that share a limited water supply. FoEME is a major player in political and ethical advocacy for communities and ecosystems along the Jordan River. The organization has also developed plans for a Peace Park on an island in the Jordan River, where Jordanians and Israelis (but not, presumably, Palestinians) could freely mingle. This is an important suggestion, because tension and sensitivity in the region endure, and the meanings of water are constructed not just by hydrological reality but also in light of nationalist narratives, religious symbolism, and historical experience. (In 2011, the State of Israel was still removing landmines from a site on the banks of the Jordan River where Jesus was purportedly baptized.)[18] Many commentators have noted that agreement about the use of fresh water is a component of any lasting peace in the Middle East.

At the time of the signing of the 1994 peace accords, Daniel Hillel offered guarded prognostications about the prospects for peace, for which he—like many in the region—understands water as a crucial middle term: "As the rivalry over common waters between neighboring states and territories intensifies, the Middle East is poised literally on a precarious watershed divide," he wrote.[19] Roughly twenty-five years have transpired since that assessment was penned. When in 2008 I asked Hillel whether he would consent to a reprinting of *Rivers of Eden*, he shook his head heavily and responded, "It was written at a different time"—a time, presumably, in which there was optimism about the peace process, a sense of multistate hydrological possibilities, and less concern about fresh water scarcity in the Jordan River basin.[20] In 2002, Allan suggested that "contention over water has proved to be subordinate to symbolic and territorial issues such as peace, Jerusalem, borders, settlements, and the return of refugees."[21] Continued cooperation—even more hopefully, a semblance of restored freshwater flows or managed aquifer recharge—will depend on many factors, such as the growth of thirsty, populous societies; the centrality of irrigated agriculture to economic development; entrenched sociopolitical realities, governance efficacy, and ideological conflicts; endemic drought in an era of global climate change; and transnational activism and education.

Religious Rhetoric and Riparian Reality

It is an awful trial to a man's religion to waltz it through the Holy Land.

—Mark Twain

Herman Melville and Mark Twain[22] were visitors to the Holy Land a decade apart in the mid-nineteenth century, and each relied on the Bible as "their main literary source" for their independent journeys to the Holy Land.[23] Presumably each man envisioned the Jordan River valley as it was described in the Hebrew Bible—"well watered everywhere, like the garden of the Lord" (Gen 13:10). Yet the gentlemen-adventurers were each chagrined to find that the Jordan was a paltry approximation of the imagined river and environs. Mark Twain's descriptions of the Holy Land and the Jordan River involved words like "puny."

That the Jordan River is degraded comes as a surprise to many travelers, especially religious pilgrims. Consider, for example, an area slightly downstream from a purported baptism site abutting the Sea of Galilee. This site, called Yardenit, is easily accessible to tourists and a primary destination for many Christian pilgrimages to Israel. Here the Jordan River appears placid and clean. Its banks are framed by stately trees, and a visitor center provides a peaceful vista as tourists imagine how the scene might have appeared in Jesus's time. Several hundred meters south of Yard-enit, the calm waters of the Jordan disappear. The river has been dammed, siphoned, redirected into underground pipes heading for Tel Aviv, and replaced by a spout of barely treated sewage that foams into a dry, rocky canal. Here, the Jordan is a limp, toxic strip of river. A warning sign conveys the hazard posed by coming into contact with this water. Still, a few hundred meters north, eager Christian pilgrims continue their ritual purifications and prayers at Yardenit, oblivious to the defiling sludge just downstream. Further downstream, close to the mouth of the Dead Sea, the river remains opaque in both complexion and status. During my visit with hydrologists in May 2008, the Jordan River measured just seven feet deep between the remaining two attested baptism sites, which are located at the same latitude on opposite banks of the river. One site is in the West Bank and the other is in Jordan. The purported baptism site in Jordan is called Al-Maghtas, or, colloquially among Christians, Bethany-Beyond-the-Jordan. The two sites are so physically proximate—just a few meters—that people standing on the opposite shore can discern one another's facial features.

The downstream site in the West Bank is known as Qasr el-Yehud. When I visited, it was accessible only under military escort. Major construction has shored up the eroding banks, and a staircase up from the water provides a pathway from the riverbank to an amphitheater. In December 2008, the Israeli government officially opened that $5 million project to the public. Across the river and in the Hashemite Kingdom of Jordan, pilgrims stretched their legs down from a dock-like platform that, hovering several feet above the water, inadvertently measures the river's continued decline in volume and its tepid flow. At this location, one cannot make out the silted, muddy bottom of the shallow river. But to leave the banks of the river, to immerse more than a toe here, to stand thigh deep—as my companion hydrologists did, in full waders and rubber gloves—requires advance permission from the governments of both Israel and Jordan. This is because the Jordan River constitutes an intently observed international border.

The three purported baptism sites in the lower Jordan River Valley vie for visitors and the designation of authenticity. In point of fact, the past is mute witness as to which bank Jesus may have stood on as John baptized him with the waters of the Jordan. Still, each nation asserts historical authenticity (Israel seems, at least implicitly, to assert it twice—once at Yardenit and once in the West Bank, at Qasr el-Yehud). The *Christian Century* aptly reports that "while the Israelis maintain that the baptism [of Jesus] took place on their side of the river, the Jordanians insist it occurred a few meters across the river on theirs."[24] The truth is that no one can definitively answer the question of exactly where Jesus was baptized, although most scholars agree that it was much more likely to be at or near one of the two baptism sites near the Dead Sea (Qasr el-Yehud or Al-Maghtas) rather than at the more touristed upstream site (Yardenit). The contestation is significant, however, for as Rachel Havrelock has noted, the competing "baptismal sites function as ciphers for national self-assertion."[25] The Jordan remains a river in which much is invested and much is at stake.

That the Jordan River of monotheistic lore could exist materially as a sluggish trickle sounds laughable to many people because of the robust riparian mythologies that have been shaped by literary and symbolic attestations from the Hebrew Bible, the New Testament, and subsequent religious, literary, and artistic expressions. To be sure, the vagaries of relying on the Bible as a historical or cartographic source have been well noted by popular writers and legions of scholars. Yet a biblically informed symbolism persists that renders the state of the Jordan River surprising, not just to bygone, pen-wielding, gentlemen-adventurers Melville and Twain, but also to visitors today. To explore the symbolism and stature of the Jordan River, one must delve not only into the sociopolitical and environmental status of the river but also its broader cultural and religious associations, a task significantly helped by recent scholarship within biblical and cultural studies.

The Jordan River in the Hebrew Bible

The Jordan River appears as a proper noun in more than eighty contexts in the Hebrew Bible. Among its noteworthy appearances, the river surfaces in Genesis. In later texts, it is often depicted as a liminal entity to be crossed. For example, Joshua establishes a memorial to the Israelites' crossing of the river with the Ark of the Covenant. King David crosses the Jordan with his triumphal retinue (Josh 3:15–17, 4:1–23; 2 Sam 19:14–19). After his famous wrestling match with an angel and his designation as "Israel," Jacob crossed the Jabbok, which is a tributary of the Jordan (Gen 32:22–28). In 2 Kings, Elijah parts the waters of the Jordan; his mantle and spirit are passed to Elisha, who also parts the river and later heals Naaman on the river's banks (2 Kings 2:6–9, 5:10–14). In the book of Judges, Gideon and his people cross the Jordan (Judg 7:24, 8:4). The famous brothers Maccabee are also said to have traversed the river (1 Macc 5:24).

Biblical scholar Jeremy Hutton has observed that a prominent motif across the texts that constitute the Hebrew Bible is the crossing of the Jordan River. He calls this literary device the "Transjordanian motif," in which a figure's crossing of the river confers a new authoritative status or effects a personal transformation. He describes how, centuries ago, "the natural environment of the Jordan River was such that easy crossings of the river could not be made at points other than at well-known fords."[26] His analysis resonates with the environmental history described by Hillel, in which the Jordan River was a formidable flow that, more often than not, resisted easy passage. So the topography of the land and the river were significant, and they were, in Hutton's words, "bound up" with a "set of emotional and cognitive relationships."[27] He adds that the productivity of the Transjordanian motif

> did not end with the closure of the corpus of Hebrew Scriptures. . . . The motif continued to be fruitful in the Jewish community, as is proved by the movement of John the Baptist to the Jordan River and of the ensuing baptism of Jesus in the Gospels. . . . Even in modern times, the Jordan holds symbolic significance and retains a certain degree of cultural and political importance.[28]

The Jordan is a material flow of water that wends its way through the land. But it also conveys robust meanings on levels that go far beyond the depleted, material riparian reality. In Hillel's aphorism, "popular lore has magnified the Jordan in the minds of millions out of all proportion to its actual size."[29]

Jewish studies scholar Rachel Havrelock, in *River Jordan: The Mythology of a Dividing Line,* concurs with the general insights of Hutton's assessment. But where Hutton emphasizes the Transjordanian motif, Havrelock traces how the river has been interpreted as an identity-generating border. She draws on the Hebrew Bible accounts of the succession of prophets, investigates the baptism of Jesus as attested in the New Testament, explores writings by later Jewish and Christian thinkers, and reflects on the contemporary sociopolitical situation. Both Hutton and Havrelock, in different ways, demonstrate how the very idea of the Jordan River can evoke associations that are loosely linked to but also radically diverge from topographical reality. What these scholars demonstrate is that even as the Jordan River is a real system, it is also a powerful, mythic landscape. But this does not necessarily mean that the "myth" is illusory or false. Quite the contrary: for Havrelock, myth is "an expression of what people hold to be most true."[30] Thinking about the mythic stature of the Jordan River enables us to decouple the material river from the imagined river. And this, in turn, helps illuminate the disjointedness of the Jordan River's sociopolitical, environmental, and religious significations. In addition to the Hebrew Bible references described earlier, the Jordan River adopts significance through New Testament depictions, as well as early Christian art and ritual practices.

The Jordan River in the New Testament, Early Christian Art, and Ritual

In the New Testament there are eleven explicit references to the Jordan River, mostly in the context of the baptism of Jesus. One cluster of New Testament texts refers to the charismatic John on the banks of the Jordan, proclaiming a baptism of repentance to people who streamed in from Jerusalem and the Judean countryside (Mt 3:5–6; Mk 1:5; Jn 1:28). The Gospels of Matthew and Mark also report the arrival of Jesus at the waters of the Jordan, his baptism by John, and the descent of the Spirit of God identifying him as "my Son, the Beloved" (Mt 3:13; Mk 1:9). The baptism of Jesus is one of the few events mentioned in all four Gospels of the New Testament. In addition, the Jordan occasionally figures as a geographic referent for events in Jesus's ministry (as in Mt 19:1; Mk 10:1; and Jn 10:40) or as a region, "beyond [or across] the Jordan," from which people came to witness Jesus's teachings (Mt 4:15, 25; Mk 10:1). Contemporary scholarship continues to explore the historical, textual, and theological significance of these references.[31]

Liturgical, artistic, and textual memories of Jesus's baptism shaped Eastern and Western forms of Christianity. Beginning "no later than the fourth century," the Jordan River "was a destination for Christian pilgrims, many of them seeking baptism, presuming its waters to be particularly blessed."[32] There is also evidence for the commemoration of Jesus's baptism, called Epiphany or Theophany, as early as the second century CE; Clement of Alexandria, for example, knew of the celebration. By contrast, the Nativity (that is, Christmas) did not gain prominence until the fourth century.[33] Origen's writings are particularly evocative with regard to the importance of the Jordan River. In historian Jean Daniélou's synopsis, for Origen, "the Jordan is a figure of the Word Himself. Thus, to plunge into the Jordan means to immerse oneself in Christ."[34] Nicholas Denysenko's historical analysis, *The Blessing of Waters and Epiphany: The Eastern Liturgical Tradition,* charts developments in these rites from the fourth through the sixteenth centuries.[35] Ancient theological and ritual commemorations of Jesus's baptism were attested by Gregory of Nyssa, Origen, and the early Christian church community at Alexandria. Daniélou explains how "the Epiphany [was] above all the feast of the Baptism of Christ, and . . . this feast focused attention especially on the water of the Jordan. . . . Furthermore, the essential rite of the day is not, as at Easter, Baptism itself, but rather the consecration of the water."[36] Still today this liturgical celebration occurs in churches worldwide, most explicitly as the Orthodox feast of Theophany in early January. The Jordan River remains a conceptual locus of the ritual. As the Orthodox prayer incants:

> Today the nature of waters is made holy, and Jordan is parted and holds back the flow of its water as it sees the Master washing himself. . . . Today the streams of Jordan are changed into healing by the presence of the Lord. Today all creation is watered by the mystical streams. . . . Today earth and sea share the joy of the world, and the world has been filled with gladness.[37]

The Jordan River is by no means an inert figure in the history of Christian liturgies and artistic representations. To the contrary, the river was vividly personified in early Christian iconographic representations of that event. Art historian Robin Jensen's work on baptismal iconography indicates that, in addition to various ways of portraying Jesus and the Holy Spirit,

most interesting is the addition of the figure that personi-
fies the Jordan River, either seated to the side emptying his
jug to provide the water or partially submerged and turning away from the momentous event. In either case he wit-
nesses the descent of the holy into his watery realm. These
details emphasize the extraordinary character of Jesus' baptism and its interpretation as a theophanic moment.[38]

Examples of this imagistic connection can be found at the Orthodox baptistery of Ravenna, where the personified Jordan River—
sporting a beard and long hair, and carrying a tall reed against
the well-defined musculature of his shoulder and bicep—is clearly
identifiable thanks to the inscription, "in bright letters, above his
head: Iordann."[39] Thus, according to Jensen, the Jordan River

> found its place in Christian iconography as nature's
> witness to Christ's baptism. . . . his [the Jordan's] pres-
> ence is an affirmation of Creation's awareness of divine
> events. . . . As candidates enter the font they symbolically
> enter that very river to receive its unique benefits.[40]

In the ancient world of the Near East, the river was "nature's
witness" to divine action. What type of witness does it offer
today in popular culture more broadly?

The river surfaces in musical lyrics and poetry, certainly in the
gospel music that was birthed from American slave experience
and found voice in spirituals. Songs such as "Deep River" or "Get
Away, Jordan" draw on the notion of crossing from one bank of
the Jordan to the other as an analogy for crossing from slavery to
liberation or suffering to eternal reward. Even beyond spiritual and
religious contexts, the symbolic stature of the Jordan River per-
vades culture generally. It has become, in Hutton's words, "a common coin of almost worldwide currency."[41] The Jordan River has
even gone prime time. For example, the television show *Crossing*

Jordan aired 117 episodes over six seasons in the United States between 2001 and 2007. This hit TV series had as its title character a forensic pathologist named Dr. Jordan Cavanaugh. Each show depicted her quest to reconstruct, mentally and often painstakingly, the events leading to a murder. In this show, Jordan literally maps the sequence of events bridging life and death: she is the one who crosses between the two realms.

Indications of the river's symbolic prominence can also be found in speeches and writings of the women of the Hashemite Kingdom of Jordan's royal family. The best-selling autobiography of Queen Noor contains a number of references to the significance of the Jordan River as a dividing line and identity marker. Similarly, the Jordan River Foundation, currently chaired by Noor's daughter-in-law, Queen Rania, "aims to promote and preserve the cultural and natural heritage of the [King Hussein Bridge] and the surrounding area" of the Jordan River, due to its importance in Jordanian culture, economy, and national identity.[42] Thus, amid the vexed history of territorial disputes, displacement, and settlement in the Middle East, the Jordan River remains a very important marker of boundary and identity. Havrelock, in particular, adroitly depicts how the Jordan River permeates identity discourse in the Middle East, especially for Israelis, Palestinians, and Jordanians living in the Jordan River basin.

Conclusion:
Bodies of Water

For centuries the Jordan River has served as a versatile, wideranging symbol and lifeblood. It is preserved in literary palimpsests and psalms as a biblical referent, personified in baptistery iconography and invoked in baptismal rites and contemporary Orthodox feast days. It is a living, slippery, polysemic flow for which simplistic or reductionist frameworks do not suffice. But it is also the case that the actual river is beset with challenges, environmentally and sociopolitically as well as ethically. Yet its mythic stature remains robust.

In the present day, a great many visitors still express outright shock at its opaque, degraded appearance, especially when visiting the lower Jordan River. In a digital age, and a century and a half after Melville's and Twain's sardonic observations, why does surprise remain such a prevalent response? It seems likely that one rather straightforward reason for the continued gap between the Jordan River's material reality and mythic stature is the preponderance of Jewish and Christian diasporas. Of course, Judaism and Christianity emerged in a particular place: the Hebrew Bible and the New Testament attest vividly to the original, ecological context of these religions. However, that physical geography is no longer the home of the majority of the world's Christians and many Jews. Moreover, many Christians and Jews have never visited the Jordan River. This means that knowledge about the Jordan River is frequently transmitted through biblical texts and cultural traditions—much more so than through experience of the physical river. As a result, religious understandings of the Jordan River, while originating in that particular ecological niche, need no longer be tightly linked to the material status of the Jordan River. What is imagined becomes as real as the actual waters of the Jordan, which is to say that the symbolism of the Jordan River is so powerful that it overrides the actual environmental status of the river.

Most Christians continually and conveniently overlook the difficult realities bearing down on the body of the Jordan River. At this disjuncture of symbolism and materiality arise a range of possible quandaries, from the epistemic to the ethical. Who or what defines the "reality" of the Jordan River? What is at stake in its narration? What is the sociopolitical, environmental, or religious value of a healthy river? By way of conclusion, three thematic immersions into the Jordan River can orient ethical reflection.

Bodies of Water

Water is life. Human beings wither and die without clean, fresh water, and the same is true of societies, nations, and ecosystems. In the valley around the Jordan River, fresh water is contested, zealously watched, and unevenly distributed. Like many other rivers worldwide, the Jordan could be a source of collaboration or a site of discord. Over the twentieth century, and now into the twenty-first, it has been both. Moreover, as Havrelock has pointed out, various narrations of the Jordan River mediate identity for Israelis and Palestinians. Both historically and in the present day, especially for Palestinians, the river "symbolizes the border between home and exile."[43] For Palestinian Christians in the region, even more is at stake in the Jordan River. In Havrelock's words, "The Jordan is doubly connected to their origin as the site of the baptism of Jesus Christ as well as a barrier crossed in the migration of their ancestors," and it plays an important contemporary religious and liturgical role.[44]

Since the waters of the Jordan saturate not only an international border but also self-understandings of bodies politic, questions and concerns about transboundary water will become ever more important: What rights and duties pertain to the issue of access to, and distribution of, fresh water? What possibilities exist for preservation of the riparian ecosystem, for the integrity of the environment and the long-term benefit of human populations? While such questions surface frequently in environmental ethics, the sociopolitical particularities of the Jordan River add a level of complexity, political history, and historical sensitivity that is, at times, daunting. It is crucial to stipulate that the distribution of water is not only a political or symbolic question; it is a deeply ethical one.

The distribution of water significantly affects the livelihoods and life possibilities of individuals, communities, and ecosystems on both sides of the river. Who is entitled to what forms of water, and for what reasons, under what conditions of justice or injustice? Toward whose benefit do these waters flow, and under whose control? Access to water is drastically uneven in Israel and the Palestinian territories. Israeli settlements are generally well equipped with water from the state water agency while Palestinian's water is rationed and controlled in massively uneven ways that imperil even subsistence agriculture and domestic uses.

Holy Waters

The Jordan is the river in which the ministry of Jesus is said to have begun. For centuries, Christian pilgrims have flocked to sites where the historical Jesus might have been baptized. Indeed, the number of tourists and pilgrims at the Jordan River's multiple purported baptism sites both reveals and helps generate the river's continued cultural significance. According to the Episcopal Diocese of Jerusalem, approximately 400,000 people visited the Bethany-Beyond-the-Jordan/Al Maghtas baptism site in one year. And on receiving permission to build a church and retreat center at the site, the Anglican Archbishop of Jerusalem noted that "we stand . . . in a region that had witnessed a great happening in Christian life and history as recorded in the Holy Scriptures."[45] Jesus's baptism is, still today, vibrant enough in religious memory to draw hundreds of thousands of pilgrims, to justify a land grant from the Kingdom of Jordan to the Anglican Diocese, to catalyze a multimillion-dollar building project at Qasr el-Yehud, and to serve as a marketing tool in a tourism economy: a newsletter about Al Maghtas recently recounted that officials have been striving "to make Epiphany and Theophany bigger events, as part of a broader effort to encourage religious tourism to the site where Jesus was baptised."[46] For Christians especially, does the river's polluted, degraded, contested state pose a theological or ethical problem?

Catholic theologian John Hart has suggested of polluted water generally that, if used in baptism, the symbolism of the ritual would be subverted by the use of the polluted water in the sacramental moment—and might well endanger the health or even life of the recipient of the sacrament. The person spiritually bathed in, blessed by, and cleansed through such water would be distracted from appreciating its spiritual significance because of its polluted material condition.[47]

But if the water of the Jordan River is polluted, pea green, and degraded, is it really so holy? One might infer that the pollution and degradation of the Jordan would—or at least, should—be of particular concern to Christians. This would seem to be especially the case given that early Christian tradition emphasized how Jesus's baptism in the Jordan *purified* the waters. Indeed, online purveyors hawk "genuine purifying Holy Water from the Jordan River."[48] One can only assume that they are speaking in spiritual terms, not hydrological ones. Still, it is strange that polluted waters persistently can be viewed as purifying.[49] As Gary Chamberlain points out, the material and symbolic status of waters may need to be drawn together more tightly if ecology is indeed a vital part of faith and religious ethics.[50]

Waters of Memory

As waters fail from a lake, and a river wastes away and dries up,
so mortals lie down and do not rise again.

—Job 14:11

Daniel Hillel's personal and professional histories with the Jordan River span most of the twentieth century and continue into the twenty-first. As a soil scientist, Hillel has written scholarly books on hydrology and agriculture; as an Israeli and self-proclaimed citizen of the region, he has witnessed the changing shape and allotments of the river. His writings also provide glimpses into what personal—not necessarily religious—memories have to do with the twentieth-century changes in the Jordan River. In the prologue to *Rivers of Eden,* Hillel recounts his experience of the Jordan River's daunting ferocity in the 1920s. During the summertime, "the ultimate in daring," he recalls,

> was to trek downstream, past the dam [just south of the Sea of Galilee], to where the river began its sinuous course. . . . In late spring, when the dam was opened, and the river was in spate and flowed full force, we would throw ourselves into the gushing current and be swept around the curve of a nearly circular meander, then grab onto the overhanging tamarisk branches. . . . The whirlpools were treacherous, . . . so the entire deed was a rather foolhardy test of youthful courage. But we did all this with sheer delight and heady abandon, completely mindless of the river's epic past and sacred significance.[51]

In 2008, I asked Dr. Hillel how the memory recounted above relates to his view of the current state of the river. He paused before describing how the demise of his old swimming site was nothing short of bewildering—even tragic. Once a fierce spot for youthful feats of bravery and adolescent invincibility, the river is now completely different. Yet, he admitted, it is that original memory—of a feisty, rollicking flow—that, despite his years of witnessing the river's decline, still shapes his sense of the Jordan.

When a river no longer exists as once it did, whether in cultural imagination or personal memory, is it something to be mourned? Resisted? Or merely accepted as a perhaps unhappy but nonetheless inevitable reality? Neither waters nor memory are uniform, singular, or static. Hillel's experiences are still partial, although uniquely broad in chronology and expertise. Yet it is worth pausing on the linkages that scholars have made between waters and memory. Cultural studies scholar Melissa K. Nelson portrays how rivers, in particular, hold a special metaphorical advantage for exploring and understanding memory. Memory is not a static phenomenon but is constantly changing depending on perspective, context, and other factors. Memories, like rivers, have sources in time and have a history . . . [for] peoples who practice an oral tradition, the land and waters hold important memories.[52]

What memories are inscribed within the waters of the Jordan River? In particular, what may individual memories of the river contribute to the conversation about its degraded environmental status? Whose memories are honored, whose stories heard?

In an era characterized by drought, uneven distribution of water resources, and environmental degradation, the memories of those individuals who have experienced a different Jordan River could form an important horizon of possibility—if only to indicate that the river can, and perhaps should, flow in a better way. Generations are growing up that will know only the limited, polluted flow of the Jordan River. Will they care? Should they? Who will tell them that it can be otherwise? The politicians will not. The environmentalists are trying. And those who remember another time, another river that used to flow, will not always be here to tell their stories. Religions have an important role to play as conduits of memory, as purveyors of ritual, and as communities of moral discernment.

CHAPTER 9

Women, Wells, and Living Water

It was about noon. A Samaritan woman came to draw water.
And Jesus said to her, "Give me a drink."

—John 4:6–7

Scholars and preachers, artists and catechists have for centuries been entranced by the story of the Samaritan woman at the well, recounted in the Gospel of John. Biblical scholar John Donahue, SJ, notes that "this narrative overflows with different meanings. . . . Bottles of ink and now printer cartridges have been expended on this interchange."[1] This is not a new insight. Centuries ago, Augustine considered this passage to be "full of mysteries, pregnant in symbols."[2] It is worth revisiting this particular well, and this particular woman, with a hydrological hermeneutic. Who was this woman? Why did Jesus speak to her? What is the significance of water in the well? And what meanings flow from their exchange?

Classical biblical interpretation has stressed the illicit, transgressive sexual status of the woman at the well. For example, in one of his homilies, Augustine frankly described how "this woman did not then have a husband, but was living with who-knows-which illicit partner, an adulterer rather than a husband."[3] The story takes place, after all, at high noon—a hot time of day to gather water; certainly no self-respecting woman would go alone to a well in the sun unmitigated by shade. In the assessment of Colin Kruse: "Normally, women came to draw water in the morning or evening, the cooler parts of the day. It is also strange that she came alone. Both these things suggest the woman felt a sense of shame and was avoiding contact with other women."[4] Indeed, continues the mainstream interpretation, the woman was a Samaritan who had worked through five husbands; she was living with yet another man but hadn't married him; surely she was no chaste moral exemplar. Rather, she must have been an adulteress, a seductress, someone on the margins of society for sexual reasons, or with—at the very least—"a dubious past."[5] Another scholar in this interpretive tradition writes, "This woman with her mind on the well . . . is also focused on a form of 'flesh'—on short-term marriages and affairs with men. She had had a whole slew of them. The situation, therefore, is not promising."[6]

In this manner generations of readers and listeners, from Augustine to the present day, have found the unnamed woman sweating through her exile, alone at the well in the middle of the day, confined to the flesh and scorned for it, when Jesus approaches her. Her sex confers a type of exile. To make matters worse, Jesus and the Samaritan woman seem to be speaking on different levels; and the Samaritan woman seems not to understand his message. When Jesus offers her living water, she asks for multiple clarifications, perhaps impudently but at the very least obtusely ("Sir, you have no bucket, and this well is deep. Where can you get this living water?"). For most of their conversation, the Samaritan woman seems to miss Jesus's point entirely. Finally, with some prodding, it begins to dawn on her: Living water! Could this be the Messiah, at Jacob's Well?

The mainstream interpretation thus yields a simplistic, value-laden conclusion. Living water, the Spirit, and Jesus are supreme and life-giving. The clairvoyance of Jesus reveals the ignorance of the woman. Living water surpasses well water. Raymond Brown provides an apt synopsis of this view: "Jesus' gifts are 'real' gifts, that is, heavenly gifts: the real water of life, as contrasted with ordinary water."[7] The syllogism provides a clean, clear, simple hierarchy of value: Jesus is to the Samaritan woman as purity is to adultery and as spiritual, living water is to ordinary well water. The problem is that this pervasive, mainstream interpretation, while tempting, is insufficient. There is more to be encountered here.

Current Biblical Hermeneutics and the Woman at the Well

Methods of biblical interpretation in the twentieth century and into the twenty-first expanded to include growing historical and archaeological knowledge of the ancient world as well as awareness of how our own cultural contexts influence our readings of these long-standing texts. As a result, nuanced forms of biblical interpretation emerged that prompted scholars around the world to articulate how readers encounter and make meaning out of texts. This allowed substantial shifts in focus and understanding. The previous approach assumed unimpeachable objectivity: texts were presumed to contain and convey clear, universally accessible truths. Sandra M. Schneiders describes how "From at least the eighteenth to the mid-twentieth century the prevailing understanding of history and of texts and their meaning was almost exclusively object-centered. The reader of the text seldom came into view, and if she or he did, the exegesis was suspect."[8] However, in the latter half of the twentieth century, scholars began to attend to the agency of the reader—due to new emphasis on subjectivity—in the production of a text's meaning. Biblical scholars began to ask: "Who is the competent reader and what kind of responsibility does the reader have to the text on the one hand and to the community on the other? And who is served by various interpretations?"[9] The ideal of one singularly authoritative, true meaning of the text gave way to questions about how text, reader, and context interact to produce meaning. During this time historical-critical methodologies and feminist theory led to fresh interpretations of biblical stories. Scholars such as Phyllis Trible and Elisabeth Schüssler-Fiorenza began to interrogate traditional, normative interpretations of texts from the Hebrew Bible and New Testament. In different ways, and with regard to different texts, these scholars sought to problematize traditional interpretations of well-known biblical texts, as well as to present women as historical agents in the formation of the early church despite the frequent invisibility of women in biblical narrative.[10]

The story of the woman at the well has been a particularly fertile site for theological reinterpretation. Theologian Peter Phan has noted that "the hermeneutical principle that texts are inherently polyvalent, and hence admit of many readings, is supremely so of this text, precisely because it can be shown to contain several layers of meaning."[11] As described above, mainstream interpretations of this story have emphasized the sexual transgressions of the woman at the well and thus the hierarchical dualisms of matter/spirit, well water/living water, Samaritan woman/Jesus. By contrast, recent reinterpretations of John 4 have emphasized the woman's prophetic role in proclaiming Jesus as the Messiah and thereby have challenged the traditional interpretation.

Consider whether the woman is significant not because she is slow to catch on but because *she eventually understands and proclaims the good news.* After all, following their exchange at the well, the woman runs into town and announces Jesus as the Messiah to any who will listen. Read in this way, it is a foreign woman (the outsider of outsiders) who is chosen to receive a revelation and empowered to spread the good news. That's a rather important role. Phan sees no lack of confidence in a woman who is boldly "self-confident enough to challenge and even reprimand Jesus for speaking to her."[12] And biblical scholar Jerome Neyrey finds that the Samaritan woman's conversation develops from a stance of questioning (Jn 4:7–15) to one of clarity: "She speaks declarative sentences and understands Jesus all too clearly. Thus, the story narrates her transformation from a Samaritan outsider who knows little and misunderstands much to that of a privileged insider who comes to know important secrets and revelations."[13] Next, like Martha in the Gospel of Luke, the woman runs into town and announces what she has experienced. Read in this way, it is a foreign woman who receives a revelation, realizes its significance, and spreads the good news.

Looking at this story in the context of the whole Gospel of John, too, the Samaritan woman with her eventual insight and proclamation stands in contrast to the disciples, who tend to be somewhat dense in their understanding of Jesus's significance. In a related way, she is a foil to Nicodemus, who in John 3 had had the opportunity to see and proclaim the Messiah but who failed to realize the import of the situation. Moreover, biblical scholars have pointed out how the symbolism of high noon in the Gospel of John should not necessarily be taken literally; instead, it is a reference to the fullness of light, that is, knowledge and truth. Neyrey, for example, observes that "we know enough not to take references to place and time literally but to read them in terms of John's symbolic world."[14] So perhaps the woman is portrayed as visiting the well at high noon because she is one who sees and understands, and then proclaims. The Samaritan woman listens, questions, realizes Jesus's significance, and shares the good news. This interpretation of John 4 is increasingly common. Schneiders has argued that the woman of John 4 actually holds a special place in the dynamics of divine revelation:

> The role of the Samaritan woman in the coming to faith of the townspeople is precisely that assigned to his disciples by Jesus himself on the night before he died. She bore witness to Jesus as the Messiah of Samaritan expectation, the "one who had told me everything" as the prophet-like Moses was to do, and through her word the hearers came to believe in him.[15]

In this interpretive trajectory, biblical commentators have even explored how the woman at the well is comparable to Moses: "someone who in the course of an ordinary day's work is made powerfully aware of the way in which slavery is challenged and broken by the divine; someone who sets out to bring that message to the people."[16]

Deconstructing and Historicizing Water

The woman at the well is polyvalent. She is much more complex than traditional, mainstream interpretations have allowed. It is therefore also worth considering that perhaps she is not obtuse: perhaps she actually knows what she's talking about when she questions Jesus. What if instead of being ignorant, she is confident and assertive and careful when she asks Jesus to clarify what he means by living water? What if she, through her own knowledge and experience as a water-gatherer, knows something that most people living in modern, industrialized Western conditions of white privilege have forgotten?

Recall, in particular, how the mainstream interpretation of the woman at the well yielded dualisms—between living water and well water, Jesus and the Samaritan woman, purity and impurity, spirit and flesh. Interpreters throughout Christian history have been tempted to value the former (purity, spirit, living water, Jesus) and devalue the latter (impurity, flesh, well water, woman). Biblical scholar Stephen D. Moore's approach is to undermine the hierarchical dualism upon which traditional interpretations of the story depend.[17] He finds in John's waters a mutual necessity. In his account, the story of the Samaritan woman at the well must be read vis-à-vis the image of Jesus thirsting on the cross. In Moore's words:

> The hierarchical opposition established at the well is inverted at the cross, the ostensibly superior, pleromatic term (living water, Spirit) being shown to depend for its

effective existence on the inferior, insufficient term (literal well-water), contrary to everything that the Gospel has led us to expect.[18]

Why is this so? Moore says that because of Jesus's thirst, "the reader arrives at the cross, then, only to be returned, in effect, to the well, carried by the current of a stream that flows equally between literality and figurality."[19] Well water and living water, matter and spirit, are all part of the same flow. Water for living and living waters depend on one another, inextricably. In this way, Moore's interpretation deconstructs old, fusty assumptions about John 4 and illuminates the polyvalent and integral relationship between spirit and matter, living water and well water, Jesus and the woman at the well.

Even so, more can be said than Moore expresses. What would it mean for biblical interpretation to historicize and contextualize understandings of fresh water? Interestingly, it is the esteemed church father Augustine of Hippo, so long associated with the above-mentioned mainstream view, who can help with this task, courtesy of his homilies. First, let us consider our own partial—that is, both incomplete and biased—knowledge. Twenty-first-century readers come to the text of John 4 with a set of assumptions and habits (implicit or explicit) surrounding fresh water. Especially for those of us at the top of the global economic pyramid—notably white, privileged Euro-Americans—water is mostly invisible, because those people who live in conditions of economic privilege in societies with advanced plumbing and sanitation infrastructure tend to be distanced from the materiality and purity of the sources of our water. The fact that water contaminations happen most frequently in underprivileged, predominantly Native American, African American, or immigrant communities in the United States points to the racialization of infrastructure systems and patterns of privilege. Many other US citizens—especially those who have benefited most from economic globalization and white privilege—experience water as unremarkable, because it flows cleanly and reliably from faucets or showers at any hour of any day. This invisibility of water is a mark of privilege, and it is linked to legacies of colonialism, racism, and economic oppression.

Where fresh water infrastructure provides clean, fresh, piped water to households—usually in wealthy neighborhoods and especially in industrialized countries—residents have a woefully incomplete picture of what fresh water provision means for most of the world's inhabitants, the majority of whom do not have access to running water or sanitation. In this way to be cognitively and physically distanced from water sources is both the result of privilege and a source of profound ignorance. This insight is true throughout historical time—for example, the economy and experience of water in Augustine's time was far more direct and explicit for most households. But it is true around the world in the current moment as well—consider, for example, the contamination and toxic legacies wrought by lead in the pipes in Flint, Michigan. Disenfranchised populations today experience water's vagaries in ways that privileged populations can blithely overlook. To ignore this fact is to preclude understanding of the Samaritan woman, her daily toil, and the quality of the water in that well.

Even though he wrote as a homilist and bishop, and not as a natural historian or water scholar, Augustine's writings can prod today's privileged readers to view fresh water differently. His homily on John 4 points toward the value of different sources of fresh water in the ancient world. But it is important to emphasize that this distinction is not the hierarchical dualism assumed by traditional interpretations of the story of the Samaritan woman at the well. For not all waters are equally potable: in antiquity, natural springs were the most salutary and desirable water source. Such waters were designated by the category of "flowing water." This well-known, frequently invoked category in the ancient world referred to water in motion, arising from springs or active sources. In the words of Augustine, it is water "which is drawn as it flows."[20]

Standing water, by contrast, refers to water that is no longer flowing, water that has been distanced from its source and is being held in some way—a pond, a dam, a cistern—and is therefore not in motion. In terms of human health, flowing water is salubrious. Standing water then, as now, is more likely to be the bearer of disease. Standing water may be acceptable, but flowing water is preferable. The catch—then as now—is that flowing water is harder to come by than standing water. Especially in the arid Near East, as in ancient Palestine and Judea, it could be very hard to come by. This was the hydrography that Augustine described several centuries after the writing of the Gospel of John, when he explained to his flock how the Samaritan woman's responses to Jesus in John 4 made perfect sense.

Augustine declares that the Samaritan woman evidently "understood *living water* . . . as the water that was in that spring"—that is, flowing water, the form of fresh water that supports life, the potable and salubrious water that is contrasted with standing well water. Thus, he continues, the Samaritan woman reasonably assumes that "living water" is "flowing water." In Augustine's own words:

> What is called living water in ordinary speech is water as it comes from a spring. I mean, water that is collected from the rain in ponds or cisterns is not called living water. Even if it has flowed from a spring and has been stored in some place, and the source from which it flowed has been cut off and its movement stopped, such that it has been separated from the spring, it is not called living water. That water is called living which is drawn as it flows. Such was the water in [the] spring. So why was Jesus promising what he was asking for?[21]

Notice here that Augustine portrays the woman's confusion as entirely reasonable. Jesus's words play directly and evocatively on the practical wisdom of water-gatherers.

The point is that this story looks different when contemporary readers examine their limited knowledge about *how water
was understood and classified in the ancient world*. What Augustine
saw clearly is largely invisible to interpreters who sit atop massive
plumbing and sanitation infrastructures. Where privileged populations are distanced from our sources of water, Augustine reminds
his audience that the woman had practical knowledge about her
sources of water. In light of the distinction between standing water
and flowing water, the Samaritan woman's objections are reasonable, even wise, based on her accumulated practical wisdom. Insofar as living, flowing water was distinct from standing water, it
must have seemed to the Samaritan woman that Jesus was the one
making the materially obvious category error. How different the
tale looks when told from this perspective.

That Jesus engages in a verbal play on the Samaritan woman's
practical wisdom is not to claim that he is acting like a dissem-
bling lout. Rather, the point is that traditional interpretations that
present the woman at the well as benighted or unreasonably con-
fused are missing a crucial point—indeed, they are missing a historical and material reality without which contemporary understandings of this story remain impoverished. They are missing
profound differences in the meaning of water's sources. Not only
that, they reveal dynamics of domination insofar as it has simply
been assumed that Jesus was right—and that the woman must be
wrong, despite her practical knowledge of the terrain and water
sources. In this way, attention to historical, hydrological context
teaches us an important distinction that alters our perceptions of
this story. This form of attention unveils insights that would have
been evident to any inhabitant of the ancient world: Standing
water is not flowing water. The people who regularly experience responsibility for obtaining clean, fresh water understand its
vitality in ways largely inaccessible to, and unacknowledged by,
people in positions of hydrosocial privilege.

There is more to be said here, for the conditions that Augustine describes also apply in some ways and some places in the

present day. To be sure, practical wisdom about water sources is mostly a historical artifact for people who live in developed, industrialized nations at the uppermost level of contemporary economic globalization. But we are few in number, relative to the global population. And it remains the case that for many—indeed, most—people, water is neither invisible nor neutral. The difference between clean water and dirty water is a living, material reality for many people worldwide. At least 1.2 billion people lack sufficient access to clean fresh water and sanitation. For them, the crucial distinction between standing and flowing water is as immediate as it was for the Samaritan woman, and for Augustine. Delving back into the story, what might now be noticeable about the woman at the well that was previously obscured?

"Her Daily Toil":
Women and Water Worldwide

The biggest distinction in today's world might very well be between those people who know what toil it is to gather clean water—whose bodies and families are shaped by carrying literal and toxic loads—and those of us in the hydro-privileged world, who have limited ideas about and no direct experience with this weighty aspect of water. We do not bear its burdens. As the saying goes, water is a very good servant but a cruel master. It is not obvious, to those living atop the pyramid of economic privilege, how water shapes the contours of one's life in the most quotidian and bodily of ways. Surely this is one lesson from the devastating failures revealed in the late coverage of the Flint water crisis. Water is the baseline substance for cooking, cleaning, bathing, agriculture, and almost any form of economic activity. If it is hard to get, it still must be procured, on foot or by wagon, regardless of cost, day after day, week after week, year after year. If it is contaminated, it still must be used if there is no other clean water source. And it is primarily women and children who are responsible for daily procurement of clean water, and thus bear its burdens when it is scarce or polluted. Even Jesus—portrayed throughout the New Testament as one who overturns social norms—was in some ways a product of his time: walking up to the well, Jesus commands the Samaritan woman: *give me a drink.*

Returning to the scene in John 4, let us presume that, at midday, the woman at the well was weary. Desiring rest, desiring shade, the woman finds herself again at the well and there, says Augustine,

> she heaved a great sigh, longing to be done with the need, longing to be done with the toil. Time and again she was constrained to come to that well, and to carry the load which met her needs, to come back again when what she had drawn was finished. This was her daily toil, because the water assuaged that need, but did not extinguish it.[22]

Water was for the Samaritan woman what it is for women throughout the world today: life-defining work. *Her daily toil.* Women across time and space find themselves walking in the heat of midday, longing for shade, bearing several kinds of burdens as a result of fresh water scarcity. What are these burdens, specifically?

First, water is literally heavy and exacting to carry: Human energy is what transports water in much of the world, where pumps and plumbing infrastructure are nonfunctioning, nonexistent, or insufficient. Water weighs more than eight pounds a gallon, but much more than one gallon must be obtained in order to satisfy the daily needs of even one person, much less a family or community or village. Since water is bulky and heavy, it shapes the musculature and skeletal structure of the women and girls who walk miles each day to procure it. And it requires caloric energy as well as mental effort to undertake this work.

Second, fresh water scarcity is a burden because it limits economic and educational opportunities for girls and women. Many girls in the developing world are deprived of education because their energies must be devoted to procuring water for domestic use. But the education of girls is a vital part of social stability and economic development: for several decades, research has demonstrated that gender equity in education is a factor in development.[23] In 2012, UNESCO's *World Atlas of Gender Equity in Education* stipulated that "gender equality is essential for protecting universal human rights and fundamental freedoms. It is also a powerful development accelerator."[24] In this way the scarcity of water shapes the future potential not only of girls and women but also of entire societies.

Third, there is the burden of embodied vulnerability linked to both age and sex. Worldwide, women do not find themselves at wells midday because they have had five husbands. Nor do they find themselves pumping bathtubs full of bottled water instead of lead-contaminated tap water as a result of their sexuality. They find themselves at wells midday, or seeking purified water from various kinds of dispensers, because they have been born female in societies that in the absence of infrastructure presume women's domestic water-gathering efforts. This is a systemic, social disenfranchisement in which the work of one sex is linked to water, such that women and girls are disadvantaged by this role that, too often, is foisted upon them. Because water supply and sufficient sanitation systems are often linked conditions, it is also the case that women and girls are disproportionately disadvantaged by the absence of sanitation facilities. As sociologist Isha Ray comments, "Male sanitation needs can be met in the course of meeting female sanitation needs, but the reverse is not true; therefore, only sanitation programs that are explicitly designed for female needs can be *adequate* 'for all,'" in the language of the United Nations' Sustainable Development Goals.[25] Ray adds that "it is clean, secure, and affordable access to latrines *outside* the home that can enable girls' education, women's mobility, and women's livelihoods," and that menstruation amplifies these needs.

Now consider polluted water supply. When water is contaminated (by insufficient sanitation infrastructure, that leads to open defecation, for example; or by carrying toxic chemical compounds), it is children, the ill, and the elderly whose bodies are most vulnerable to disease and long-term effects. Again, in Flint, the biggest long-term effects are borne by children whose cognitive development is permanently stultified because of environmentally racist structures and decisions. The public health crisis that has narrowed their future trajectories is hardly a matter of free, individual choice, and it is linked to structures of racism and exclusion that rendered the Flint population particularly vulnerable. Some outcomes are not, in fact, a matter of choice or free will. Unsurprisingly, it is primarily women in these communities who are responsible for obtaining clean water—through donations of bottled water or other means, but not the pipes—and for making sure that their affected offspring are well cared for now and into the future. None of these burdens were chosen.

Did the woman in John 4 choose to go to the well to gather water? We can only conjecture. A good wager would be: yes and no. Yes, the Samaritan woman probably chose to go to a certain well at a certain time, and not to some other water source at some other time. But it is highly unlikely that she chose—in that sense of ultimate freedom and vocation—to be a water-gatherer. It was simply her lot. This is water's burden as a factor of gender: It is an unrelenting necessity, borne disproportionately by women. What, then, do we make of the linkage between sexual sin and the Samaritan woman's slog to the well at midday? Were her choices of well and time of day limited by social opprobrium of her lascivious behavior? What we do know is that if the woman at the well was a seductress, then she is an exception and not the norm. In the present day at least, the siren song of the seductress at the well is a fallacy. To the contrary: women water-gatherers are frequently the victims of rape and assault.[26] They are attacked while walking great distances to gather water, wash clothing, or bathe. There is indeed a link between sexual sin and water gathering, but it is a link based on the vulnerability of women while going about their "daily toil," and the sin rests with the predations of strong, powerful men. It is inaccurate and unhelpful to blame the victim for her vulnerability. To ignore or disavow the structural factors that disempower women who gather water is to evade some of the most potent meanings that can surface from this text.

This reading of the Samaritan woman at the well suggests several conclusions. It is time to dispense with the salacious, dualistic reading of John 4 that has for so long characterized biblical interpretation about this woman and the well. As it turns out, she likely knew quite a bit about water sources; it is generally white, privileged, industrialized demographics that are experientially ignorant of the operative distinction between flowing (safe, healthy) and standing (unsafe, contaminated) water. Moreover, gathering water is still a gender-bound task that precludes many possibilities, including education. It correlates to socioeconomic status. It comes with the risk of physical and sexual assault. It remains, in Augustine's words, a constraint, a daily toil. Then as now, hydrology is destiny—especially for women and others living in poverty.

Conclusion: Thirst

Imagine an arid land. Dust simmers beneath short-shorn bushes. Hot winds blow under the unrelenting afternoon sun. Atop a hill, at a little distance, the Jordan River is an unruly ribbon on the horizon. A few disciples and women stand around, speaking in hushed tones, or not at all.

On the cross is Jesus.

As the life seeps out of him, Jesus whispers his last words: *I thirst.*

The women, unsurprised, affirm: *We know.*

One by one the women turn away and go to gather water.

Another time, another place: A woman is cast into the desert with her infant son, exiled into the wilderness with only some bread and a flask of water. Stumbling through hot sand and sharp brush, without any specific destination and without aid, she is tired and thirsty and alone, beyond the physical protection afforded by society. The dynamics of social and political power dictate that she cannot return to the place from which she came. But the reality of the wilderness is hardly compensation; it is, in many ways, a death sentence. After several days of exposure to searing sun, she is losing focus. Her tongue expands in her mouth, and she stumbles as the relentlessly incremental processes of sustained dehydration slowly choke her. She has no options. And thus, the book of Genesis tells us, *When the water was gone, she cast the child under one of the bushes*; and as she sat opposite him, *she lifted up her voice and wept.*

Perhaps she closed her eyes from despair or delirium, or the searing sun and burning sand. But then, miraculously, God provides the one thing minimally necessary for survival: water. As the book of Genesis reports, after Hagar lays the infant Ishmael under some sparse bramble, she can do nothing more than sit a small distance away, unable to bear the sight of her dying son. But *God opened her eyes and she saw a well of water. She went, and filled the skin with water, and gave the boy a drink.* Hagar and Ishmael live, and the story of Ishmael's lineage is by no means lost to history.[27]

There are many types of wilderness, literal and figurative; there are many types of thirst, material and spiritual. But fresh water is the only substance that sustains life in conditions of scarcity; its presence or absence shapes human lives. Thus the story of exile and thirst ends differently for many men, women, and children who take to the wilderness by choice or by force in the present day. Hagar the post-parturition slave was cast into the wilderness by jealous, threatened owners; many more women, men, and children are cast into deserts by economic and social need.

One such present-day desert lies within the borders of the United States. Here, in the Sonoran wilderness of southern California and Arizona, on the reservation of the Tohono O'odham tribe, are the remains of the 150–250 people a year who die of dehydration while trying to reach safety, their families, or economic opportunity. These migrants are not US citizens. To many Americans, they are a threat and a scourge on the economy. To the government, they lack legal status. But they are also known, on both sides of the border, as mother, father, sister, friend. And so to relief workers—many of whom are Christian, many of whom have no religious creed—they are people who need help. In theological terms, they are neighbors who deserve to be fed, clothed, and given water for the journey—*for as you did to these the least of them,* says Jesus in the Gospel of Matthew, *so you did it to me.* Water, in particular, has become a battleground in the Sonora. Humanitarian relief workers store caches of water in gallon-sized jugs in the Sonora in the hopes that immigrants will stumble upon them, their thirst momentarily relieved. How many of these voyagers will have the luck of Hagar, who *opened her eyes and saw a well of water,* and lived?

It is impossible to say who will survive and who will not. What is certain is that the desert of southern Arizona is one place where the realities of human migration, social and political power, and bodily thirst form a fierce knot of iniquity. Here, as elsewhere, women bear a particular burden. Author Ananda Rose straight-forwardly explains the reality of female migrants: "Many suffer atrocious abuse at the hands of their smugglers: they are robbed, sexually assaulted or simply abandoned in the desert."[28] And she quotes a matter-of-fact exhortation by an aid worker in Arizona: "The question is not *if* a female migrant will be raped, . . . but when and how often."[29] The devastating reality is that exile, thirst, and vulnerability are more than historical memories: they are constant realities for many women worldwide.

The burden of water is gendered. The opprobrium of exile, the weight of water, and the force of assault is foisted upon women and girls. In the present-day Sonora, as in the time of the Samaritan woman, it is a masculinist fallacy to imagine the exiled, thirsty woman as the seductress. So too with Hagar, who was pregnant by forced sex with her master and exiled into the wilderness. *She lifted up her eyes and wept.*

Women throughout history and around the world bear water's burdens. Then, as now, they are exiled and vulnerable quite plainly because there is no other choice. It is a matter of survival and therefore her lot, her daily toil; and like the task of gathering water, some stories never end, even when consistently overlooked.

Lessons in Liquidity

My intention in this book has been to make visible some of the more pressing aspects of global fresh water scarcities while presenting theological and ethical resources that, with critical and constructive engagement, can help shape the growing global discourse on fresh water and ethics. I summarize key insights here.

Fresh water is universal, but it is not uniform. It is a transboundary resource that evades containment by virtue of the hydrological cycle and its persistent pursuit of the path of least resistance. Dynamic and shape-shifting on all levels, from the molecular to the glacial, water requires us to think locally and globally at the same time. In the twenty-first century, it will become an increasingly scarce and contested resource, as groundwater is depleted and climate change amplifies regional patterns of aridity or deluge.

How might global, pluralistic humanity sustain the integrity of our rapidly diminishing global fresh water resources in ways that also promote justice? The question is central since fresh water is both sui generis and a sine qua non condition for the survival and flourishing of human beings and ecosystems. Among those who lack sufficient clean water—those whose lives, contexts, and possibilities are circumscribed by its natural scarcity, pollution, cost, or inequitable distribution—water is a fundamental event. At worst it can be, in Edward Schillebeeckx's phrase, a "negative contrast experience" of suffering. In the twenty-first century, access to clean water tends to correspond to geographic position, military might, economic prowess, hydraulic expertise, and socially mediated forms of privilege. Put simply, there remains truth in the adage that *clean water flows toward power*. Fresh water is not merely a matter of hydrology; hydrosocial cycles are also determinative of social dynamics and questions of justice in access to fresh water. People living in poverty and other forms of structurally embedded vulnerability are most affected by fresh water's absence, especially women and children, as well as groups structurally and historically disenfranchised due to race, class, and legacies of settler colonialism in the United States and abroad.

What is to be done, given the scale and pervasiveness of the problem? There is no one-size-fits-all solution. The facts demonstrate that less than 10 percent of global fresh water is used for domestic purposes, which means that individual water-saving efforts—while an important part of water conservation—will not solve global fresh water crises. Fresh water is a collective challenge, and an urgent need is to articulate and implement ethically informed long-term policies that treat water not just as a commodity or even a right, but also as a public good or public trust, in ways that resonate with Catholic social teaching's notions of the common good. Scholars, lawyers, and policy makers need to parse and advocate better arrangements of the political economy of fresh water, including property regimes. Economists and policy makers need to develop robust notions of fresh water as a public good and ways to incorporate the externalities that beset contemporary late-capitalist uses of fresh water as an invisible form of natural capital. Governments and corporations need to take those specifications seriously in regulation and business practices. Socially oriented or not, businesses should include fresh water responsibility riders as a limiting condition of their investment portfolios and practices. Agricultural and industrial corporations, which represent many consumptive uses of fresh water, must be held accountable for overextraction of ground and surface water, as well as the pollution of water sources.

Everyone—individuals, governments, and the contrived, legal "persons" called corporations—bears responsibility for the preservation and wise use of this unique and essential resource, and this in turn requires action at collective, regional, and transnational levels. Because hydrology, climate, geography, population, culture, and political economy differ profoundly around the world, ethical discernment must be central to a process that relies on careful, steady awareness of context, lessons learned from history, and up-to-date social analysis and scientific data. There is no one-size-fits-all solution, but there are better and worse ways of proceeding. Each chapter in this volume has attempted to demonstrate how ethical analyses can proceed in light of several key convictions:

- Fresh water's status as sui generis and sine qua non for life must be recognized and considered as a first principle of ethical reasoning.
- The principles of water justice and water sustainability for current and future generations should shape the management and provision of fresh water. Here the preferential option for the poor obtains in a special way, and women and children deserve focused attention, since they bear multiple burdens associated with fresh water.
- Access to fresh water is a fundamental human right, yet other moral concepts are needed too, including the language of nonnegotiable duties to future generations and the continued development of the insight that fresh water is a public good.
- The life-sustaining qualities of fresh water forestall a reductive equivalence between fresh water's value and price. Economic valuation must be subordinated to equity in distribution for individuals, future generations, and ecosystem services (on which the sustainability of human

societies fundamentally depends). Privatization of water supply may be considered, but only insofar as equity of access (for current and future generations) is always sought and ensured before corporate profit. Public regulation of the water sector is necessary to ensure that negative externalities are absorbed by the corporation (and shareholders), not by downstream stakeholders.

- Technology has an important role to play in mitigating the effects of fresh water scarcity, but hydraulic technologies are not a panacea, as they are always deployed within a broader framework, which must be shaped by the preceding principles.

- Because of the vital significance of groundwater, there must be full disclosure of any toxic compounds involved in technologies that may have negative downstream consequences, whether in agriculture or industry (especially but not exclusively in fossil fuel extraction).

- With regard to agriculture: in most places worldwide, consumptive water uses are unsustainable. At a bare minimum, irrigation systems must be made maximally efficient (for example, by moving away from center-pivot irrigation to drip irrigation). Governmental subsidies to industrial agriculture should also be examined and revised if they encourage profligate water extraction, excessive application of toxic chemicals, and the planting of soil-exhausting monocultures.

Amid the diversity of fresh water quandaries that characterize human experience, human beings remain watery, embodied creatures; like most other living things, we depend on water for survival. These are basic insights yet not simplistic: they are fundamental. "Water is a verb," wrote Craig Childs in *Orion Magazine*.[1] Water as a verb—or an entity that shape-shifts between noun and verb—is dynamic and, far from inert; it is a source of life and site of economic and social control, an occasion for activism, and an enduring if shape-shifting substance that refracts multiple notions of morality and the sacred. Although water is everywhere vital, it is never "just water." Universal yet not uniform; foundational yet not monolithic; fresh waters are apt substances for capturing the slipperiness of twenty-first-century ontology, anthropology, and ethics—which cannot proceed except in light of plurality and contextuality, and ongoing revisability. The journey is ever unfinished.

> We walk, and in the desert
> we grow wiser
> and don't say: "Because the wilderness is perfection"
>
> But our wisdom needs a song
> with a lively tempo
> so that hope doesn't flag
>
> How far is far?
> How many ways to get there?
>
> —Mahmoud Darwish,
> "How Far Is Far?" in *A River Dies of Thirst*[2]

Notes

Chapter 1
Theology and Ethics for the New Millennium

[1] Vatican Council II, *Gaudium et Spes* (1965), no. 4.

[2] James F. Keenan, SJ, *A History of Catholic Moral Theology in the Twentieth Century: From Confessing Sins to Liberating Consciences* (London: Continuum, 2010), 6.

[3] Karl Rahner, *The Love of Jesus and the Love of Neighbor* (New York: Crossroad, 1983), 73. It can be argued that Rahner's facility in making this claim is strongly informed by the critical work of his most famous student, J. B. Metz.

[4] Ibid.

[5] Ibid., 70–71.

[6] Keenan, *A History of Catholic Moral Theology*, 219.

[7] Jon Sobrino, "Systematic Christology," in *Mysterium Liberationis: Fundamental Concepts in Liberation Theology*, ed. Ignacio Ellacuría and Jon Sobrino (Maryknoll, NY: Orbis Books, 1993), 459.

[8] Ignacio Ellacuría, "Salvation History and Salvation in History," in *Freedom Made Flesh* (Maryknoll, NY: Orbis Books, 1976), 18. See also Michael E. Lee, ed., *Ignacio Ellacuría: Essays on History, Liberation, and Salvation* (Maryknoll, NY: Orbis Books, 2013).

[9] Ellacuría, "Salvation History," 15.

[10] Among many other sources, see, for example, Gustavo Gutiérrez, "Option for the Poor," in *Mysterium Liberationis*, 248.

[11] Sobrino, "Systematic Christology," 453.

[12] Henri Nouwen, foreword to Gustavo Gutiérrez, *We Drink from Our Own Wells: The Spiritual Journey of a People* (Maryknoll, NY: Orbis Books, 1984), xvii.

[13] Ellacuría, "Salvation History," 12.

[14] For a comparative overview see Curt Cadorette, "Liberation Theology: Context and Method," in *Liberation Theology: An Introductory Reader,* ed. Curt Cadorette, Marie Giblin, Marilyn J. Legge, and Mary Hembrow Snyder (Maryknoll, NY: Orbis Books, 1992), 1–10. See also Maureen O'Connell, *Compassion: Loving Our Neighbor in an Age of Globalization* (Maryknoll, NY: Orbis Books, 2009).

[15] Elizabeth A. Johnson, *Quest for the Living God: Mapping Frontiers in the Theology of God* (New York: Continuum, 2007), 86.

[16] Benedict XVI, "Blessed Are the Peacemakers," Message for the World Day of Peace (January 1, 2013).

[17] Johnson, *Quest,* 87.

[18] O'Connell, *Compassion,* 198.

[19] Marjorie Keenan, *From Stockholm to Jerusalem: An Historical Overview of the Concern of the Holy See for the Environment, 1972–2002* (Vatican City: Vatican, 2002). The majority of this section is taken from Christiana Zenner Peppard, "Commentary on *Laudato Si',*" in *Modern Catholic Social Teaching,* rev. ed., ed. Kenneth J. Himes, OP (Washington, DC: Georgetown University Press, 2017).

[20] Sean McDonagh, *The Greening of the Church* (Maryknoll, NY: Orbis Books, 1990), 175–76. Noting that "at last the Church is beginning to wake up to what is at stake," McDonagh also identified the problematic endurance of "domination theology" and observed that a universalizing "anthropocentric bias" permeates Vatican II documents.

[21] John Paul II, *Message for World Day of Peace,* Vatican website (www. vatican.va), January 1, 1990, 6.

[22] Ibid., 7.

[23] Ibid., 9.

[24] John Paul II and Ecumenical Patriarch Bartholomew I, "Common Declaration on Environmental Ethics," Vatican website, June 10, 2002.

[25] Ibid.

[26] Pontifical Council for Justice and Peace, *Compendium of the Social Doctrine of the Church,* Vatican website, May 26, 2005, chap. 10.

[27] For analysis of Benedict XVI's contributions to environmental notions, see the essays in *Environmental Justice and Climate Change: Assessing Pope Benedict XVI's Vision for the Church in the US,* ed. Tobias Winright and Jame Schaefer (Lanham, MD: Lexington, 2013).

[28] See the commentary on *Caritas in Veritate* by Meghan J. Clark in *Modern Catholic Social Teaching: Commentaries and Interpretations,* rev. ed., ed. Kenneth J. Himes (Washington, DC: Georgetown University Press, 2018).

[29] Pope Francis, "Address of the Holy Father Pope Francis," Vatican website, March 16, 2013.

[30] Pope Francis, *Laudato Si'*, 96.

[31] For detailed analysis of the content, context, and implications of the encyclical *Laudato Si'*, see Peppard, "Commentary on *Laudato Si'*."

[32] Sean McDonagh, *Catholic Teaching and the Environment*, Part I in *On Care for Our Common Home: Laudato Si', The Encyclical of Pope Francis on the Environment* (Maryknoll, NY: Orbis Books, 2016), xvi.

[33] Francis, *Laudato Si'*, 3.

[34] See, for example, the essays in *The Challenge of Global Steward-ship: Roman Catholic Responses*, ed. Maura Ryan and Todd Whitmore (Notre Dame, IN: University of Notre Dame Press, 1997); Elizabeth Johnson, *Ask the Beasts: Darwin and the God of Love* (New York: Bloomsbury Academic, 2014); Ilia Delio and Keith Douglass Warner, *Care for Creation: A Franciscan Spirituality of the Earth* (Cincinnati, Ohio: St. Anthony Messenger, 2006); Denis Edwards, *Ecology at the Heart of Faith* (Maryknoll, NY: Orbis Books, 2006); Leonardo Boff, *Cry of the Earth, Cry of the Poor* (Maryknoll, NY: Orbis Books, 1997); and McDonagh, *Greening of the Church*. For an overview of these trends, see Christiana Zenner Peppard, "An Ethic of Aridity: Theology, Ecology, and Planetary Change," *Proceedings of the Catholic Theological Society of America* 72 (2017), 1–13.

[35] "The Global Catholic Population," Pew Research Center, February 13, 2013, www.pewforum.org.

[36] "Religion in Latin America: Widespread Change in a Historically Catholic Region," Pew Research Center, November 13, 2014, www.pewforum.org.

[37] Michael Lipka, "Key Findings about American Catholics," Pew Research Center, September 2, 2015, www.pewresearch.org.

[38] Traci C. West, *Disruptive Christian Ethics: When Racism and Women's Lives Matter* (Louisville, KY: Westminster John Knox, 2006), 37.

[39] Edward Schillebeeckx, "How Experience Gains Authority," in *The Schillebeeckx Reader*, ed. Robert J. Schreiter (London: T&T Clark, 2001), 42.

[40] Edward Schillebeeckx, foreword to *Constructing Local Theologies*, by Robert J. Schreiter (Maryknoll, NY: Orbis Books, 1985), xi.

[41] In the parlance of ethical theory, the distinction Schillebeeckx makes is between "permanent human impulses and orientations, values, and spheres of value," on the one hand, and the context-dependent

articulation of universal norms, on the other. See Schillebeeckx, "System of Coordinates for an Anthropology," in *Schillebeeckx Reader,* 29.

[42] Ibid.

[43] Ibid.

[44] Louis-Marie Chauvet, *The Sacraments: The Word of God at the Mercy of the Body* (Collegeville, MN: Liturgical Press, 2001), 114.

[45] Denis Edwards, *Ecology at the Heart of Faith: The Change of Heart That Leads to a New Way of Living on Earth* (Maryknoll, NY: Orbis Books, 2006), 7.

[46] Johnson, *Quest*, 184.

[47] Schillebeeckx, "System of Coordinates," 29.

[48] He observes that "man can have an influence on his ecological position in nature, though he depends on it, as becomes clear above all when he destroys the conditions under which he lives." In an important theological statement, Schillebeeckx further claims that "Christian salvation is also connected with ecology and with the conditions and burdens which particular life (here and now) lays on men. To say that all this is alien to the meaning of 'Christian salvation' is perhaps to dream of a salvation for *angels,* but not for *men.*" Schillebeeckx, "System of Coordinates," 31, 32.

[49] Ibid., 29.

[50] Susan A. Ross, *Extravagant Affections: A Feminist Sacramental Theology* (New York: Continuum, 1998), 46. See also Susan A. Ross, *For the Beauty of the Earth* (New York: Paulist Press, 2006).

[51] Sallie McFague, *The Body of God* (Minneapolis: Fortress Press, 2000), 96. Morally, McFague says, one upshot is that nature should be viewed as "the new poor."

[52] Ivone Gebara, *Longing for Running Water: Ecofeminism and Liberation* (Minneapolis: Fortress Press, 1999), 29.

[53] Ibid.

[54] Ibid., 62.

[55] See, for example, Carolyn Merchant, *The Death of Nature: Women, Ecology, and the Scientific Revolution,* repr. ed. (San Francisco: HarperOne, 1990). For a theological interpretation, see Cristina L. Traina, *Feminist Ethics and Natural Law: The End of the Anathemas* (Washington, DC: Georgetown University Press, 1999) and Christiana Z. Peppard, "Denaturing Nature," *Union Seminary Quarterly Review* 63, no. 1–2 (Spring–Summer 2011): 97–120.

[56] Charles Darwin, *On Evolution,* ed. Thomas F. Glick and David Kohn (Indianapolis: Hackett, 1996), 269.

[57] Christiana Z. Peppard, "Poetry, Ethics, and the Legacy of Pauli Murray," *Journal of the Society of Christian Ethics* 30, no. 1 (2010): 36.

[58] Emilie M. Townes, *Womanist Ethics and the Cultural Production of Evil* (New York: Palgrave Macmillan, 2006), 12.

[59] Margaret A. Farley, "A Feminist Version of Respect for Persons," *Journal of Feminist Studies in Religion* 9, no. 1–2 (1993): 183.

Chapter 2
A Primer on Global Fresh Water Crises

[1] Hillary Rodham Clinton, "Remarks in Honor of World Water Day," Department of State (March 22, 2012), www.state.gov.

[2] UN-Water, "Statistics," www.unwater.org.

[3] Ibid.

[4] UN-Water, "International Decade for Action: Water for Life, 2005–2015," www.un.org.

[5] Peter Rogers and Susan Leal, *Running Out of Water: The Looming Crisis and Solutions to Conserve Our Most Precious Resource* (New York: Palgrave Macmillan, 2010), 6.

[6] See the Circle of Blue infographic, www.circleofblue.org.

[7] Ibid.

[8] Brian Richter et al., "Tapped Out: How Can Cities Secure Their Water Future?" *Water Policy* 15 (2013): 337.

[9] Igor A. Shiklomanov and John C. Rodda, *World Water Resources at the Beginning of the Twenty-First Century,* International Hydrology Series (Cambridge: Cambridge University Press, 2004); Richter et al., "Tapped Out."

[10] Jeremy J. Schmidt, "Water Ethics and Water Management," chap. 1 in *Water Ethics: Foundational Readings for Students and Professionals,* ed. Peter G. Brown and Jeremy J. Schmidt (Washington, DC: Island Press, 2010), 3.

[11] Derrick Jensen, "Forget Shorter Showers: Why Personal Change Does Not Equal Political Change," *Orion* (July–August 2009): 18–19.

[12] Robert Glennon, *Unquenchable: America's Water Crisis and What to Do about It* (Washington, DC: Island Press, 2009), 151.

[13] Ibid., 159.

[14] William deBuys, *A Great Aridness: Climate Change and the Future of the American West* (New York: Oxford University Press, 2011), 37.

[15] See the fact sheets from UN-Water, www.unwater.org and www.un.org.

[16] See the UNICEF Fact Sheet on Water and Sanitation, www.unicef.org.

[17] See the UNIFEM Fact Sheet on Climate Change, www.unifem.org.

[18] See Farhana Sultana and Alex Loftus, *The Right to Water: Politics, Governance, and Social Struggles* (London: Earthscan/Routledge, 2012).

[19] To reduce by half the number of people without access to clean water and sanitation by the year 2015 was the aim of Millennium Development Goals (MDG) 7c, codified by the United Nations in 1990 as a subset of the overall aim of sustainability.

[20] Pontifical Council for Justice and Peace, "Water, an Essential Element for Life—An Update," Letter of the Holy See to the Sixth World Water Forum in Marseilles, France (March 2012).

[21] Peter Gleick, quoted in Brian Richter, *Chasing Water: A Guide for Moving from Scarcity to Sustainability* (Washington, DC: Island Press, 2014), 77.

[22] J. R. McNeill, *Something New under the Sun: An Environmental History of the Twenty-First Century World* (New York: W. W. Norton, 2000), 128.

[23] Jamie Linton and Jessica Budds, "The Hydrosocial Cycle: Defining and Mobilizing a Relational-Dialectical Approach to Water," *Geoforum* 57 (November 2014): 170–80; Rutgerd Boelens et al. expand the notion to "hydrosocial territories as spatial configurations of people, institutions, water flows, hydraulic technology and the biophysical environment that revolve around the control of water" (see Boelens et al., "Hydrosocial Territories: A Political Ecology Perspective," *Water International* 41, no. 1 [2016]: 1–14).

[24] Margreet Z. Zwarteveen and Rutgerd Boelens, "Defining, Researching, and Struggling for Water Justice: Some Conceptual Building Blocks for Research and Action," *Water International* (March 19, 2014): 143–58.

Chapter 3
Water: Human Right or Economic Commodity?

[1] Michael Sandel, "What Isn't for Sale?" *Atlantic*, April 2, 2012. See also Sandel, *What Money Can't Buy: The Moral Limits of Markets* (New York: Farrar, Straus and Giroux, 2012), chap. 1.

² For thorough treatments of bottled water, see Peter Gleick, *Bottled and Sold: The Story behind Our Obsession with Bottled Water* (Washington, DC: Island Press, 2010); Elizabeth Royte, *Bottlemania: How Water Went on Sale and Why We Bought It* (New York: Bloomsbury, 2008); and Maude Barlow and Tony Clarke, *Blue Gold: The Fight to Stop the Corporate Theft of the World's Water* (New York: New Press, 2002), esp. chap. 6. See also the award-winning documentary film *Flow*, written and directed by Irena Salina (2008), www.flowthefilm.

³ Annie Leonard, "The Story of Bottled Water," The Story of Stuff Project (2010), www.storyofstuff.org.

⁴ Ibid.

⁵ Ibid.

⁶ Royte, *Bottlemania*, 169.

⁷ FIJI Water, "The Water," www.fijiwater.com.

⁸ Ibid.

⁹ Ibid.

¹⁰ Gleick, *Bottled and Sold*, 170.

¹¹ Ibid.

¹² Royte, *Bottlemania*, 154.

¹³ Gleick, *Bottled and Sold*, 175.

¹⁴ Royte, *Bottlemania*, 33.

¹⁵ Since 2007, Aveda has been committed to avoiding the use of fur and bottled water and to providing organic foods backstage at Fashion Week. The New York City Department of Environmental Protection has launched a tap water campaign, complete with an androgynous, anthropomorphic bird mascot, called "Birdie."

¹⁶ "Take Back the Tap," www.foodandwaterwatch.org.

¹⁷ "A Refreshing Way to Recycle," www.dasani.com.

¹⁸ For a good analysis of whether such efforts can be ethical in any meaningful way, see Gleick, *Bottled and Sold*.

¹⁹ Royte, *Bottlemania*, 173.

²⁰ Gleick, *Bottled and Sold*, 180.

²¹ My emphasis. The full text of the document is available at www.un-documents.net. For a strong critique of the Dublin Statement, see Barlow and Clarke, *Blue Gold*, chaps. 4–5.

²² My emphasis.

²³ Among the many accounts and interpretations of the Cochabamba conflict, the most reliable is that by Jim Shultz of the Democracy Center in Bolivia. See Jim Shultz, "The Cochabamba Water Revolt and Its

Aftermath," chap. 1 in *Dignity and Defiance: Stories from Bolivia's Challenge to Globalization,* ed. Jim Shultz and Melissa Crane Draper (Berkeley: University of California Press, 2008).

²⁴ United Nations Department of Public Information, "International Year of Freshwater 2003 Backgrounder: The Right to Water," February 2003, Doc. No. DPI/2293F (2003), General Comment No. 15, "on the implementation of Articles 11 and 12 of the 1966 International Covenant on Economic, Social, and Cultural Rights." For a helpful legal analysis of prospects and challenges, see Eric Bluemel, "The Implications of Formulating a Human Right to Water," *Ecology Law Quarterly* 31, no. 4 (2004).

²⁵ United Nations, "Backgrounder: The Right to Water."

²⁶ Ibid.

²⁷ "Declaration of the Rights of Mother Earth" (2010), http://pwccc.wordpress.com.

²⁸ For a brief but insightful history of the quest for the UN Right to Water, see Maude Barlow, "Our Right to Water: A People's Guide to Implementing the United Nations' Recognition of the Right to Water and Sanitation," *Council of Canadians* (June 2011), http://www.canadians.org.

²⁹ For Barlow and Rifkin's Global Water Commons Treaty Initiative, "Global fresh water supply is a shared legacy, a public trust, and a fundamental human right, and therefore, a collective responsibility," see Barlow and Clarke, *Blue Gold,* xvii. Vandana Shiva identifies six principles of water democracy and maintains that because water is the source of life, "all species and ecosystems have a right to their share of water on the planet," and humans have a commensurate "duty to ensure that our actions do not cause harm to other species and other people"; thus, selling water for profit "denies the poor of their human rights." Vandana Shiva, *Water Wars: Privatization, Pollution and Profit* (Cambridge, MA: South End, 2002), 35.

³⁰ A prominent example of this position is James Gustave Speth, especially *America the Possible: Manifesto for a New Economy* (New Haven: Yale University Press, 2012).

³¹ Text of the Treaty Initiative is reproduced in Barlow and Clarke, *Blue Gold,* xviii.

³² Fred Pearce, *When the Rivers Run Dry: Water—The Defining Crisis of the Twenty-First Century* (Boston: Beacon Press, 2006), 308.

Chapter 4
A Right-to-Life Issue for the Twenty-First Century

[1]   Kenneth R. Himes, OFM, introduction to *Modern Catholic Social Teaching: Commentaries and Interpretations,* ed. Kenneth R. Himes, OFM (Washington, DC: Georgetown University Press, 2005), 4. For commentaries on *Caritas in Veritate* by Meghan Clark and on *Laudato Si'* by yours truly, please see the 2018 second edition from Georgetown University Press.

[2]   David J. O'Brien and Thomas A. Shannon, introduction to *Catholic Social Thought: The Documentary Heritage,* ed. O'Brien and Shannon (Maryknoll, NY: Orbis Books, 1992), 5.

[3]   For the purposes of this chapter I am largely unconcerned about gradations in authoritative status, because the emerging realities of fresh water scarcity do not fall neatly under the aegis of theological dogma, for which the question of authoritative status has become very important indeed in recent decades. For a fuller explication of authoritative documents in Catholic social thought and my methodology, as well as an extended discussion of each of the eight interpretive keys, see Christiana Z. Peppard, "Fresh Water and Catholic Social Teaching—A Vital Nexus," *Journal of Catholic Social Thought* 9, no. 2 (Summer 2012): 325–51.

[4]   Pontifical Council for Justice and Peace (PCJP), "Water, An Essential Element for Life" (Kyoto, 2003) and "Water, An Essential Element for Life—An Update" (Mexico City, 2006). Unless otherwise noted, magisterial documents quoted in this chapter are available at www.vatican.va.

[5]   Bishops of the Columbia River Watershed Region, *The Columbia River Watershed: Caring for Creation and Our Common Good* (January 8, 2001), http://thewscc.org.

[6]   PCJP, "Water" (2003).

[7]   Pontifical Council for Justice and Peace, *Compendium of the Social Doctrine of the Church* (Vatican City: Pontifical Council for Justice and Peace, 2004), no. 466; see also no. 470.

[8]   Paul VI, "Address to the Stockholm Conference on Human Environment" (June 1, 1972), in Marjorie Keenan, *From Stockholm to Johannesburg: An Historical Overview of the Concern of the Holy See for the Environment, 1972–2002* (Vatican City: Pontifical Council for Justice and Peace, 2002).

[9]   PCJP, "Water" (2006).

[10]   Pope Francis, *Laudato Si',* 20. Hereafter cited as *LS.*

[11] Ibid., 28.

[12] *Columbia River Watershed*, 9.

[13] Catholic Earthcare Australia, endorsed by the Bishops of the Murray-Darling Basin, *The Gift of Water* (North Sydney: Catholic Earthcare Australia, 2013), 1.

[14] *Gaudium et Spes* (1965), no. 69.

[15] World Synod of Catholic Bishops, *Justitia in Mundo* (1971), no. 8.

[16] John Paul II, "Address of His Holiness John Paul II to the Diplomatic Corps" (January 13, 2003), no. 4. He adds that in this situation, it is morally unacceptable to "cocoon" oneself inside "a privileged social class or a cultural comfort which excludes others," especially the poor and vulnerable, and future generations.

[17] PCJP, "Water" (2006).

[18] PCJP, *Compendium*, chap. 10, no. 484.

[19] Benedict XVI, "If You Want to Cultivate Peace, Protect Creation," Message for the World Day of Peace (2010), no. 8.

[20] UN-Water, "SDG Indicators and the Tiering System" (May 22, 2017), http://www.unwater.org.

[21] PCJP, *Compendium*, chap. 10, no. 485.

[22] *LS*, 30.

[23] PCJP, "Water" (2006).

[24] PCJP, *Compendium*, chap. 10, no. 485.

[25] PCJP, "Water" (2003, 2006); see also PCJP, *Compendium*, chap. 10, no. 485.

[26] UNICEF, "Child Survival: Water and Sanitation," (2018), www.unicefusa.org/mission/survival/water.

[27] PCJP, *Compendium*, chap. 10, no. 484.

[28] PCJP, "Water" (2006).

[29] PCJP, *Compendium*, no. 473.

[30] *LS*, 186–87.

[31] Benedict XVI, *Caritas in Veritate*, no. 16.

[32] *LS*, 185.

[33] PCJP, "Water" (2003).

[34] *LS*, 139.

[35] John L. Allen Jr., *The Future Church: How Ten Trends Are Revolutionizing the Catholic Church* (New York: Crown, 2009).

[36] See Cindy Wooden, "Promote Life by Protecting, Sharing Clean Water, Pope Says," *Catholic News Service*, February 24, 2017,

http://www.catholicnews.com. See also Pope Francis's address to the gathering: https://press.vatican.va.

[37] Alessandro Speciale, "Pope Francis Says Atheists Can Be 'Allies' for the Church," *Washington Post*, March 20, 2013.

Chapter 5
The Agriculture/Water Nexus

[1] UN News Center, "UN Projects World Population to Reach 8.5 Billion by 2030, Driven by Growth in Developing Countries," http://www.un.org (July 2015).

[2] Water Footprint Network, "Introduction," www.waterfootprint.org.

[3] Kai Olson-Sawyer, "Beef Has a Big Water Footprint. Here's Why," Grace Communications Foundation (March 14, 2017), http://www.gracelinks.org.

[4] Lukas Thommen, *An Environmental History of Ancient Greece and Rome* (Cambridge: Cambridge University Press, 2012 [Munich:Verlag C. H. Beck, 2009]), 33.

[5] John Bellamy Foster, Brett Clark, and Richard York, *The Ecological Rift: Capitalism's War on the Earth* (New York: Free Press, 2010), 45–46.

[6] See Donald Worster, *Nature's Economy: A History of Ecological Ideas*, 2nd ed. (New York: Cambridge University Press, 1994).

[7] See Roxane Dunbar-Ortiz, *An Indigenous Peoples' History of the United States* (Boston: Beacon Press, 2015).

[8] Donald Worster, *Rivers of Empire: Water, Aridity and the Growth of the American West* (New York: Pantheon, 1985), 130–31, 162. After the completion of sales of public lands, the main source of revenue for subsidizing irrigation for agriculture came from the sale of hydropower from large dams.

[9] Donald Pisani, *Water and American Government: The Reclamation Bureau, National Water Policy, and the West, 1902–1935* (Berkeley: University of California Press, 2002), 243.

[10] Ibid., 272–73; Jessica Teisch, *Engineering Nature: Water, Development, and the Global Spread of American Environmental Expertise* (Chapel Hill: University of North Carolina Press, 2011), 180.

[11] Alexis de Tocqueville, *Democracy in America,* trans. Harvey C. Mansfield and Delba Winthrop (Chicago: University of Chicago Press, 2000), I.2.9.

[12] Pisani, *Water and American Government,* 277.

[13] Ibid., 281.

[14] Robert Glennon, *Water Follies: Groundwater Pumping and the Fate of America's Fresh Waters* (Washington, DC: Island Press, 2002), 25.

[15] Ibid., 26.

[16] Robert Glennon, *Unquenchable: America's Water Crisis and What to Do about It* (Washington, DC: Island Press, 2010), 122.

[17] Gilbert White, *Science and the Future of Arid Lands* (Paris: UNESCO, 1960), 37–38.

[18] Donald Worster, for example, suggests several "unstated premises" in the adoption of the doctrine of prior appropriation: "that the West should in fact be growing crops and building up its population, that it should be cut up into private property, that its water or any other resource should be exploited to its maximum economic potential." Worster, *Rivers of Empire*, 92.

[19] Lynton Keith Caldwell, "Implications of a World Economy for Environmental Policy and Law," in *The Economics of Transnational Commons,* ed. Partha Dasgupta, Karl-Göran Mäler, and Alessandro Vercelli (Oxford: Clarendon Press, 1997), 222.

[20] Although she is not credited, Paul Ehrlich's wife, Anne Ehrlich, co-authored the book.

[21] Paul Ehrlich, *The Population Bomb* (1968; Cutchogue, NY: Buccaneer Books, 1971).

[22] Wil S. Hylton, "Broken Heartland: The Looming Collapse of Agriculture on the Great Plains," *Harper's Magazine*, July 2012.

[23] Former World Bank economist Ismail Serageldin bluntly states that "the amount of subsidies in agriculture are notorious." See "Conversation with Ismail Serageldin," *World Policy Journal* 26, no. 4 (Winter 2009–10): 30.

[24] Richard Misrach and Kate Orff, *Petrochemical America* (New York: Aperture, 2012), 183.

[25] Michael Pollan, *The Omnivore's Dilemma: A Natural History of Four Meals* (New York: Penguin, 2006), 45.

[26] Katherine Gustafson, *Change Comes to Dinner: How Vertical Farmers, Urban Growers, and Other Innovators Are Revolutionizing How America Eats* (New York: St. Martin's Griffin, 2012), 201–2.

[27] Misrach and Orff, *Petrochemical America*, 183.

[28] Ibid., 189.

[29] Given the EU's ban on atrazine, it is ironic that the potent herbicide is patented and manufactured by Syngenta Corporation, which

is headquartered in Switzerland (with offices in the United States, of course).

[30] See, for example, the meta-study and commentary by Jennifer Beth Sass and Aaron Colangelo, "European Union Bans Atrazine, while the United States Negotiates Continued Use," *International Journal of Occupational and Environmental Health* 12, no. 3 (2006): 260–67.

[31] Natural Resources Defense Council, "Atrazine: Poisoning the Well," www.nrdc.org.

[32] Sandra Steingraber, *Living Downstream: An Ecologist Looks at Cancer and the Environment*, 2nd ed. (Boston: Da Capo, 2010).

[33] See, for example, Thomas Pogge, *World Poverty and Human Rights*, 2nd ed. (Boston: Polity, 2008), as well as a succinct op-ed by the executive director of the UN Food Programme, Josette Sheeran, "We Can End Hunger: 10 Ways to Feed the World," *Huffington Post*, October 1, 2010.

[34] Social ethicist John Sniegocki's presentation of negative effects is noteworthy: "Industrial farming methods have contributed, for example, to massive soil erosion as a consequence of the impacts of mechanized plowing and the abandonment of many traditional soil conservation practices. These modern farming methods have led also to seriously declining levels of organic matter and nutrient levels in the soil due to exclusive reliance on chemical fertilizers. The widespread use of modern irrigation methods has led to serious problems of soil salinization and waterlogging. A recent UN study has found that in South Asia, one of the pioneer areas in Green Revolution agriculture, nearly 50 percent of the land has suffered 'serious degradation' from soil erosion, declining soil fertility, salinization, waterlogging, and/or other ecological problems." John Sniegocki, *Catholic Social Thought and Economic Globalization* (Milwaukee: Marquette University Press, 2009), 200.

[35] Wes Jackson, *New Roots for Agriculture* (Lincoln: University of Nebraska Press, 1980), 14.

[36] Charles Bowden, *Killing the Hidden Waters* (1977; Austin: University of Texas Press, 2005), 19.

[37] Fred Pearce, *When the Rivers Run Dry: Water—The Defining Crisis of the Twenty-First Century* (Boston: Beacon, 2007), 201.

[38] Ibid. For the NASA image, see online Earth Observatory, http://earthobservatory.nasa.gov.

[39] Ibid., 201.

[40] For discussion of the destruction of the Aral Sea, see ibid., chap. 23, "Aral Sea: The End of the World."

[41] White, *Science,* 20.

[42] Karl Wittfogel, *Oriental Despotism: A Comparative Study of Total Power* (New Haven: Yale University Press, 1957), 19.

[43] Pearce, *Rivers,* 133.

[44] See, for example, Jacques Leslie, *Deep Water: The Epic Struggle over Dams, Displaced People, and the Environment* (New York: Picador, 2006); Patrick McCully, *Silenced Rivers: The Ecology and Politics of Large Dams,* updated and revised ed. (London: Zed Books, 2001); Rob Nixon, *Slow Violence and the Environmentalism of the Poor* (Cambridge, MA: Harvard University Press, 2011).

[45] World Commission on Dams, *Dams and Development: A New Framework for Decision-Making* (London: Earthscan, 2000), xxviii.

[46] "Three Gorges Dam," International Rivers Network, www.internationalrivers.org.

[47] Brett Walton, "Texas High Plains Prepare for Agriculture without Irrigation," *Circle of Blue Water News,* April 5, 2013.

[48] Glennon, *Unquenchable,* 123.

[49] Hylton, "Broken Heartland."

[50] "Conversation with Ismail Serageldin," 28–29.

[51] Jackson, *New Roots,* 1.

[52] Ibid.

[53] Aldo Leopold, *For the Health of the Land: Previously Unpublished Essays and Other Writings,* ed. J. Baird Callicott and Eric T. Freyfogle (Washington, DC: Island Press, 2001), 218.

[54] Wendell Berry, *The Unsettling of America: Culture and Agriculture,* preface to the 1986 edition (San Francisco: Sierra Club, 1986), viii.

[55] Ellen Davis, *Scripture, Culture, and Agriculture: An Agrarian Reading of the Bible* (New York: Cambridge University Press, 2009), 8.

[56] Norman Wirzba, *Food and Faith: A Theology of Eating* (New York: Cambridge University Press, 2011), 2.

[57] Mark E. Graham, *Sustainable Agriculture: A Christian Ethic of Gratitude* (Eugene, OR: Wipf and Stock, 2009).

[58] Fred Kirschenmann, "Theological Reflections while Castrating Calves," chap. 1 of *Cultivating an Ecological Conscience: Essays from a Farmer-Philosopher,* by Fred Kirschenmann, ed. Constance Falk (Louisville: University Press of Kentucky, 2010), 20.

[59] Ibid., 17.

[60] Ibid., 20.

[61] Matthew Whelan, "The Grammar of Creation: Agriculture in the Thought of Pope Benedict XVI," paper presented at the Catholic Consultation on Climate Change, Catholic University of America, Washington, DC, November 8–10, 2012.

[62] Pontifical Council for Justice and Peace, *Compendium of the Social Doctrine of the Church* (2004), chap. 6, no. 299.

[63] United States Conference of Catholic Bishops, *Economic Justice for All* (1985), no. 217.

[64] Ibid., no. 227.

[65] John Paul II, "Message to Jacques Diouf, Director General of the Food and Agriculture Organization of the United Nations, on the Occasion of World Food Day" (October 13, 2002). As stipulated in the *Compendium*, chap. 10: "Human interventions that damage living beings or the natural environment deserve condemnation, while those that improve them are praiseworthy. *The acceptability of the use of biological and biogenetic techniques is only one part of the ethical problem*: as with every human behaviour, it is also necessary to evaluate accurately the real benefits as well as the possible consequences in terms of risks. In the realm of technological-scientific interventions that have forceful and widespread impact on living organisms, with the possibility of significant long-term repercussions, it is unacceptable to act lightly or irresponsibly" (no. 473).

[66] Pontifical Council for Justice and Peace, "Water, an Essential Element for Life," letter from the Holy See to the Third World Water Forum in Kyoto, Japan (March 2003).

[67] Catholic Earthcare Australia, endorsed by the Bishops of the Murray-Darling Basin, *The Gift of Water* (North Sydney: Catholic Earthcare Australia, 2013).

[68] Bishops of the Columbia River Watershed Region, *The Columbia River Watershed: Caring for Creation and Our Common Good* (January 8, 2001), 15–16, http://thewscc.org.

[69] Catholic Earthcare Australia, *The Gift of Water,* 13.

[70] Laura M. Hartman, *The Christian Consumer: Living Faithfully in a Fragile World* (New York: Oxford University Press, 2011), 190–91.

[71] Jackson, *New Roots,* 4.

Chapter 6
Climate Change and Water in the Anthropocene

[1] Zafar Adeel, "Climate Change Is All about Water," www.unwater.org.

[2] For an evocative description of some of these developments in light of the idea of planetary consciousness and emerging earth community, see Mary Evelyn Tucker and Brian Swimme, *Journey of the Universe* (New Haven: Yale University Press, 2011).

[3] See, for example, Andreas Malm, *Fossil Capital: The Rise of Steam Power and the Roots of Global Warming* (Brooklyn: Verso Books, 2016).

[4] Holmes Rolston III, *Science and Religion: A Critical Survey*, 20th Anniversary Edition (Philadelphia: Templeton Foundation Press, 2006), xi.

[5] Jan Zalasiewicz, Mark Williams, Will Steffen, and Paul Crutzen, "The New World of the Anthropocene," *Environmental Science and Technology* 44, no. 7 (2010): 2228–31.

[6] Ibid.

[7] International Commission on Stratigraphy, http://www.stratigraphy.org.

[8] Comprehensively, scientist Johan Rockström and his team identified many of these in a 2009 article in *Nature* as "planetary boundaries," a notion considerably updated by Will Steffen and colleagues in 2015. Shorter-term impacts include changes to geomorphology (for example, the shape of the earth's surface is affected by urbanization, agriculture, and mountaintop removal for coal mining). Longer-term impacts include changes to biology (for example, biodiversity loss as well as human manipulation of genetic materials) and alterations in earth chemistry (including changes to the nitrogen cycle, for example, as a result of industrial agriculture; as well as climate change and its multiple impacts, such as sea level rise and ocean acidification). Scholars point out that among these earth systems dynamics, it is anthropogenic climate change that is most commonly and quickly seen as both symptom and cause of the Anthropocene (closely followed, perhaps, by rampant species extinction). Johan Rockström et al., "A Safe Operating Space for Humanity," *Nature* 461 (September 2009): 472–75; Will Steffen et al., "Planetary Boundaries: Guiding Human Development on a Changing Planet," *Science* 347, no. 6223 (February 2015).

[9] "Welcome to the Anthropocene," *Economist*, May 26, 2011.

[10] Michael Northcott, *A Political Theology of Climate Change* (Grand Rapids, MI: W. B. Eerdmans, 2013), 73.

[11] Andreas Malm and Alf Hornborg, "The Geology of Mankind? A Critique of the Anthropocene Narrative," *Anthropocene Review* 1, no. 1 (2014): 62.

[12] Ibid., 63.

[13] Ibid., 64.

[14] Ibid.

[15] Some people endeavor to deny human-induced climate change. This particularly vocal subset of people in the United States, which insists that recent climatic fluctuations are merely a natural part of Earth's history, unfortunately also has a willing political audience. To be sure, many geological and tectonic realities persist independent of human influence: stratigraphic records from millions upon millions of years of planetary history certainly indicate a range of climatic fluctuations. On this single point, climate change deniers are correct about one thing: the planet has warmed and cooled over vast periods of time, and the atmospheric carbon dioxide concentration has even risen and fallen dramatically over some of these periods. However, that single point must be viewed in tandem with the many other data points about climate change of the last two centuries. Although it is true that climate systems have always fluctuated more and less dramatically, it is simultaneously true that climate changes of recent centuries have been dramatically amplified due to human activity. To restate the vital point: climate scientists do not argue that the climate systems have always been stable. Rather, scientists point out how human societies have amplified climatological patterns in ways that have never been seen in human history, in ways that track onto legacies of industrialization, and in ways that may not be remediable within a humanly meaningful time frame. Director of the California Academy of Sciences Jon Foley puts it pithily: "In several aspects, especially climate, land, biodiversity, and geochemical flows, it is now clear that human activities have changed the planet beyond what was normally experienced in our geologic epoch." Jonathan Foley, "Living by the Lessons of the Planet: How Can Human Societies Thrive within Earth's Physical and Biological Limits?" *Science* 356, no. 6335 (April 21, 2017): 251.

[16] Environmental Protection Agency, "Overview of Greenhouse Gases: Carbon Dioxide," www.epa.gov. (As of access date February 15, 2018.)

[17] Bill McKibben, "Global Warming's Terrifying New Math," *Rolling Stone*, July 19, 2012.

[18] International Monetary Fund, "Energy Subsidy Reform: Lessons and Implications" (January 28, 2013), www.imf.org.

[19] John Paul II, Message for World Day of Peace (1990), no. 6.

[20] Margaret Thatcher, Speech at 2nd World Climate Conference (1990), http://www.margaretthatcher.org.

[21] For a historical perspective see J. R. McNeill, *Something New under the Sun: An Environmental History of the 20th-Century World* (New York: W. W. Norton, 2001).

[22] Zalasiewicz, Williams, Steffen, and Crutzen, "New World."

[23] Vandana Shiva, *Water Wars: Privatization, Pollution and Profit* (Boston: South End, 2002), 50.

[24] Amitav Ghosh, *The Great Derangement: Climate Change and the Unthinkable* (Chicago: University of Chicago Press, 2016), 153.

[25] Ibid., 159.

[26] Suzanne Goldberg, "U.S. Military Warned to Prepare for Consequences of Climate Change," *Guardian*, November 9, 2012.

[27] National Academy of Sciences, National Academy of Engineering, Institute of Medicine, and National Research Council, *America's Climate Choices: Advancing the Science of Climate Change* (Washington, DC: National Academies Press, 2010).

[28] National Center for Atmospheric Research, "Taking a Systemic Look at Characteristics of the Global Hydrologic Cycle," http://ncar.ucar.edu.

[29] NRC 2010 report on climate change, http://dels.nas.edu.

[30] "Water Vapor Confirmed as Major Player in Climate Change," *NASA* (November 17, 2008), www.nasa.gov.

[31] Kenneth E. Kunkel et al., "Probable Maximum Precipitation (PMP) and Climate Change," *Geophysical Research Letters* (2013).

[32] Shiva, *Water Wars*, 49.

[33] Jim Stipe, "Report: Climate Change Threatens One Million Maize and Bean Farmers in Central America," *CRS Newswire*, October 9, 2012.

[34] For a discussion of this topic in a theological vein, see Richard W. Miller, "Global Climate Disruption and Social Justice: The State of the Problem," in *God, Creation, and Climate Change: A Catholic Response to the Environmental Crisis* (Maryknoll, NY: Orbis Books, 2010), 9–13.

[35] See the discussion of this concept and its significance for the United States in William deBuys, *A Great Aridness: Climate Change and the Future of the American Southwest* (New York: Oxford University Press, 2011).

[36] Danielle Nierenberg, "How to Save Water on World Water Day," *Miami Herald*, March 21, 2013.

[37] Norman Myers, "Environmental Refugees: A Growing Phenomenon of the Twenty-first Century," *Philosophical Transactions of the Royal Society of London* 357 (2002): 609.

[38] Ibid.

[39] Ibid.

[40] See, for example, *Climate Change and the Arab Spring*, ed. Caitlin Werrell and Francesco Femia, with a preface by Anne-Marie Slaughter (Washington, DC: Center for American Progress, 2013).

[41] Alon Tal, *Pollution in a Promised Land: An Environmental History of Israel* (Berkeley: University of California Press, 2002), 199–200.

[42] Diane Raines Ward, *Water Wars: Drought, Flood, Folly, and the Politics of Thirst* (New York: Riverhead Books, 2002), 188.

[43] See the infographic, "Why Palestinians Have No Water—And No, It's Not That Palestine Has No Water" (March 22, 2013), http://www.commondreams.org.

[44] The Pacific Institute timeline is available at http://www.worldwater.org, and the podcasts are at http://pacinst.org.

[45] Hussein A. Amery and Aaron Wolf, *Water in the Middle East: A Geography of Peace* (Austin: University of Texas Press, 2000).

[46] Kader Asmal, preface to World Commission on Dams, *Dams and Development: A New Framework for Decision-Making* (London: Earthscan, 2000), v.

[47] International Rivers Network, World Commission on Dams, *Dams and Development: A New Framework for Decision-Making* (London: Earthscan, 2000), xxviii.

[48] "Why Is Eutrophication Such a Serious Pollution Problem?" United Nations Environment Programme, *Newsletter on Lakes and Reservoirs,* vol. 3.

Chapter 7
Water from Rock: Standing Rock and *Laudato Si'*

[1] A version of this chapter first appeared as "*Laudato Si'* and Standing Rock: Water Justice and Indigenous Ecological Knowledge," chapter 12 in *Theology and Ecology Across the Disciplines: On Care for Our Common Home*, ed. Celia Deane-Drummond and Rebecca Artinian-Kaiser (New York: Bloomsbury, 2018).

[2] I have written elsewhere about how Pope Francis's remarks in *Laudato Si'* (hereafter cited as *LS*) overlap with or are challenged by the Declaration of the Rights of Mother Earth. See Christiana Z. Peppard,

"Hydrology, Theology, and *Laudato Si'*," *Theological Studies* 77, no. 2 (June 2016): 416–35.

[3] Special thanks are joyfully due to Seattle University, where I first articulated normative implications of Pope Francis's turn to indigenous knowledge in the Catholic Heritage lectures series through the Institute for Catholic Thought and Culture in February 2016; to Barry University for hosting me as their Founder's Day Distinguished Lecturer in November 2016, where these ideas were further developed; and to Stephen Payne and Meg Stapleton-Smith of Fordham University for stupendous research assistance.

[4] Testimony of Charles W. Murphy, in "Water Problems on the Standing Rock Sioux Reservation," U.S. Senate Committee of Indian Affairs (November 18, 2004), 2–3.

[5] Testimony of Senator Tim Johnson, ibid., 5.

[6] Testimony of Kent Conrad, ibid., 8.

[7] Senator Byron Dorgan, ibid., 14, 16.

[8] Senator Daniel Inouye, ibid., 22.

[9] Standing Rock Sioux Tribe, "Stand with Standing Rock" (2017). Available online at http://standwithstandingrock.net.

[10] Indigenous Environmental Network (2017). Available online at www.ienearth.org.

[11] Jack Healy, "I Want to Win Someday: Tribes Make Stand against Pipeline," *New York Times*, September 9, 2016.

[12] Indigenous Environmental Network (2017).

[13] Sacred Stone Camp, "DAPL easement suspended but the fight's not over," December 5, 2016, http://sacredstonecamp.org. Doug Hayes, "What's Next for Standing Rock and the Dakota Access Pipeline Fight?" *The Planet* by the Sierra Club, December 13, 2016.

[14] ACLU of North Dakota, "Stop Government Suppression of the Right to Protest in North Dakota." Available online at https://action.aclu.org.

[15] Louise Erdrich, "Holy Rage: Lessons from Standing Rock," *New Yorker*, December 22, 2016.

[16] Ibid.

[17] Roxanne Dunbar-Ortiz, *An Indigenous People's History of the United States* (Boston: Beacon Press, 2014), 7.

[18] David Archambault II, "Taking a Stand at Standing Rock," *New York Times*, August 24, 2016.

[19] Bill McKibben, "After 525 Years, It's Time to Actually Listen to Native Americans," *Grist*, August 22, 2016, http://grist.org.

[20] Jennifer Veilleux, "Income Maps of the Native Americans Living in the Missouri River Basin," *The Way of Water* (December 19, 2016), http://jveilleux.blogspot.com.

[21] Michigan Civil Rights Commission, "The Flint Water Crisis: Systemic Racism through the Lens of Flint" (February 17, 2017), www.michigan.gov.

[22] Marion Grau, "'The Camp Is a Ceremony': A Report from Standing Rock," *Religion News Service*, November 25, 2016.

[23] Erdrich, "Holy Rage."

[24] Ibid.

[25] For a fuller exposition and analysis of this development, see Christiana Zenner Peppard, "*Laudato Si*'," in *Modern Catholic Social Teaching: Commentaries and Interpretations*, ed. Kenneth Himes, OFM (Washington, DC: Georgetown University Press, 2017).

[26] Bill McKibben, "The Pope and the Planet," *New York Review of Books*, August 13, 2015.

[27] See Zenner Peppard, "*Laudato Si*'," in *Modern Catholic Social Teaching*.

[28] Nado Aveling, "Don't Talk about What You Don't Know: On (Not) Conducting Research with/in Indigenous Contexts," *Critical Studies in Education* 54, no. 2 (2013): 206.

[29] John Thavis, "Standing Rock Activists See Pope Francis as Spiritual Ally," *Religion News Service*, December 2, 2016, http://religionnews.com.

[30] This section is adapted from Zenner Peppard, "Theology, Hydrology, and *Laudato Si*'" as well as my commentary on *Laudato Si*' in *Modern Catholic Social Teaching*.

[31] See chapter 4 in this volume, and Christiana Z. Peppard, "Fresh Water and Catholic Social Teaching: A Vital Nexus," *Journal of Catholic Social Thought* 9, no. 2 (2012): 325–51.

[32] *LS*, 30.

[33] Ibid., 145.

[34] Thavis, "Standing Rock Activists See Francis as a Spiritual Ally."

[35] *LS*, 146.

[36] Mark Silk, "The Disappointing Victory at Standing Rock," *Religion News Service* (December 6, 2016), http://religionnews.com.

[37] US Jesuit Conference, "US Jesuits, Red Cloud Indian School, and St. Francis Mission Call Dakota Access Pipeline Decision 'Morally Unacceptable'" (February 22, 2017), https://jesuits.org.

[38] Silk, "Disappointing Victory."

[39] Eric Martin, "At Standing Rock and Beyond, What Is to Be Done?" The Stone, *New York Times*, November 25, 2016.

[40] Grau, "The Camp Is a Ceremony."

[41] See, for example, www.culturalsurvival.org.

[42] Jeremy J. Schmidt, *Water: Abundance, Scarcity, and Security in the Age of Humanity* (New York: New York University Press, 2017).

[43] *LS*, 185.

Chapter 8
The Jordan River

[1] Denis Edwards, *Ecology at the Heart of Faith: The Change of Heart That Leads to a New Way of Living on Earth* (Maryknoll, NY: Orbis Books, 2006), 48.

[2] Daniel Hillel, *Rivers of Eden: The Struggle for Water and the Quest for Peace in the Middle East* (New York: Oxford University Press, 1994), 147.

[3] Ibid., 155.

[4] Anne Gunkel and Jens Lange, "New Insights into the Natural Variability of Water Resources in the Lower Jordan River Basin," *Water Resources Management* 26, no. 4 (2012): 963–80; Rana Samuels, Alon Rimmer, and Pinhas Alpert, "Effect of Extreme Rainfall Events on the Water Resources of the Jordan River," *Journal of Hydrology* 375, no. 3–4 (2009): 513–23.

[5] Pre-twentieth-century flows of the river are estimated at roughly 1.2 billion cubic meters per year. Only once in the past twenty years has the annual flow reached 350 million cubic meters (MCM). More frequently, it hovers closer to 100 MCM. Until recently, scientific models and overviews of surface water availability were limited.

[6] Hillel, *Rivers of Eden*, 166.

[7] K. David Hambright et al., "Exploitation and Destabilization of a Warm, Freshwater Ecosystem through Engineered Hydrological Change," *Ecological Applications* 18, no. 7 (2008): 1591.

[8] Rana Samuels et al., "Extreme Value Indicators in Highly Resolved Climate Change Simulations for the Jordan River Area," *Journal of Geophysical Research* 116, no. D24 (2011): 17.

[9] "Living Conditions in Gaza 'More and More Wretched' over Past Decade, UN Finds," *UN News Center*, July 11, 2017, http://www.un.org.

[10] Hillel, *Rivers of Eden*, 156–57.

[11] Jordan River Foundation, "Crossing the River Jordan," www.jordanriver.jo (2002).

[12] Miriam Lowi, "The Politics of Water: The Jordan River and the Riparian States," *McGill Studies in International Development* no. 35 (1984); Lowi, *Water and Power: The Politics of a Scarce Resource in the Jordan River Basin* (Cambridge: Cambridge University Press, 1993); Hillel, *Rivers of Eden*; Munther Haddadin, *Diplomacy on the Jordan: International Conflict and Negotiated Resolution* (Dordrecht: Kluwer Academic, 2002).

[13] For two interpretations of the issue, see Amnesty International's report "Water Is a Human Right," in *Thirsting for Justice: Palestinian Access to Water Restricted* (October 2009), http://www.amnesty.eu; and the response by Alon Tal, *Israel Journal of Foreign Affairs IV: 2* (2010): 59–73. See also Alon Tal, ed., *Water Wisdom: Preparing the Groundwork for Cooperative and Sustainable Water Management in the Middle East* (New Brunswick, NJ: Rutgers University Press, 2010).

[14] William deBuys, *A Great Aridness: Climate Change and the Future of the American Southwest* (New York: Oxford University Press, 2011), 37–38.

[15] Alon Tal, *Pollution in the Promised Land: An Environmental History of Israel* (Berkeley: University of California Press, 2002), 199.

[16] J. Anthony Allan, "Hydro-Peace in the Middle East: Why No Water Wars? A Case Study of the Jordan River Basin," *SAIS Review* 22, no. 2 (Summer–Fall 2002): 260.

[17] Ibid., 258, 256.

[18] Judith Sudilevsky, "Israel Removes Landmines from Jesus Baptism Site," *Christian Century*, June 14, 2011.

[19] Hillel, *Rivers of Eden*, 283.

[20] Interviews were conducted in May 2008, in Israel and Jordan.

[21] Allan, "Hydro-Peace," 259.

[22] The epigraph for this section is from Mark Twain, *The Innocents Abroad* (London: Wordsworth Editions, 2010). For an engaging biographical rendering of Twain's voyage and religious views, see William E. Phipps, *Mark Twain's Religion* (Atlanta: Mercer University Press, 2003).

[23] Phipps, *Mark Twain's Religion*, 79.

[24] Sudilevsky, "Israel Removes Landmines."

[25] Rachel Havrelock, *River Jordan: The Mythology of a Dividing Line* (Chicago: University of Chicago Press, 2011), 281.

[26] Jeremy Hutton, *The Transjordanian Palimpsest: The Overwritten Texts*

of Personal Exile and Transformation in the Deuteronomistic History (Berlin: Walter deGruyter, 2009), 5–6, 44.

[27] Ibid., 35.

[28] Ibid., 45.

[29] Hillel, *Rivers of Eden,* 156.

[30] Havrelock, *River Jordan,* 156.

[31] See, for example, Douglas S. Earl, "'(Bethany) beyond the Jordan': The Significance of a Johannine Motif," *New Testament Studies* 55, no. 3 (2009): 279–94.

[32] Robin Jensen, *Living Water: Images, Settings and Symbols of Early Christian Baptism* (Leiden: Brill, 2011), 121.

[33] Hermann Usener, *Religionsgeschichtliche Untersuchungen: Erster Theil: Das Weihnachtsfest* (Bonn, 1899).

[34] Jean Daniélou, SJ, *The Bible and the Liturgy* (Notre Dame, IN: University of Notre Dame Press, 1956), 101.

[35] Nicholas Denysenko, *The Blessing of Waters and Epiphany: The Eastern Liturgical Tradition* (Farnham: Ashgate, 2012).

[36] Daniélou, *The Bible and the Liturgy,* 100.

[37] I am indebted to Timothy Brunk of Villanova University for drawing my attention to this quotation from the Service of the Great Blessing of the Waters, in his article "Water: Liturgical Symbol of Life from Death," unpublished paper delivered at Villanova University (September 2008), 11. See also Denysenko, *The Blessing of Waters and Epiphany.*

[38] Jensen, *Living Water,* 88. She adds that in several of these contexts, "the personification of the Jordan bears similarities to the figure of Neptune or the river god," but she disagrees with previous interpreters who would read the figure of the Jordan as a competing deity (95).

[39] Spiro Kostof, *The Orthodox Baptistery of Ravenna* (New Haven: Yale University Press, 1965), 85.

[40] Jensen, *Living Water,* 123.

[41] Hutton, *Transjordanian Palimpsest*, 47.

[42] Jordan River Foundation, "Crossing the River Jordan."

[43] Havrelock, *River Jordan*, 261.

[44] Ibid., 245.

[45] "Jordan's King Donates Land for Church at Baptismal River Site," *Christian Century*, May 6, 2008.

[46] Baptism Site Commission, "Thousands Attend Epiphany at Baptism Site" (2012), www.baptismsite.com.

[47] John Hart, *Sacramental Commons: Christian Ecological Ethics* (Lanham, MD: Rowman and Littlefield, 2006), 90.

[48] Crown of Thorns (2012), www.crown-of-thorns.com (site accessed May 7, 2012, but no longer active).

[49] For a comparative, ethnographic perspective on this issue of environmental degradation and religious purity, see the important book by David Haberman, *River of Love in an Age of Pollution: The Yamuna River of Northern India* (Berkeley: University of California Press, 2006).

[50] Gary Chamberlain, *Troubled Waters: Religion, Ethics, and the Global Water Crisis* (Rowman and Littlefield, 2007).

[51] Hillel, *Rivers of Eden*, 4.

[52] Melissa K. Nelson, "Rivers of Memory, Lakes of Survival: Indigenous Water Traditions and the Anishinaabeg Nation," chap. 4 in *Deep Blue: Critical Reflections on Nature, Religion and Water,* ed. Sylvie Shaw and Andrew Francis (London: Equinox, 2008), 79.

Chapter 9
Women, Wells, and Living Water

[1] John R. Donahue, SJ, "High Noon," *America*, February 25, 2002.

[2] Augustine, *Homilies on the Gospel of John 1–40,* vol. I/12, trans. Edmund Hill, OP, ed. and with an annotated introduction by Allan D. Fitzgerald, OSA, in *The Works of St. Augustine: A Translation for the 21st Century* (Hyde Park, NY: New City Press, 2009), Homily 15, p. 277.

[3] Augustine, *Homilies on John,* no. 15, 286.

[4] Colin Kruse, *John: The Tyndale New Testament Commentaries* (Grand Rapids, MI: Eerdmans, 2004), 128.

[5] Daniel J. Harrington, SJ, "Spiritual Thirst," *America*, February 18, 2008.

[6] Thomas L. Brodie, *The Gospel of John* (New York: Oxford University Press, 1993), 214. Other traditional interpreters have argued that the five husbands are not literal men but allegories for geographical locations, aspects of Samaritan theology, correspondences to the Pentateuch, or—in Augustine's allegorical rendering—the five senses.

[7] Raymond E. Brown, SS, *An Introduction to the Gospel of John,* ed., updated, introduced and concluded by Francis J. Moloney, SDB (New York: Doubleday, 2003), 236. Brown later adds that the trope of misunderstanding or confusion—so evident in this pericope—can be seen to function similarly to the parables in the Synoptic gospels, or in relation to Johannine Christology (see 289).

[8] Sandra M. Schneiders, "The Gospels and the Reader," in *The Cambridge Companion to the Gospels,* ed. Stephen C. Barton (New York: Cambridge University Press, 2006), 97.

[9] Ibid., 98.

[10] This approach to biblical interpretation, in the words of Schüssler-Fiorenza, "It seeks to bring about change by repudiating the 'common-sense' cultural premise of historical invisibility of most women and dis-enfranchised men in dominant historiographies"; it "seeks to interrupt this positivist ethos of biblical studies which claims that historians are able to tell readers 'what the text meant' or to give an accurate descrip-tion, objective reflection, and value-free report on the past." Elisabeth Schüssler-Fiorenza, *In Memory of Her* (New York: Continuum, 1983), xxiii.

[11] Peter C. Phan, "An Interfaith Encounter at Jacob's Well: A Missio-logical Interpretation of John 4:4–42," *Mission Studies* 27, no. 2 (2010): 160.

[12] Ibid., 163.

[13] See Jerome Neyrey, SJ, *The Gospel of John,* The New Cambridge Bible Commentary (New York: Cambridge University Press, 2007), 87.

[14] Ibid., 88.

[15] Sandra M. Schneiders, *Written That You May Believe: Encountering Jesus in the Fourth Gospel* (New York: Herder and Herder, 1999), 143–44.

[16] Brodie, *The Gospel of John,* 214.

[17] Stephen D. Moore, "Are There Impurities in the Living Water That the Johannine Jesus Dispenses? Deconstruction, Feminism, and the Samaritan Woman," chap. 13 in *The Interpretation of John,* 2nd ed., ed. John Ashton (Edinburgh: T. & T. Clark, 1997).

[18] Ibid., 288.

[19] Ibid., 292.

[20] Augustine, *Homilies on John,* 281. The text is Homily 15, which was preached in the summer of 407 C.E.

[21] Ibid., 281–82.

[22] Ibid., 283.

[23] See, for example, Aaron Benavot, "Education, Gender and Eco-nomic Development: A Cross-National Study," *Sociology of Education* 62, no. 1 (January 1989): 14–32.

[24] United Nations Educational, Scientific, and Cultural Organiza-tion, *World Atlas of Gender Equity in Education* (Paris: UNESCO, 2012), 1.

[25] Isha Ray, "Public Spaces, Private Acts: Toilet Access and Gender Equity," *Just Environments,* Social Science Research Council (May 20, 2017), http://items.ssrc.org.

[26] See the "Facts and Figures on Global Climate Change" published by UN-WOMEN (UNIFEM), www.unifem.org; see also the 2010 report by the gender-and-development organization Newcourse, "Women, Natural Resource Management and Poverty: A Review of Issues and Opportunities," www.actforconservation.org.

[27] Delores S. Williams's vital book *Sisters in the Wilderness: The Challenge of Womanist God-Talk* (Maryknoll, NY: Orbis Books, 1995) poses and interprets the story of Hagar as an ongoing revelation of forced surrogacy, racial privilege, and a theology that looks not for liberation but for mere baseline survival. The hydrological hermeneutic that I offer corroborates and intensifies Williams's claims.

[28] Ananda Rose, "Death in the Desert," *New York Times*, June 21, 2012. See also Rose, *Showdown in the Sonoran Desert: Religion, Law and the Immigration Controversy* (New York: Oxford University Press, 2012), and Kristin Heyer, *Kinship across Borders: A Christian Ethic of Immigration* (Washington, DC: Georgetown University Press, 2012).

[29] Rose, "Death in the Desert."

Coda
Lessons in Liquidity

[1] Craig Childs, "The Birthplace of Water," *Orion Magazine*, January/February 2016.

[2] Mahmoud Darwish, "How Far Is Far?" in *A River Dies of Thirst: Journals*, trans. Catherine Cobham (Brooklyn: Archipelago Books, 2016), 30.

Further Resources

This selected bibliography identifies texts and other resources that can aid further exploration of key themes and ideas presented in *Just Water*.

General Interest and Background Information

Ball, Philip. *Life's Matrix: A Biography of Water.* Berkeley: University of California Press, 2001.

Black, Maggie, and Jannet King. *The Atlas of Water: Mapping the World's Most Critical Resource.* 2nd ed. Berkeley: University of California Press, 2009.

Chellamy, Brahma. *Water, Peace, and War: Confronting the Global Water Crisis.* Lanham, MD: Rowman and Littlefield, 2013.

Circle of Blue Water News: www.circleofblue.org.

deVilliers, Marq. *Water: The Fate of Our Most Precious Resource.* New York: Mariner Books, 2001.

Gleick, Peter. *The World's Water,* vol. 7: *The Biennial Report on Freshwater Resources.* Washington, DC: Island Press, 2011.

Peppard, Christiana Z. "Where We Get Our Fresh Water" and "An Introduction to the Global Water Crisis." TED-Ed (2013). www.ed.ted.com.

Reisner, Marc. *Cadillac Desert: The American West and Its Disappearing Water.* Rev. ed. New York: Penguin Books, 1993.

Shilomanov, Igor A., and John C. Rodda. *World Water Resources at the Beginning of the Twenty-First Century.* International Hydrology Series. Cambridge: Cambridge University Press, 2004.

Hydraulic Expansion in the Twentieth Century

Glennon, Robert. *Water Follies: Groundwater Pumping and the Fate of America's Fresh Waters.* Washington, DC: Island Press, 2002.

Hoekstra, Arjen, and Ashok Chapagain. *Globalization of Water: Sharing the Planet's Freshwater Resources.* Malden, MA: Blackwell, 2008.

Leslie, Jacques. *Deep Water: The Epic Struggle over Dams, Displaced People, and the Environment.* New York: Picador, 2006.

McCully, Patrick. *Silenced Rivers: The Ecology and Politics of Large Dams.* Updated and revised edition. London: Zed Books, 2001.

Pearce, Fred. *When the Rivers Run Dry: Water—The Defining Crisis of the Twenty-First Century.* Boston: Beacon Press, 2007.

Pisani, Donald. *From the Family Farm to Agribusiness: The Irrigation Crusade in California, 1850–1931.* Berkeley: University of California Press, 1984.

————. *Water and American Government: The Reclamation Bureau, National Water Policy, and the West, 1902–1935.* Berkeley: University of California Press, 2002.

Solomon, Steven. *WATER: The Epic Struggle for Wealth, Power, and Civilization.* San Francisco: Harper, 2010.

Teisch, Jessica. *Engineering Nature: Water, Development, and the Global Spread of American Environmental Expertise.* Chapel Hill: University of North Carolina Press, 2011.

Worster, Donald. *Rivers of Empire: Water, Aridity, and the Growth of the American West.* New York: Pantheon, 1985.

Water and Conflict

"Bolivia: Leasing the Rain." NOW with Bill Moyers. PBS (June 2002). www.pbs.org.

Delli Priscoli, Jerome, and Aaron Wolf. *Managing and Transforming Water Conflicts.* International Hydrology Series. Cambridge: Cambridge University Press, 2009.

Raines Ward, Diane. *Water Wars: Drought, Flood, Folly, and the Politics of Thirst.* New York: Riverhead Books, 2002.

Scholz, John T., and Bruce Stiftel, eds. *Adaptive Water Governance and Water Conflict: New Institutions for Collaborative Planning.* Washington, DC: Resources for the Future, 2005.

Shultz, Jim, and Melissa Crane Draper, eds. *Dignity and Defiance: Stories from Bolivia's Challenge to Globalization.* Berkeley: University of California Press, 2008.

Bottled Water

Barlow, Maude, and Tony Clarke. *Blue Gold: The Fight to Stop the Corporate Theft of the World's Water.* New York: New Press, 2002.

Didier, Susan. "Water Bottle Pollution Facts." *National Geographic.* http://greenliving.nationalgeographic.com.

Gleick, Peter. *Bottled and Sold: The Story behind Our Obsession with Bottled Water.* Washington, DC: Island Press, 2010.

Leonard, Annie. "The Story of Bottled Water." Oakland: The Story of Stuff Project, 2010. www.storyofstuff.org.

Royte, Elizabeth. *Bottlemania: How Water Went on Sale and Why We Bought It.* New York: Bloomsbury, 2008.

Salina, Irena. *FLOW.* 2008. www.flowthefilm.com.

Fresh Water as a Human Right and Justice Issue

Bakker, Karen. *Privatizing Water: Governance Failure and the World's Urban Water Crisis.* Ithaca, NY: Cornell University Press, 2010.

Barlow, Maude. *Blue Covenant: The Global Water Crisis and the Coming Battle for the Right to Water.* New York: New Press, 2009.

Barlow, Maude, and Tony Clarke. *Blue Gold: The Fight to Stop the Corporate Theft of the World's Waters.* New York: New Press, 2005.

Nixon, Robert. *Slow Violence and the Environmentalism of the Poor.* Cambridge, MA: Harvard University Press, 2011.

Pontifical Council for Justice and Peace. *The Compendium of the Social Doctrine of the Church,* chapter 10. Vatican City: Pontifical Council for Justice and Peace, 2004.

Shiva, Vandana. *Water Wars: Privatization, Pollution, and Profit.* Boston: South End, 2002.

Sultana, Farhana, and Alex Loftus, eds. *The Right to Water: Politics, Governance, and Social Struggles.* London: Earthscan, 2012.

Agriculture

Berry, Wendell. *The Unsettling of America: Culture and Agriculture.* San Francisco: Sierra Club, 1986.

Bowden, Charles. *Killing the Hidden Waters.* 1977. Austin: University of Texas Press, 2005.

Davis, Ellen. *Scripture, Culture, and Agriculture: An Agrarian Reading of the Bible.* New York: Cambridge University Press, 2009.

Graham, Mark. *Sustainable Agriculture: A Christian Ethic of Gratitude.* Eugene, OR: Wipf and Stock, 2009.

Gustafson, Katherine. *Change Comes to Dinner: How Vertical Farmers, Urban Growers, and Other Innovators are Revolutionizing How America Eats.* New York: St. Martin's Press, 2012.

Jackson, Wes. *Altars of Unhewn Stone: Science and the Earth.* San Francisco: North Point Press, 1987.

———. *New Roots for Agriculture.* Rev. ed. Lincoln: University of Nebraska Press, 1980.

Kirschenmann, Fred. *Cultivating an Ecological Conscience: Essays from a Farmer-Philosopher.* Edited by Constance Falk. Louisville: University Press of Kentucky, 2010.

The Land Institute (Salina, Kansas). www.landinstitute.org.

The Leopold Center for Sustainable Agriculture at Iowa State University (Ames, Iowa). www.leopold.iastate.edu.

Pollan, Michael. *The Omnivore's Dilemma: A Natural History of Four Meals.* New York: Penguin, 2006.

The Stone Barns Center for Food and Agriculture (Pocantico Hills, NY). www.stonebarnscenter.org.

Wirzba, Norman, ed. *The Essential Agrarian Reader: The Future of Culture, Community, and the Land.* Louisville: University Press of Kentucky, 2003.

Climate Change and the Anthropocene

DeBuys, William. *A Great Aridness: Climate Change and the Future of the American Southwest.* New York: Oxford University Press, 2011.

Field, C. B., et al., eds. *Climate Change 2007: Impacts, Adaptation and Vulnerability.* Contribution of Working Group II to the Fourth Assessment Report of the Intergovernmental Panel on Climate Change (pp. 617–52). Cambridge: Cambridge University Press, 2007.

Heinberg, Richard, and Daniel Lerch, eds. *The Post Carbon Reader: Managing the Twenty-first Century's Sustainability Crises.* Healdsburg, CA: Watershed Media, 2010.

Lenton, Timothy, et al. "Tipping Elements in the Earth's Climate System." *Proceedings of the National Academy of Sciences* 105, no. 6 (February 12, 2008): 1786–93.

Powell, James Lawrence. *Dead Pool: Lake Powell, Global Warming, and the Future of Water in the West.* Berkeley: University of California Press, 2008.

"Welcome to the Anthropocene." *The Economist*, May 26, 2011.

Zalasiewicz, Jan. *The Earth after Us: What Legacy Will Humans Leave in the Rocks?* New York: Oxford University Press, 2009.

Zalasiewicz, Jan, Mark Williams, Will Steffen, and Paul Crutzen. "The New World of the Anthropocene." *Environmental Science and Technology* 44, no. 7 (2010): 2228–31.

The Jordan River

Allan, J. Anthony. "Hydro-Peace in the Middle East: Why No Water Wars? A Case Study of the Jordan River Basin." *SAIS Review* 22, no. 2 (Summer–Fall 2002).

Haddadin, Munther. *Diplomacy on the Jordan: International Conflict and Negotiated Resolution.* Dordrecht: Kluwer Academic, 2002.

Havrelock, Rachel. *River Jordan: The Mythology of a Dividing Line.* Chicago: University of Chicago Press, 2011.

Hillel, Daniel. *Rivers of Eden: The Struggle for Water and the Quest for Peace in the Middle East.* New York: Oxford University Press, 1994.

Hutton, Jeremy. *The Transjordanian Palimpsest: The Overwritten Texts of Personal Exile and Transformation in the Deuteronomistic History.* Berlin: Walter deGruyter, 2009.

Lowi, Miriam. *Water and Power: The Politics of a Scarce Resource in the Jordan River Basin.* Cambridge: Cambridge University Press, 1993.

Peppard, Christiana Z. "Troubling Waters: The Jordan River between Religious Imagination and Environmental Degradation." *Journal of Environmental Studies and Sciences* 3, no. 2 (2013): 110–19.

Tal, Alon. *Pollution in the Promised Land: An Environmental History of Israel.* Berkeley: University of California Press, 2002.

Zeitoun, Mark. *Power and Water in the Middle East: The Hidden Politics of the Palestinian-Israeli Water Conflict.* London: I. B. Tauris, 2008.

Ecology, Public Health, and Synthetic Chemicals

Carson, Rachel. *Silent Spring.* New York: Houghton Mifflin, 1962.

Misrach, Richard, and Kate Orff. *Petrochemical America.* New York: Aperture, 2012.

Schrader-Frechette, Kristin. *Taking Action, Saving Lives: Our Duties to Protect Environmental and Human Health.* New York: Oxford University Press, 2007.

Steingraber, Sandra. *Living Downstream: An Ecologist's Personal Investigation of Cancer and the Environment.* 2nd ed. Boston: Da Capo, 2010.

Hydraulic Fracturing

Andrews, Anthony, et al. "Unconventional Gas Shales: Development, Technology, and Policy Issues." Washington, DC: Congressional Research Service, 2009.

Cooley, Heather, and Krista Donnelly. *Hydraulic Fracturing and Water Resources: Separating the Frack from the Fiction*. Oakland: Pacific Institute, 2012. www.pacinst.org.

Manning, Richard. "Letter from Elkhorn Ranch: Bakken Business." *Harper's Magazine* 26, no. 1954 (March 2013).

Steingraber, Sandra. "Each Other—Where We Are" (see especially her several columns on hydraulic fracturing). *Orion Magazine*. www.orionmagazine.org.

Western Resource Advocates. "Fracking Our Future." Boulder, CO: Western Resource Advocates, 2012. www.westernresources.org.

Catholic Social Teaching, Theology, and Water

Allman, Mark. "Theology H2O: The World Water Crisis and Sacramental Imagination." Chapter 19 in *Green Discipleship: Catholic Theological Ethics and the Environment*, edited by Tobias Winright. Winona, MN: Anselm Academic, 2011.

Catholic Relief Services. "Water and Sanitation." www.catholicrelief.org.

Chamberlain, Gary. *Troubled Waters: Religion, Ethics, and the Global Water Crisis*. Lanham, MD: Rowman and Littlefield, 2007.

Hart, John. *Sacramental Commons: Christian Ecological Ethics*. Lanham, MD: Rowman and Littlefield, 2006.

Korten, David C. "Catholic Social Teaching and Globalization: End of Empire and the Step to Earth Community." *Journal of Catholic Social Thought* 2, no. 1 (2005): 209–20.

Miller, Richard W., ed. *God, Creation, and Climate Change: A Catholic Response to the Environmental Crisis*. Maryknoll, NY: Orbis Books, 2010.

Peppard, Christiana Z. "Fresh Water and Catholic Social Teaching: A Vital Nexus." *Journal of Catholic Social Thought* 9, no. 2 (Summer 2012): 325–52.

Schaefer, Jame. *Theological Foundations for Environmental Ethics: Reconstructing Patristic and Medieval Sources*. Washington, DC: Georgetown University Press, 2009.

Sniegocki, John. *Catholic Social Teaching and Economic Globalization: The Quest for Alternatives.* Milwaukee: Marquette University Press, 2009.

Philosophy, Social Theory, and Water

Brown, Peter, and Jeremy J. Schmidt. *Water Ethics: Foundational Readings for Students and Professionals.* Washington, DC: Island Press, 2010.

Linton, Jamie. *What Is Water? The History of a Modern Abstraction.* Vancouver: University of British Columbia Press, 2010.

Ward, Colin. *Reflected in Water: A Crisis of Social Responsibility.* London: Cassell, 1997.

Water and Environmental Policy for the Twenty-First Century

Barnett, Cynthia. *Blue Revolution: Unmaking America's Water Crisis.* Boston: Beacon Press, 2012.

Gleick, Peter, and Juliet Christian-Smith. *A Twenty-First Century US Water Policy.* New York: Oxford University Press, 2012.

Glennon, Robert. *Unquenchable: America's Water Crisis and What to Do about It.* Washington, DC: Island Press, 2009.

Rogers, Peter, and Susan Leal. *Running Out of Water: The Looming Crisis and Solutions to Conserve Our Most Precious Resource.* New York: Palgrave Macmillan, 2010.

Speth, James Gustave. *The Bridge at the End of the World: Capitalism, the Environment, and Crossing from Crisis to Sustainability.* New Haven: Yale University Press, 2009.

———, ed. *Worlds Apart: Globalization and the Environment.* Washington, DC: Island Press, 2003.

Index

absolute water scarcity, 43–44
Adeel, Zafar, 118, 135, 140
agribusiness, 43, 88, 94, 96, 98–99, 136
agriculture
    agricultural subsidies, 136
    Catholic Social Teaching on, 113–16
    in China, 138, 144
    crop hydration, 41, 134
    dam projects and agricultural
        policies, 105
    displacement of the indigenous
        for agricultural projects, 162
    drought, effects on, 29, 43, 129, 135
    ecological agriculture, 112, 117
    fresh water devoted to, 33–34,
        35–37, 87, 174, 210
    high-yield agriculture in Green
        Revolution, 95–100
    history of, 89–91
    Jordan River and agricultural
        runoff, 169
    Lake Kinneret, as supplying
        agricultural water, 170–71
    nineteenth-century U.S. agriculture,
        91–95
    toxic pollution from agricultural
        chemicals, 111–12
    twentieth-century agricultural
        expansion, 106
    See also industrial agriculture
Aguas del Tunari, 62, 63
al-Abdullah, Raina, 184
al-Hussein, Noor, 184
Allan, J. Anthony, 87, 174, 175–76
Allen, John, Jr., 83
Al-Maghtas baptism site, 177, 178, 187
Alternative World Water Forum
    2012, 61
American Civil Liberties Union

(ACLU), 153
American West
    history of conflict over water, 140
    hydraulic development, 36, 91–93
    overuse of water, 111
    Southwest water concerns, 43,
        110, 145
ammonium nitrates, 97, 100
Amu Darya River, 103–4
Anthropocene
    Anthropocene ethics, primary
        question of, 131
    anthropogenic climate change,
        119–20, 125–26, 129–30, 146
    climate deniers and, 124, 125
    equal responsibility of all humanity,
        not implying, 122, 123
    fresh water as a key term, 145
    Geological Society, considering
        official formulation of term, 121
anthropogenic climate change, 119–20,
    121–23, 124–26, 129–30, 146
anthropological constants, 18–19, 21
anti-environmentalism, 127
Aquafina water, 52
aquifers
    depletion of, 29, 79, 137
    in Fiji, 54
    fossil water of ancient aquifers,
        106, 133
    industrial agriculture, negative
        effect on, 101, 110, 117
    in Jordan River region, 170, 174
    as non-renewable, 32, 38, 107, 134
    Ogallala Aquifer, 37, 107–8, 109
    over-extraction of water from, 82,
        134
    Palestinian access as restricted,
        140, 171

aquifers *(continued)*
    as previously untapped, 37
    rotary pumps, providing access
        to deeper aquifers, 94
    salinization of, 132, 134
Arab League, 139
Aral Sea, 102–4
Archambault, David, II, 154, 156,
    161
Arizona, 1, 36, 206–7
Army Corps of Engineers,
    148–50, 152, 160, 162
Arrhenius, Svante, 124
Arrowhead water, 57
Asmal, Kader, 140
Aswan Dam, 145
atrazine herbicide, 99, 177
Augustine, Saint, 24, 191, 197–201,
    202, 205
Australia, bishops of, 75, 114
Aveda corporation, 57
Aveling, Nado, 158

Bakken oil shale, 150–51
baptism
    baptistry iconography, 184
    of Jesus, 175, 178, 180, 181–83, 186
    Jordan River, baptism sites on,
        176–78
    polluted water used for, 187–88
Barlow, Maude, 65, 66, 141
Bartholomew, Patriarch, 11–12
Bechtel corporation, 62, 63
Belo Monte dam, 105, 144
Benedict XVI, Pope
    Caritas in Veritate, 12–13, 71, 77,
        78, 82, 131
    Congregation for the Doctrine
        of the Faith, directing, 8
    ecological issues, addressing, 11,
        22, 130
    on integral development as elusive,
        70
    on water rights, 77, 83, 159
    World Day of Peace messages,
        9–10, 76
Berry, Wendell, 111, 112, 115

Bethany-Beyond-the-Jordan, 177, 187
Bible
    biblical hermeneutics and the
        woman at the well, 193–96
    biblical stories, connecting
        to water concerns, 168
    fresh water, contextualizing
        understanding of, 197
    Hebrew Scriptures as
        land-centered, 112
    on the Jordan River, 176, 178,
        179–81, 181–84, 185
Blessing of Waters and Epiphany
    (Denysenko), 182
Blue Nile River of Ethiopia, 105
Blue Planet Project, 30
Body of God (McFague), 22
Boelens, Rutgerd, 48
Boff, Leonardo, 14
Book of Nature, 72–74
Bottled and Sold (Gleick), 58
bottled water
    as an economic commodity, 59
    as a fetishized commodity, 52, 56
    FIJI water, 54–56, 57
    problems with, 58
    sales as steady, 28–29, 53
Bowden, Charles, 101–2
Brazil, 60, 105, 144
bridge fuel, 146–47
Brown, Raymond, 192–93

Caldwell, Lynton Keith, 95
California
    brown bear extinction, 1
    Central Valley farming region,
        36, 107
    desalination plants, 42
    droughts in, 29
    salinity plume of Los Angeles, 134
    San Francisco mayor, eschewing
        bottled water, 57
    Sonoran desert deaths from
        dehydration, 206
Cambrian Explosion, 118
carbon dioxide, 119, 123, 124–25,
    127, 129, 143

carbon neutrality, 55, 57, 131
Caritas in Veritate (Benedict XVI)
  environmental degradation,
    12–13, 131
  local involvement in decision-
    making, 82
  on water rights, 71, 72, 77, 78
Catholic Agency for Overseas
    Development (CAFOD), 71, 85
Catholic Church
  embodiment and ecology focus,
    19–23
  environmental justice, stand on,
    162–64
  fresh water access as a human
    right, 60, 61, 65, 67, 165, 168
  Millennium Development Goal,
    45, 77
  theology in the twentieth century,
    2–5, 5–8
  See also Catholic Social Teaching
Catholic Coalition on Climate
    Change, 131
Catholic Relief Services (CRS), 71,
    85, 114, 134
Catholic Social Teaching (CST)
  on agriculture, 113–16
  appeal of, 70–71
  Catholic environmentalism, as
    an expression of, 68–69
  the common good and, 50, 210
  ecological degradation as a
    central theme, 22
  environment and ecology in, 10–13
  fresh water insights, CST
    exploring, 72–84, 85, 159–60,
    163, 165, 168
  on indigenous knowledge, 157–59
  liberation theology, insights woven
    into, 9–10
  See also Laudato Si'
Centesimus Annus encyclical, 11
Chamberlain, Gary, 188
Chauvet, Louis-Marie, 19
Chenu, M. D., 5
children
  clean water procurement,

    responsibility for, 201–2
  in deserts of U.S. border, 206
  in the global South, 25
  poor children, suffering from
    water scarcity, 59, 80, 114, 211
  as vulnerable, 15, 204, 210
  waterborne diseases, deaths from, 44
Childs, Craig, 212
China
  Beijing aquifer, 37, 38
  dams, desire for, 104
  environmental refugees, 138
  North China Plain as a key
    farming region, 107
  Three Gorges Dam, 105, 144
  water footprint as increasing, 33
Circle of Blue think tank, 30, 107
Clark, Brett, 91
Clean Ocean Action, 57
Clement of Alexandria, 181
climate change
  adaptation to, 136
  anthropogenic climate change,
    119–20, 121–23, 124–26,
    129–30, 146
  causes of, 123, 147
  dams, amplifying effects of, 144
  diminished agricultural productivity,
    leading to, 134
  drought as a new normal, 43, 110,
    133, 135
  fresh water scarcity, worsening, 46, 80
  Jordan River, expected effects on,
    171
  in *Laudato Si'*, 130–31
  need to address, 127
  NRC report on, 132
  People's Conference on Climate
    Change, 64
  as a security threat, 28
climate science, 124–26
Clinton, Hillary, 29
Coastal Aquifer, 171
Coca-Cola corporation, 52
Cochabamba, Bolivia, 52, 62–65
Colorado River, 29
Columbia River, bishops of, 73, 75

Columbia River Watershed: Caring for Creation and Our Common Good (Bishops of the Columbia River Watershed), 73
commodity, water as. *See* bottled water
Common Declaration on Environmental Ethics, 12
common good, 9, 50, 66, 76, 147, 210
Compendium of the Social Doctrine of the Church
   advocacy for clean water access, 71
   agriculture, on changes needed in, 113–14
   Catholic Social Teaching and the environment, 12
   fresh water reserves, on the risks to, 74
   magisterial authority chain, at the top of, 72
   the poor, on access of water for, 79
   technological-scientific interventions, cautious attitude towards, 81
   universal destination of goods as applying to water, 76
   water as merely an economic good, rejecting, 78
Conrad, Kent, 149
consumptive use of water. *See under* water use
contextual epistemology, 23
La Coordinadora community group, 62
"Coordinates for an Anthropology" (Schillebeeckx), 17
crops
   climate change, affecting, 110, 129, 134–35
   crop resilience, need for, 102, 109
   drip irrigation, 41, 174
   ecological agriculture, crop rotation in, 117
   in Green Revolution, 96–97
   hydraulic technology, increasing crop yield, 90–91, 94–95
   for non-human consumption, 86
   organic crops as a Catholic ideal, 115

   petrochemical use, 98–99
   regionally specific crops, 90, 136
   as vulnerable, 101
   water-intensive crops, Israel importing, 87
   in western United States, 36
Crossing Jordan (television series), 183–84
Crutzen, Paul, 120, 129, 130
culpable ignorance, 117
culture of water as an invitation and challenge, 83–84

Dakota Access Pipeline (DAPL)
   Bakken oil shale, transporting fuels from, 150, 151
   Catholic bishops, silence on, 162
   indigenous values, not honoring, 148, 158
   leakage, concern over, 142
   legal actions, 147
   #NODAPL movement, 155, 156, 161, 165
   protest pushback, 153
   tribal approval for project as disputed, 152
   See also Standing Rock; water protectors
dams
   agricultural expansion, role in, 91, 94–95
   in the American West, 93
   climate change, large dams amplifying effects of, 144–45
   displacement due to dam construction, 138
   Global Commission on Large Dams, report findings, 143–44
   impoundment storage in wet season, 36
   at Jordan River, 189
   at Lake Kinneret, 170
   noneconomic costs, 82
   resistance to large dams, 104–5
   twenty-first-century interest in large dams, 106, 139
Dams and Development: A Framework

for Decision-Making (World
Commission on Dams), 105
Daniélou, Jean, 182
Darwin, Charles, 24, 95, 119, 121
Dasani, 52, 57
Davis, Ellen, 112
Day of Prayer for the Environment,
12
Daza, Victor Hugo, 62–63
Dead Sea, 169, 170, 173, 177, 178
DeBuys, William, 43, 173
"Declaration of the Rights of
Mother Earth," 64, 66
deconstruction of water, 196–201
Deere, John, 91–92
deforestation, 74, 124, 128, 137, 170
Denysenko, Nicholas, 182
desalination, 41–42, 80, 135, 173
desertification, 74, 96, 133, 134, 137
Donahue, John, 191
Dorgan, Byron, 149–50
drip irrigation, 41, 110, 174, 212
drought
    climate change, link with, 76, 110,
        132
    distribution problems resulting
        from, 149
    environmental refugees, creating,
        137–38
    fresh water supply in drought-
        prone areas, 133
    in Jordan River region, 170, 190
    megadroughts, 135
    in North America, 29, 39, 134
    the poor as severely affected, 129
    small-scale producers,
        challenged by, 136
    social scientific research
        on, 139–40
    twenty-first century, lengthier
        droughts of, 43
    water collection in developing
        countries, 44
dry farming, 90, 110
Dublin Statement on Water and
    Sustainable Development, 60
Dunbar-Ortiz, Roxanne, 154

earth-systems, 2, 120, 121, 122
ecological agriculture, 112, 117
ecological conscience, 113
ecological theology, 14, 20–23
economic globalization
    environmental degradation,
        linked with, 12, 66, 68–69
    fresh water scarcity, exacerbating, 46
    privilege and the unremarkability
        of water, 197–98, 201
    public good in the era of, 141
    in twentieth century, 1
Economic Justice for All pastoral
    letter, 114
Economist, 28, 121
education, water scarcity affecting,
    44, 47, 79, 202–3, 205
Edwards, Denis, 14, 21, 168
Egypt, 90, 104, 139–40, 145
Ehrlich, Paul, 95–96
Ellacuría, Ignacio, 6–7, 8
embodiment in Christian theology,
    19–20
Energy Transfer Partners, 150–51
environmental degradation
    "Common Declaration on
        Environmental Ethics,"
        addressing, 12
    consumer discomfort, offsetting, 58
    CST, as a central theme of, 22, 68,
        69, 70, 74
    economic globalization, linked to, 66
    environmental refugees, resulting
        from, 137
    fossil fuel economy leading to,
        122
    Jordan River as degraded, 176–77,
        185, 187–88, 190
    Laudato Si', taking a stand against,
        131
    magisterial reflection on, 14
    Paul VI as first pope to address,
        10–11
    petrochemical fertilizers as a
        cause of, 98
    in South America, 13

environmental migrants, 137–38, 144
Environmental Protection Agency, 124, 127
environmental sustainability, 20, 91, 147
Epiphany, 181–82, 187
Erdrich, Louise, 153
Essay on the Principles of Population (Malthus), 95
Ethos Water, 57
Europe
    atrazine ban, 99
    bottled water, fondness for, 52
    colonization, 1, 154, 157, 172
    decline of Christianity, 3, 15
    European theology, speaking for all humanity, 17–18
    Industrial Revolution and, 122, 126
    Israeli pioneers, evoking European aesthetic, 173–74
eutrophication, negative effects of, 98, 144
Evangelium Vitae encyclical, 11
evaporation, 41, 110, 135, 145
Evian water, 52

faith, 8, 70, 131, 163, 165, 195
Farley, Margaret, 26
feedback cycles, 123, 125–26, 133
feminist theology, 20, 22, 23, 24–25
fertilizer, 88, 96, 97–98, 100, 102
FIJI water, 52, 54–56, 57
Firestein, Stuart, 125
Flint, Michigan
    bottled water use, 53
    contaminated water, 155, 204
    lead contamination, 47, 198
    lesson learned from water crisis, 201
    water inequality, perpetuating, 28
flooding, 105, 132, 135, 138, 169
flowback water, 142
flowing water, 198–201, 205
Food and Water Watch, 30, 57, 109
food deserts, 100
FoodTank, 109, 136
fossil fuels
    anthropogenic climate change, role in, 120, 126, 145

Dakota Access Pipeline, transporting, 150
downstream consequences of fossil fuel extraction, 212
fossil fuel emissions required for transport, 57
global capitalist economy, driving, 121–22
industrial agriculture, linked to fossil fuel economy, 116
in Industrial Revolution, 119, 124
negative externalities, 130
in nitrogen fertilizer production, 97, 98
pollution caused by, 29, 128
subsidies to fossil fuel companies, 125, 126
sustainable energy options, 129, 142–43
United States, fossil fuel use in, 123, 146–47
water contamination in fossil fuel extraction, 141–42
fossil water, 37, 106, 133
Foster, John Bellamy, 91
Francis, Pope
    Catholic Social Teaching, inheriting legacy of, 68–69
    Day of Prayer for the Environment, as co-founder, 12
    "Dialogue on Water," hosting, 162
    fresh water access as fundamental human right, 29, 69, 77, 163
    homeless of Rome, establishing Vatican showers for, 84
    indigenous claims, resonance with, 165
    liberation theology orientation, 9, 157
    the poor, focus on, 13
    preferential option for the poor, guided by, 79
    Standing Rock, not addressing directly, 161
    theology and ethics as theme of leadership, 10

universal destination of goods, including in encyclicals, 76
   See also Laudato Si'
Francis of Assisi, 68
free market, skepticism *vs.* faith in, 60
fresh water
  access as a human right, 29, 60, 61, 65, 67, 69, 77, 163
  agriculture, devoted to, 33–34, 35–37, 87, 174, 210
  Bible, contextualizing understanding of, 197
  Catholic Social Teaching on, 72–84, 85, 159–60, 163, 165, 168
  in drought-prone areas, 133
  extraction rates as unsustainable, 32, 100
  fresh water infrastructure, 198
  groundwater as a fresh water source, 32, 94
  Israel, fresh water control in, 139–40, 172–73
  as a key term in the Anthropocene, 145
  Lake Kinneret as a fresh water source, 170–71
  as a matter of justice, 46, 52, 59–60, 150, 209–10
  Middle East peace, fresh water as a component of, 140, 175
  Pope Francis, advocating for, 82, 84, 166
  technological innovation, 40–43
  women, burdened by fresh water scarcity, 44, 59, 201–5, 208, 210, 211
  See also water use
Friedman, Milton, 69
Friends of the Earth Middle East (FoEME), 175
furrow-to-furrow monoculture, 96, 100

Gaudium et Spes pastoral constitution, 3, 75
Gaza, 134, 171
Gebara, Ivone, 14, 23

genetic modification, 88–89, 96
Geological Society of London, 120–21
Geological Time Scale (GTS), 121
geology, processes of, 119–20
Ghosh, Amitav, 130
girls. *See* women and girls
Gleick, Peter, 45, 55–56, 58
Glennon, Robert, 41–42, 94, 107
Global Commission on Large Dams, 143–44
global commons, fresh water as part of, 59
global warming. *See* climate change
globality, expansion of, 2
globalization. *See* economic globalization
Goldtooth, Tom, 152
"Good Water Neighbors" program, 175
Graham, Mark, 112
Grau, Marion, 156, 164
gray water, 41
Green Revolution, 91, 95–97, 100–102, 103, 108, 109
greenhouse gases, 100, 123, 127, 133
greenwashing, 55
Gregory of Nyssa, 182
groundwater
  in bottled water production, 56
  contamination of, 53, 98, 142
  depletion of, 38, 100–108, 209
  downstream consequences, 142, 212
  extraction of, 36–37, 88, 96, 97, 100, 106, 211
  as a fresh water source, 32, 94
  groundwater rights, sales of, 141
  in Israel, 87
  in Jordan River region, 171
  sustainability of, 40
  See also aquifers
Gulf of Mexico, 29, 98
Gustafson, Katherine, 97–98
Gutiérrez, Gustavo, 6, 14

Hagar, 205–7
harnessing demand of domestic water habits, 39

Hart, John, 14, 187–88
Hartman, Laura, 116
Havrelock, Rachel, 178, 180, 184, 186
Hebrew Bible, 112, 176, 178, 179–81,
    185, 194
Hillel, Daniel, 169–70, 171–72, 175,
    179–80, 188–89
Himes, Kenneth, 70
historical-critical methodologies, 193–94
history
    of agriculture, 89–91
    anthropogenic climate change,
        historical origins of, 122–23
    baptism sites of Jesus, historical
        authenticity of, 178
    ecological knowing, developing
        out of historical moments, 23
    historical default, 165–66
    historical memory, 127–28
    historization of water, 28, 166,
        196–201
    history of earth, human place in,
        119–20
    Jordan River, environmental history
        of, 169–71, 179, 186
    liberation theology on salvation
        as a historical event, 8
    love of neighbor, historicity of, 4–5
    new stage of, human race in, 3
    revelation of God in history, 6
    Schillebeeckx on changing
        historical realities, 19
Hoekstra, Arjen, 87
Hoover, Herbert, 92–93
Hoover Dam, 104, 145
Hornborg, Alf, 122–23
human nature, 10, 16, 18, 24, 26, 80
human rights
    access to water as a right-to-life
        issue, 29, 67, 78–79
    Charter of Human Rights, 11
    fresh water as a human right
        in Catholic social teaching,
            77–78, 83, 159–60, 163, 165,
            168
        fresh water as a common good,
            211

    Pope Francis, advocating for, 82,
        84, 166
    United Nations on water rights
        as human rights, 61, 63–64,
        65, 66
    gender equality as linked to
        universal human rights, 203
    human rights vs. economic
        commodities, 59–60
    as a twentieth-century concept, 1
humility, 25, 49, 73, 165
hunger, global, 100
Hutton, Jeremy, 179–80, 183
hydraulic fracturing, 53, 142
hydraulic optimism, 36, 37, 104
hydraulic technologies
    in American West, 92–95
    control over water, amplifying, 90,
        97
    crop hydration through drip
        irrigation, 41
    desalination, issues with, 42
    groundwater exploitation,
        making possible, 106
    hydrological optimism,
        generating, 36–37
    not a panacea, 212
    twentieth-century enthusiasm for,
        104
hydrocarbons, 155
hydrologic cycle, 132
hydrological reality, 107, 109–12
hydrology as destiny, 205
hydropower, 93, 105, 142, 143
hydrosocial cycle, 45–48, 49–50, 210
hydrosocial privilege, 200–201
Hylton, Wil S., 96, 107–8

Ignorance: How it Drives Science
    (Firestein), 125
impoundment of seasonal
    precipitation, 36
incarnation as an on-going process, 113
India
    aquifer stress in Gangetic Plain, 107
    dam construction, 104, 138, 144
    droughts in, 43

industrial agriculture development, 91
irrigation in, 36
water footprint of middle class, 33
Indigenous Environmental Network, 151–52, 156, 161
Indigenous People's History of the United States (Dunbar-Ortiz), 154
industrial agriculture
  Catholic Social Teaching, reflecting on, 113
  detrimental effects of, 96, 104, 117, 134, 136
  as economically unstable, 111
  Green Revolution, association with, 91, 100–101, 108
  long-term externalities, not incorporating, 110
  massive corporate profits, generating, 99
  origin of, 97
  as pervasive, 97–98
  pollution, generating, 29, 144
  population growth, facilitating, 100, 107
  short-term focus, 101–2
  U.S. subsidies, 116, 212
industrial economy, 40, 116, 146
Industrial Revolution, 91, 119, 122, 124–26
industrialization
  alternative energy challenges, 142–43
  Anthropocene era, link to, 122
  criterion for farming productivity in industrial societies, 101–2
  dams, importance to industrializing nation-states, 106, 144
  as fossil fuel-driven, 119, 121, 147
  fresh water infrastructure, 198
  ignorance, 205
  Industrial Revolution as shaping agriculture, 91
  industry, water use devoted to, 33
  massive economic growth, Industrial Revolution leading to, 119
Inouye, Daniel, 150

integral development, 12, 70, 77, 82, 166
International Monetary Fund, 36, 126, 143
International Mother Earth Day, 64
International Rivers Network, 105
irrigation
  in the American West, 92–93
  Aral Sea decline, irrigation choices leading to, 104
  costs of, 82
  dams, directing water towards irrigation, 143
  drip irrigation, 41, 110, 174, 212
  environmental impact assessment, calls for, 114
  expansion of agriculture, as part of, 95, 96, 97
  groundwater irrigation from Ogallala Aquifer, 108
  in ideal agricultural operations, 115
  irrigation canals, 36, 37, 90–91, 94, 109, 110
  Jordan River as a source for, 170
  Mississippi River as a source for, 151
  soil pollution and, 101
  transnational development loans and, 105
Ishmael, 205–6
Israel
  access to water, 187
  aquifer undergird, 37, 134, 171
  desalination plants, 42
  fresh water control, 139–40, 172–73
  gray water use, 41, 174
  industrial agriculture, 91
  Lake Kinneret, use of, 170–71
  landmine removal along Jordan River, 175
  water-intensive crops, importing, 87
  Yardenit baptism site, 176–78
Israel-Jordan Peace Treaty, 172

Jackson, Wes, 101, 109, 115, 116
Jensen, Derrick, 39–40
Jensen, Robin, 182–93

Jesus Christ
  baptism of, 175, 178, 180, 181–83,
    186, 187–88
  ecology, strengthening link to, 168
  in liberation theology approach, 7
  Samaritan woman, interaction with,
    191–93, 194–95, 196–201, 202
  thirst, experiencing on cross,
    196–97, 205
John Paul II, Pope
  2003 Address to Diplomatic Corps, 76
  climate change as a crisis, 130
  environmental advocacy, 127–28
  fresh water access, recognizing
    importance of, 159
  integral development concept,
    endorsing, 70
  Patriarch Bartholomew, collaboration
    with, 11–12
  water resources for the poor, 114
Johnson, Elizabeth, 8–9, 10, 14
Johnson, Tim, 149
Jordan
  crops grown in, 174
  fresh water access as a contentious
    issue, 140
  international border with Israel,
    172, 177–78
  Qasr el-Yehud baptism site, 187
  "Red-Dead" water deal, 173
  royal family, writings of, 184
  in Six Day War, 139
Jordan River
  as a baptismal site, 86, 176–78
  environmental aspects, 169–71
  in Hebrew Bible, 179–81
  imagery in the arts, 183–84
  Israel, water diverted to, 139
  memories linked to, 188–90
  mythic stature and present day
    realities, 185
  in New Testament, 181–83
  Palestinian access as restricted, 140
  as polluted, 187–88
  sociopolitical aspects, 171–76
Jordan River Foundation, 184
justice

  in Catholic Social Teaching, 70,
    79–80, 148
  climate justice, 129
  distributive justice, 76, 80
  fresh water access as a matter of
    justice, 46, 52, 59–60, 150, 209–10
  in liberation theology, 7, 8–9, 157
  social justice focus on fresh water, 71
  See also water justice
Justice in the World (Synod
  of Bishops), 76

Kalamazoo River, 151, 155
Keenan, James, 4, 5
Keenan, Marjorie, 10–11
Kesicki, Tim, 162–63
Kirschenmann, Fred, 112–13, 115
Kruse, Colin, 192

Lake Erie, 29
Lake Kinneret, 170–71. *See also* Sea
  of Galilee
Lake Oahe, 149, 152, 154
Lakota Sioux, 142, 148–53, 154,
  161–62, 165
Land Institute, 101, 109
Landry, Candace, 155
Laudato Si' (LS)
  climate change, addressing, 130, 131
  CST, as part of, 22, 66, 71, 72, 148,
    159–60
  ecclesial and social context of
    launch, 15
  ecological charism of Patriarch
    Bartholomew, inspiring, 12
  on ecological relationships, 20–21
  economic gain as a sole criterion,
    not accepting, 78, 81
  on fresh water rights, 74–75, 77–78,
    82, 166
  integrated approach as goal, 83
  the local and the indigenous,
    respecting, 13, 157, 158, 160, 163
  meat, lessening reliance on not
    addressed, 116
  the poor, as affected by lack of
    fresh water, 80

Pope Francis as author, 68, 85
  Standing Rock and, 161–63, 165
  Twitter, encyclical quotes released
    on, 14
Leal, Susan, 33
Leo XIII, Pope, 70
Leopold, Aldo, 111
liberation theology, 6–10, 13–14, 17,
  19, 79, 157
living water, 192–93, 196–97, 199
local/regional focus
  bottled water and local rights of
    access, 54–55
  in contextual epistemology, 23
  decision making, local communities
    participating in, 82–83, 157
  local agriculture, 91, 136–37
  localized water challenges, 109
  negative externalities, local
    communities bearing cost of, 56
  non-monetary costs of fossil fuel
    consumption, locals bearing, 147
  Schillebeeckx and attention to the
    local, 19
Longing for Running Water (Gebara), 23
love of neighbor, 4–5, 7, 8, 113
Malm, Andreas, 122–23
Malthus, Robert Thomas, 95
Maori understanding of river water,
  66–67
marginalization, 25, 47, 155, 158, 166
Martin, Eric, 163
Marx, Karl, 6, 91
McDonagh, Sean, 11, 14
McFague, Sallie, 22
McKibben, Bill, 154–55, 157
McNeill, J. R., 46
meat consumption, 33, 88, 115–16
megadrought, persistence of, 135
Melville, Herman, 176, 178
memories of water, 188–89
Message for the World Day of Peace
  papal speeches, 9–10, 11
Metz, Johann Baptist, 5
Mexico City aquifer, 37, 38
microchips, water footprint of, 33
Middle East

fresh water use as a component of
    peace, 140, 175
  identity discourse in, 184
  Israel, water use in, 139
  Lake Kinneret as fresh water
    source, 170–71
  virtual water workaround, 87, 174
Misrach, Richard, 98
Mississippi River, 29, 98, 99, 151
Missouri River, 148, 149–56
mni wiconi water claim, 142, 156,
  161–62, 165, 167
monoculture crops
  downstream effect, as a result of,
    88–89
  increase in agricultural production,
    role in, 95
  in the Midwest, 98
  as nutrient-poor, 117
  post-war technology making
    possible, 96
  as soil-exhausting, 100, 136, 212
  synthetic fertilizer opening the
    way to, 97
Moore, Stephen D., 196–97
Morales, Evo, 64–65
Mountain Aquifer, 171
Murphy, Charles, 149
Murray-Darling Basin, 75, 114–15

Narmada dams of India, 144
NASA, 102, 133, 171
National Academy of Sciences, 132
National Catholic Rural Life Confer-
    ence (NCRLC), 71, 85, 114, 131
National Center for Atmospheric
    Research, 132
National Oceanic and Atmospheric
    Administration, 133
National Reclamation (Newlands)
    Act, 92, 94
National Resource Council (NRC),
    132, 133
natural law theory in Catholic
    theology, 72
Natural Resources Defense Council
    (NRDC), 99

natural springs as a water source, 198
Nebraska, 36, 37, 109
negative externalities, 56, 129, 130, 147, 212
neighbor, love of, 4–5, 7, 8, 113
Nelson, Melissa K., 189–90
Nestlé corporation, 52, 57
New York Times, 151–52, 163
Newlands Act, 92
Neyrey, Jerome, 194–95
Nierenberg, Danielle, 136
nongovernmental organizations, 29, 61, 65
nonrenewable groundwater sources, 32, 38, 82
Northcott, Michael, 121
no-till agriculture, 99
la nouvelle théologie movement, 5

Obama, Barack, 152
O'Brien, David, 70–71
O'Connell, Maureen, 10
Octogesima Adveniens encyclical, 11
Ogallala Aquifer, 37, 107–8, 109
Omnivore's Dilemma (Pollan), 97
Orff, Kate, 98
Origen, 182
Origin of Species, 119
Orthodox Church, 12, 182, 183, 184
Oslo Accords, 173

Pacific Institute on water conflicts, 140
Palestinian Water Authority, 172–73
Palestinians, 140, 171, 175, 184, 186–87, 199
Paris Climate Accords, 126–27
particularity and universality, 26, 27
Patasco Aquifer, 37, 134
Paul VI, Pope, 10–11, 74, 77
Pearce, Fred, 67, 102–3, 104
People's Conference on Climate Change and the Rights of Mother Earth, 64
PepsiCo, 52
Perrier water, 52
Petrochemical America (Misrach/Orff), 98

petrochemicals, 88, 95–100, 111, 117, 134
petroleum, 119, 142
Phan, Peter, 194
Pisani, Donald, 93–94
planetarity concept, 2
Poland Spring, 52, 54, 57
political theology, 5–6
Pollan, Michael, 97
pollution
    in the American West, 111
    atmospheric pollution, 129
    corporate responsibility, 210–11
    dams and irrigation contributing to, 82
    Economic Justice for All, discussing, 114
    health problems, linked to, 122
    in the Jordan River, 188
    large-scale pollution, 29, 110
    petrochemical use and, 98, 117
    urban population growth as a factor, 91
    water pollution as a sign of the times, 74
Pontifical Academy of Sciences, 84, 130, 132, 159, 162
Pontifical Council for Justice and Peace (PCJP), 71, 72, 76, 78, 79–80, 83. *See also Compendium of the Social Doctrine of the Church*
the poor
    in Catholic Social teaching, 69, 82
    climate change, disproportionately affecting, 129, 135, 145
    environmental degradation, linked to, 68, 69, 137
    as environmental refugees, 129
    fresh water access concerns, 44, 46, 59, 83, 114, 159–60, 210
    global poverty, Pope Francis critiquing, 14
    liberation theology and focus on the poor, 6–8
    preferential option for the poor, 7, 9, 13, 79–80, 211
Population Bomb (Ehrlich), 95–96
population growth

aquifer factor, 107
  in China, 144
  deep groundwater access making
    possible, 106
  farmland, cutting into, 138
  fresh water scarcity and, 46, 80
  industrial agriculture, facilitating, 100
  rate of, as disproportionate to
    agricultural production, 95–96
Populorum Progressio encyclical, 70, 77
precautionary principle, 81
privatization water supply, 52, 58–59,
  62–63, 66, 141, 212
produced water, 142
public good, water as a, 59, 141, 210, 211

Qasr el-Yehud baptism site, 177–78, 187
queens of Hashemite Kingdom of
  Jordan, 184

Rahner, Karl, 4–5
rain, 36, 104, 132, 199. *See also* drought
rainforests, 124
Ratzinger, Joseph. *See* Benedict XVI,
  Pope
Ravenna bapistry, 183
Ray, Isha, 203
relativism, 18, 19, 25, 27, 166
renewable energy sources, 142–43
renewable water supply. *See* surface
  water
Renewing the Earth pastoral letter, 74
Rerum Novarum encyclical, 70
reservoirs, 36, 105, 106, 110, 144, 170
resource nationalism of Bolivia, 64
revelation, 6–7, 194–95
right-to-life issue of fresh water, 29,
  65, 67, 69, 77–79, 83, 164
*River Jordan: The Mythology of a
  Dividing Line* (Havrelock), 180
Rivers of Eden (Hillel), 171–72, 175, 189
Rogers, Peter, 33
Rolston III, Holmes, 120
Roman Catholic Church. *See* Catholic
  Church
Rose, Ananda, 207
Ross, Susan, 22

Royte, Elizabeth, 55, 58
Ruether, Rosemary Radford, 14, 22

Sabbath ecology, 112
salt water, 32, 41–42
Samaritan woman at the well
  hierarchical dualism of interpre-
    tations, 193, 196, 198, 205
  Jesus, conversing with, 194–95, 202
  as a seductress, 191–92, 204, 207
  standing and flowing water,
    distinguishing between, 199–201
Sandel, Michael, 51
sanitation
  as a basic right, 61, 65
  children as susceptible to poor
    sanitation, 44
  female sanitation needs, 47, 203
  lack of access to, 79, 198, 201
  sanitation infrastructure, distancing
    users from water sources, 197
  UN Sustainable Development Goals,
    as a major initiative of, 45, 77
Sarawak Dam, 105–6
Schillebeeckx, Edward,
  17–19, 21, 209–10
Schmidt, Jeremy J., 38, 165–66
Schneiders, Sandra M., 193, 195
Schüssler-Fiorenza, Elisabeth, 194
science
  agricultural productivity, suc-
    cessfully application to, 96
  Anthropocene as a scientific
    category, 121
  anthropogenic climate change,
    scientific consensus on, 146
  climate science, 124–26
  CST attitude towards, 73, 81
  ethical discernment in analysis of
    scientific data, 211
  NASA, confirming water
    absorption hypothesis, 133
  optimism for scientific progress in
    arid America, 93
  scientific cosmology, 21
  Vatican summits on scientific
    topics, 84

Sea of Galilee, 170–71, 176, 189
seawater intrusion into aquifers, 38,
    132, 134
Second Vatican Council. *See* Vatican II
seeds, modification of, 88, 95, 96
Senate Committee on Indian Affairs,
    148, 150
Serageldin, Ismael, 108, 109
shale oil, 150, 151
Shannon, Thomas, 70–71
shareholders *vs.* stakeholders, 55, 60,
    82, 147, 212
Shiva, Vandana, 65, 66, 129, 134, 141
signs of the times, 3, 5, 7, 8, 72, 74, 84
Silk, Mark, 162, 163
Singapore, 41
Six Day War, water as an igniting
    factor, 139
Six Principles of Water Democracy, 66
Sobrino, Jon, 6, 7
soil
    agricultural revolution and atten-
        tion on soil health, 102, 109, 117
    crop yield, soil quality affecting, 90
    depletion and erosion of, 111, 114,
        136, 137
    diminished water content, 43
    irrigation canals and dry soils, 36
    Jordan River area, exposed soil of,
        169
    Marx on restoration of soil
        metabolism, 91
    saline soil, 103, 110
    soil degradation, 99, 117, 134
    soil exhaustion, 96, 212
    synthetic fertilizer use as polluting,
        97–98, 100
    virgin soil of the American West, 93
    water retention capabilities, 88
solar power, 142–43
solidarity, 9, 13, 25, 156, 159, 163, 165
Sollicitudo Rei Socialis encyclical, 11
Sonoran desert region, 206–7
soul and body, dualism between, 24
Soviet water policies, 102–4
Standing Rock, 142, 148–55, 159,
    161–64, 165

standing water, 199–201, 205
Starbucks, 58
stewardship of the natural world,
    74–75
Stoermer, Eugene, 120
Stone Barns Center for Food and
    Agriculture, 109
sub-Saharan Africa, 15, 43, 138
subsidence as linked with sinkholes, 38
subsidiarity principle in CST, 82
surface water
    dams as collecting, 139, 143
    groundwater connection, 106
    industrial agriculture and, 110
    in Jordan River basin, 174
    long-term sustainability, 40
    over-extraction of, 211
    as a renewable water suply, 32
    snowmelt as a source of, 29
*Sustainable Agriculture: A Christian
    Ethic of Gratitude* (Graham), 112
Synod of Bishops, 76
Syr Darya River, 103
Syria, 139–40

"Take back the tap" campaigns, 29, 57
Tal, Alon, 139, 173–74
tap water, 52–53, 56–57, 203
Teisch, Jessica, 93
Texas, 29, 36, 37, 107, 109
Thatcher, Margaret, 128
Thavis, John, 159, 161
"Theological Reflections while
    Castrating Calves" (Kirschenmann),
    112–13
*Theology of Liberation: History, Politics,
    Salvation* (Gutiérrez), 6
theology of twentieth century, 2–5,
    5–10, 19–23, 70, 72. *See also*
    Catholic Social Teaching
Theophany, 181–82, 183, 187
Thommen, Lukas, 89–90
Three Gorges dam, 105, 144
Tocqueville, Alexis de, 93
Tohono O'odham tribal land, 206
Townes, Emilie, 26
toxicity

desalination, leaving behind toxic
  brine salts, 42
from fossil fuel extraction, 142, 212
of Jordan River, 177
of lead pipes in Flint, Michigan, 198
of soil in Aral Sea region, 100
toxic chemical pollutants, 29, 53,
  99, 111, 204
toxicology findings, 21, 98
transboundary water, 186
Transjordanian motif, 179–80
transpiration and high temperatures, 135
Treaty Initiative to Share and Protect
  the Global Water Commons, 66
Trible, Phyllis, 194
Trump, Donald, administration
  of, 124, 126, 127, 128, 152
Twain, Mark, 140, 176, 178, 185
Twitter, encyclical quotes released
  through, 14

United Nations Educational, Scientific
  and Cultural Organization
  (UNESCO), 63, 203
United Nations Conference on
  Environment and Development
  (Rio), 60–61
United Nations Convention on the
  Rights of the Child, 64
United Nations Environment
  Programme, 144
United Nations General Assembly, 64
United Nations General Convention,
  61, 65
United Nations Millennium
  Development Goal, 45, 77
United Nations Sustainable Devel-
  opment Goals, 45, 77, 203
United States
  agricultural subsidies, 116, 136
  American Catholics, focus on
    reproductive issues, 69, 78
  bottled water consumption, 53–58
  Convention on the Rights of
    the Child, not a signatory, 64
  crop declines, 134–35
  dam development, 105, 143

food production, 114, 116
fossil fuel use, 123, 146–47
fresh food, differentials in access, 100
immigrant communities, 197
Laudato Si', addressing, 131
Midwest region, 29, 92, 98–99,
  107–8, 111, 134
nineteenth-century U.S.
  agriculture, 91–95
Paris Climate Agreement,
  withdrawal from, 126–27
settler colonialist legacy, 154, 210
Sonoran desert, migrants crossing,
  206–7
water footprint as world's largest, 33
See also American West
Universal Declaration of Human
  Rights, 64, 65
universalism, 3, 27, 157
universality, 17, 18, 23, 26
U.S. Conference of Catholic Bishops,
  74, 131, 162

Vatican, 8, 74, 77–78, 84, 131
Vatican Ecological Task Force, 83
Vatican II
  CST, guiding, 70
  Gaudium et Spes pastoral
    constitution, 3, 75
  signs of the times, imperative to
    engage in, 3, 5, 7, 84
  World Day of Peace, referenced in, 9
Veilleux, Jennifer, 155
virtual water, 33, 87, 115, 174

Ward, Diane Raines, 139
Water Follies (Glennon), 107
Water Footprint Network, 87–88
water footprints, 33, 87–88
water justice
  advocacy organizations and
    individuals, 30, 65–66
  defining, 47–48
  ethics of, 84, 166–67
  preferential option for the poor and,
    79–80, 211
  at Standing Rock, 161–64, 165

water mining, 37
water protectors
  Catholic establishment, not fully
    supporting, 164
  hybrid identities and aptitudes, 156
  indigenous claims, 165
  mni wiconi as rallying cry, 142, 162,
    167
  moral claims, 148
  Pope Francis, reverence for, 161
  strength of heart, expressing, 153
  support for, 163
water quality, 35, 86, 110, 115, 132, 144
water sustainability, 45–48, 50, 51, 211
water use
  in agriculture, 86, 90, 174, 212
  consumptive use of water
    affluence as driving up
      consumption, 33
    in agriculture, 34–35, 40, 86,
      89–91, 114, 210–11
    fresh water extraction rates as
      unsustainable, 32, 100
    personal consumption,
      reducing, 38–39
  nonconsumptive use of water, 34, 3
    5, 39
  water footprint and indirect water
    use, 88
  water withdrawals, 32, 34–35, 39,
    86, 174
water vapor, 133, 135, 145
water virtue, 39
water war of Bolivia, 62–67
waterborne diseases, 44, 79
wateriness of food, 86–87
water-stressed regions, defining, 44
Weisenberger, Arthur Van, 53–54
wells, 53, 90–91, 106, 107, 142. *See
  also* Samaritan woman at the well
West, Traci, 16
West Bank, 37, 171, 173, 177–78
Whanganui River as a living entity,
  66–67

Whelan, Matthew, 113
White, Gilbert, 94–95, 103–4
White Bull, Brenda, 153
wind power, 142–43
windmills, 90, 143
Wirzba, Norman, 112
Wittfogel, Karl, 104
Wolf, Aaron, 140
women and girls
  education challenges, 44, 47
  female migrants, plight of, 207
  fresh water scarcity, as burdened
    by, 44, 59, 201–5, 208, 210, 211
  gaps in theological and moral
    anthropology, women filling, 24
  in the global South, 25
  indigenous women as water
    protectors, 156
  invisibility of women in biblical
    narrative, 194
  Jordan's royal family, women of, 184
  orders of women religious and
    focus on water justice, 71
  theological discourse, women
    claiming a place in, 3
  trafficking of, 70
*World Atlas of Gender Equity in
  Education* (UNESCO), 203
World Bank, 36, 62, 126, 143
World Commission on Dams, 105, 140
World Conservation Union, 143
World Food Day, 113
World Water Council, 60
World Water Day, 29, 61
World Water Forums, 45, 60–61, 71,
  73, 79–80, 83
Worster, David, 92

Yardenit baptism site, 176–77, 178
Yellowstone River, 151, 155
York, Richard, 91

Zwarteveen, Margreet, 48